MW00994265
66
64
250
244
71
220
94
168
72
CALIFORNIA, NORTH
SITE LOCATIONS INDICATED BY PAGE NUMBER.
213
162
98
30
50
205
47
156
206
202
37
177
120
189
113
222

THE VISIONARY STATE

BY ERIK DAVIS

Photographs by
MICHAEL RAUNER

THE VISIONARY STATE

A JOURNEY THROUGH CALIFORNIA'S SPIRITUAL LANDSCAPE

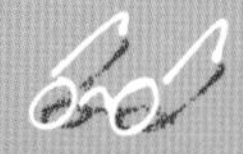

CHRONICLE BOOKS
SAN FRANCISCO

PAGES 2–3: LABYRINTH, SIBLEY VOLCANIC REGIONAL PRESERVE, OAKLAND

Library of Congress Cataloging-in-Publication Data available.
ISBN-10: 0-8118-4835-3
ISBN-13: 978-0-8118-4835-0

Manufactured in China.
Designed by Shawn Hazen.

Distributed in Canada by Raincoast Books
9050 Shaughnessy Street
Vancouver, British Columbia V6P 6E5

10 9 8 7 6 5 4 3 2 1

Chronicle Books LLC
85 Second Street
San Francisco, California 94105
www.chroniclebooks.com

CONTENTS

INTRODUCTION

ENVISIONING CALIFORNIA

When I'm abroad, I usually tell people I am from California rather than the United States. I'm not just trying to be clever, or to slough off the increasingly heavy load of being an American in foreign climes. I actually identify that way. I was born in the Bay Area in June of the Summer of Love and grew up in Del Mar, a town of university profs, oddballs, and longhairs name-dropped by the Beach Boys in "Surfin' U.S.A." When I was a teenager, my family moved to Rancho Santa Fe, into a rambling ranch house that lay about a mile from the Spanish Revival mansion where the Heaven's Gate UFO cult later committed mystic suicide. Since 1995, I have lived in San Francisco, where in the fortuitous year of 1847 my great-great-great-grandfather I. C. C. Russ disembarked with his family from the *Loo Choo*. My roots are here, in this rootless place.

When I tell people I'm Californian rather than American, I'm also letting them know something about the forces that shaped me. Like Texas and New York City, California seems in some ways separate from the rest of the United States, a realm apart. Even as a little kid, I knew that my home was different: the granola state, the land of fruits and nuts, the space-case colony with a moonbeam governor that collected, like a dustbin, everything in America that wasn't firmly rooted

SWAMI'S, ENCINITAS

down. Time has not dulled this reputation. We Californians are still routinely mocked for our flakiness, our self-obsession, our fondness for fads and health regimens and strange notions. But the familiar jokes also reflect something much more substantial about the place: its intensely creative and eccentric spiritual and religious culture. If the American West is, as Archibald MacLeish once said, a country of the mind, then California is clearly a state of mind—an altered state, for sure, or, better yet, a visionary one.

When the United States seized the territory from Mexico in 1848, California became the stage for a strange and steady parade of utopian sects, bohemian mystics, cult leaders, psychospiritual healers, holy poets, sex magicians, fringe Christians, and psychedelic warriors. There are many and complex reasons for this efflorescence of marvels. Between its Edenic bounty and multicultural mix, its wayward freedoms and hungry dreams, California quickly became an imaginative frontier exceptional in the history of American religion. Less a place of origins than of mutations, California served as a laboratory of the spirit, a sacred playground at the far margins of the West. Here, deities and practices from across space and time became mixed and matched, refracted and refined, packaged and consumed anew. Such spiritual eclecticism is not novel, of course, and similar scenes have popped up throughout history, often with more rigor and depth. But nowhere else in the modern world has such unruly creativity come as close to becoming the status quo. I call this loose spiritual ethos "California consciousness": an imaginative, experimental, and often hedonistic quest for human transformation by any means necessary.

Defining California consciousness is no easier than defining the New Age. Though world faiths like Buddhism and Christianity have marked the West Coast's alternative spirituality in fundamental ways, many of the paths that cross California are, in the words of the religious scholar Robert Fuller, "spiritual, but not religious." Even that wan word *spirituality* barely helps, since many paths crisscross the realms of sacred and profane, and look more like diets or art or crazy fun than sacred pursuits. But that is the point, since the quest for insight, experience, and personal growth can take you anywhere: a mountaintop, a computer, a yoga mat, a rock 'n' roll hall.

In his book *The Varieties of Religious Experience,* William James defined religion as "the feelings, acts, and experiences of individual men in their solitude, so far as they apprehend themselves to stand in relation to whatever they may consider the divine." California seekers could be said to have taken the bait that James dangled. For James, the cornerstone of religion was personal experience, a perspective that decoupled the religious life from questions of dogma and institution, and brought it into the sphere of the individual. This shift also opened up the *wunderkammer* of consciousness, redefining mysticism and so-called altered states as valid points of departure. Experimenting with psychedelic compounds like peyote and nitrous oxide, James argued that exalted states of consciousness had to be integrated into any philosophy worth its salt. Though James's approach hardly exhausts our understanding of religion, it certainly helps illuminate California consciousness. Solitude, especially, is key: though California has hosted scores of sects and cults, seekers are often driven by the sneaking suspicion that, in many ways, they are on their own. In California, though, James's "individual men" are as often as not women—the feminization and even "queering" of the sacred being one of California's defining, and most controversial, characteristics.

Although I was not raised within the bosom of religion, my adolescence was shaped by a variety of religious experiences. Like most of my peers, I received only the most garbled version of the good word that has sustained most Westerners for centuries. Neither baptized nor churched, I learned the gospel from obsessive and repeated listenings to my mom's beat-up LP copy of *Jesus Christ Superstar.* For the most part, the world around me was defined by skate parks, *Star Wars,* Led Zeppelin, and pot. But because I grew up when and where I did, I was also surrounded by the spent fuel rockets of the spiritual counterculture. By the time school beckoned me east, I had met and broken bread with teen witches, born-again surfers, Hare Krishnas, wandering Christian mendicants, Siddha yogis, est seminar leaders, psychedelic Deadheads, and a spindly metaphysician who taught English at my junior high and read my aura after class.

Years later, in a time of existential freefall, I yearned for something more: I wanted to be rooted in an authentic religious tradition. I was envious of the people I knew who had been raised with faith, for they at least had something formative to wrestle with, something they had no choice but to engage. I had nothing but what sociologists call "the religious marketplace"—the vast array of books, gurus, practices, paths, and healing modalities that burdens the modern seeker with choice. Conversion felt too much like consumerism; real religion, it seemed to me, should lie at the root of the self, before choice enters the matter. But then it dawned on me: what if California was my tradition? Like Hinduism, which is really just a catchall term for a riot of sects and paths and teachings, California consciousness is a great polytheistic collage. It is essentially pluralistic, even contradictory, although it speaks so much of wholeness and the One. To study this heterodox tradition, then, was to take it all in: transplanted religions, self-help systems, nature mysticism, Jesus freaks, creepy cults, tools of ecstasy.

California consciousness, I came to see, is like the landscape of the state: an overlapping set of diverse ecosystems, hanging, and sometimes quaking, on the literal edge of the West. This landscape ranges from pagan forests to ascetic deserts to the shifting shores of a watery void. It includes dizzying heights and terrible lows, and great urban zones of human construction. Even in its city life, California insists that there are more ways than one, with its major urban cultures roughly divided between the San Francisco Bay Area and greater Los Angeles. Indeed, Northern and Southern California are considered by some to be so different as to effectively constitute different states. But that is a mistake. California is not two: it is bipolar.

If California consciousness is a kind of landscape, then it makes sense for a student of this tradition to hit the road. And so I traveled across the state, visiting monasteries and mountaintops, churches and homes, storefronts and desert arroyos. I found that, while so many of California's spiritual subcultures have come and gone, many relics remain, preserving traces of spiritual passage in physical space. Some of these traces are well-known structures, monuments to God or Art or both; others are marginal places, slipping into oblivion or disguised by later owners. I found nearly all of these spots to be beautiful and strange, and they brought to life, if only for a spell, the people and stories that created them and that continue to shape the spirit of the West. My research began to take the form of a psychogeography: a dreamlike movement through space that uncovers subliminal stories and symbolic connections. This book is a reflection of those trips.

Accompanying me on the journey was photographer Michael Rauner. Like me, Michael is a native Californian. He grew up Catholic and was educated by nuns at Our Lady of the Sacred Heart in the polycultural environs of east San Diego. Another teenage seeker, Michael would come to explore the liminal zone between sacred and profane in his art. When we first met, he showed me two books of photography he had shot and designed, one about the Mission San Diego de Alcalá, and a more ambitious project devoted to California's hidden world of amateur bullfighting—a bloodless ritual with mythic roots. An earlier project, *Reliquary DNA,* offered a mystical take on genetic research. Michael not only resonated with the vision I was pursuing but also brought a tremendous and sympathetic sensitivity to the task of capturing the unusual character of the state's spiritual landscape.

The Visionary State is not a general overview of religion in California. I have not spent as much time as I would have liked on the Native American and Mexican roots of California, nor with the mainline faiths that shape the lives of millions, from the synagogues of Los Angeles to the evangelical churches of the Central Valley. With some important exceptions, *The Visionary State* focuses on the restless, heretical edge of the Anglo American experience as it probes the inside and outside of religious institutions. And even here, *The Visionary State* only scratches the surface.

What ties together the sites we have chosen is their visionary quality. What do I mean by *visionary?* It is a singular seeing, rooted in imagination and personal experience. The visionary person sees farther, or sees differently, and then draws others into the dream. Such visions are not inherently sublime—they can be tacky or mad or even terrifying. Disneyland was a vision of sorts, as was Hearst Castle, and McDonald's. What is important in the life of California is the interplay between the visionary imagination and cultural invention, and how this creative fancy introduced an enchanted and sometimes sacred dimension to an often tacky world of cheap thrills, commerce, and trash. As a place that has always been imagined as much as it has been lived, California is, perhaps, inherently visionary. The Gold Rush was a vision, and so was Los Angeles, which bootstrapped itself into being through self-mythology and hype. In this sense, California's colorful and unique spiritual culture is simply one aspect of the creative mania that has made the state the great American exception. But it also reveals something deeper: the continuing call of spirit at the frayed edges of the modern world, a call that demands novelty and reinvention, and the equal invocation of ancient ways.

Welcome, then, to California's theme park of the gods.

SUNSET STATE BEACH, SANTA CRUZ COUNTY

ARCADIA

COYOTE TRACKS

In 1906, following the earthquake that ruined San Francisco, an anthropologist working near the Sacramento Valley asked a Wintu shaman what he thought had happened. The man said that originally the world had been much smaller than it was at present. As the population of the world's original inhabitants increased, Coyote Old Man—the trickster and culture hero who scampers through countless California myths—had to stretch the world in order to make more room. When the whites started pouring in, Coyote had to stretch it some more, and finally the world ripped. Worse lay ahead, according to the shaman. The quake was only the beginning of a catastrophe that would destroy the Indians and all living things, flattening the earth and rendering it a realm of the dead.

Given the depredations suffered by California's Native Americans, one can hardly blame the fellow for his apocalyptic sentiments. By his time, there were around twenty thousand Indians left in the state, down from the three hundred thousand or so who had inhabited the territory when the Spanish first arrived, bringing their guns, germs, and God. Indians lived all across the state at the time, a testament, at least in part, to the natural abundance of the land. Though varied to the extreme, premodern California was inexpressibly fertile, overrun with fish and rabbits, lush grasses and acorn-bearing oaks. Outside the southern Colorado River region, few native Californians bothered to practice much agriculture at all, though some cultivated tobacco, for reasons, presumably, of both power and pleasure. Because of their reliance on foraging, California Indians were called Diggers by many nineteenth-century Americans, who believed the tribes they encountered were about as brutish and crude as Indians got. But the wilderness that so amazed the white folks was in some important ways a product of native ingenuity. Meadows were weeded and sown, forests pruned, salmon hunts regulated. When the Western Mono burned hillsides to encourage growth, they mimicked the pattern of lightning strikes.

Native Californians were, for the most part, exceptionally mellow, and avoided elaborate political federations and extreme social hierarchies. Most people lived in small autonomous groups that Arthur Kroeber, the great anthropologist from the University of California, Berkeley, called "tribelets." These small communities tended to move around within relatively small chunks of territory whose boundaries were jealously guarded. This separatism may help explain the tremendous linguistic diversity found in California, which featured something like twenty-one distinct language families and hundreds of mutually incomprehensible dialects. Cultural differences were significant as well. Anthropologists routinely divide the state into six major cultural zones, some of which overlap other major cultures, like the Pacific Northwest potlatch societies and the maize growers of the southwestern pueblos. California's core cultural zone stretched across the bulk of the state, from the northern Central Valley down to Los Angeles, and reached its technocultural florescence in the Chumash territories near present-day Santa Barbara. Reaping the abundant seas from plank canoes steered with double-bladed paddles, the Chumash constructed the kinds of social hierarchies and urban densities associated with settled agricultural societies, even as they maintained their hunting and gathering ways.

Native Californians practiced a number of distinct religious traditions. In Central California, the masked secret societies associated with the Kuksu cult often gathered in nifty subterranean pit houses not unlike hobbit holes. Along the northwestern coast, village fat cats sponsored yearly World Renewal ceremonies in order to rebalance a creation always threatening to fall out of whack. Underlying all

BLYTHE GEOGLYPH, BLYTHE

California religion, though, was the intense and idiosyncratic power of the shaman. Often called Doctor or the Man of Power, the shaman had direct access to a shifty zone of spirit guides and cosmic forces that could be used both to heal and to hex. There were bear shamans and rattlesnake shamans and weather wizards. To gain allies and spiritual power, shamans traveled to supernaturally charged areas of the earth: rock outcroppings, springs, caves, mountain peaks. They induced visionary states of consciousness through dancing or fasting or dream cultivation. Plant allies were also part of the sacred tool kit. Along with the widespread use of potent tobacco, many native Californians smoked or drank concoctions of jimsonweed, or *Datura meteloides,* a noxious and potentially fatal hallucinogen. Generally taken by males for group initiations and puberty rites, jimsonweed was also used in some areas in a more elective fashion by both men and women.

Shamanism in some form or another most likely inspired the most visible trace that native Californians have left on the landscape: the graven glyphs and painted designs of rock art. Some of the earliest rock art in the region—a handful of spiky red motifs in a Mojave Desert cave—may be over nine thousand years old, while some rather similar designs in Riverside County are quite recent, probably rendered during girls' puberty rites within the last few hundred years. The meaning of these images eludes us, but it is pretty safe to say that at least some of California's extraordinary rock art reflects visionary experience. It is impossible to encounter the fiery pinwheels and jagged lozenges of Chumash sites like Painted Cave and not sense the presence of uncanny forces, if not the literal reflections of hallucinatory geometries. The earliest dime-store legends told about Painted Rock, a famous Chumash site located inland on Central California's Carizzo Plain, link it to warring shamans. Before the site was wrecked by target practice and modern graffiti, Painted Rock unrolled like a sacred cartoon of seals and canoes; even the fragments that remain suggest a dreamlike incandescence. The location of the site also demonstrates how native artists, who may well have been shamans themselves, folded their work into the landscape. The pictographs at Painted Rock mostly line the interior of a vulvalike outcrop in the midst of an empty plain; the California rock-art specialist David Whitley speculates that the rock shape may reflect sexual metaphors for entering trance.

TULARE PAINTED ROCK,
TULE RIVER INDIAN RESERVATION

The abstract designs that characterize so much rock art may have even more direct connections to altered states of consciousness. A number of scholars argue that the zigzags, cross-hatches, and spirals that appear in rock art across the world reflect entoptic phenomena—basic visual patterns hardwired into the human optic system and often stimulated by mind-altering drugs. In this view, much rock art may have served as a trip report about a particular shaman's voyage into the other world. The abstract designs may signify the dizzying onset of hallucination, while the representational images may reflect the spirit helpers and dangerous beasts encountered in the depths of trance. One fabulous and comparatively recent Yokuts site in the Tule River Indian Reservation features a mix of geometric motifs and surreal creatures painted in red, white, yellow, and black. A shallow cave formed by large boulders in the river valley of the western Sierra Nevada foothills, Tulare Painted Rock includes stylized pictographs of beavers, frogs, lizards, and one large and striking centipede. The most mysterious figure is a barrel-shaped, hirsute monster with its arms spread wide. Though it resembles a grizzly bear, the creature has also been linked by some tribal elders to Yokuts stories about a shaggy giant called the Hairy Man. A few freelance researchers have in turn linked this figure to Bigfoot, the elusive Yeti-like creature who earned his name after a bulldozer operator in Humboldt County found enormous apelike footprints in the forest mulch in 1958.

Other examples of California rock art are equally enigmatic. A number of animal and human figures are etched directly into the ground near the town of Blythe, in the Colorado Desert, near the Arizona border. Yuman-speaking peoples created these desert intaglios, which may be a thousand years old, by scraping away the surface rock and exposing the lighter earth beneath. A handful of these geoglyphs are huge and, like the famous Nazca Lines in Peru, can be appreciated only from the air—a vantage point that their makers presumably did not possess (unless the UFOs that began swooping across the Southern California desert in the mid-twentieth century actually dropped by much earlier). But perhaps the most mysterious rock art in California is the Hemet Maze, a complex grid—more a labyrinth than a maze—neatly inscribed on an isolated rock in Riverside County. Archaeologists have no idea who made the ornate design or why. A small swastika recently etched in one corner of the maze may be a footnote pointing out the central figure's resemblance to that ancient Indo-European symbol. Or it may be a neo-Nazi graffiti tag—not altogether surprising in this area of the state, a hotbed of Aryan supremacy.

One message of California's rock art seems clear: humanity's most fundamental sacred space is nature itself, that rustling tabernacle of canyons and creeks and star-studded skies. Although some native Californians built decently fortified dwellings, one suspects they did not recognize the extreme cleavage between architecture and natural landscape that characterizes the modern sense of space. This sharp divide certainly intensifies the power

of "civilized" architecture, especially in its sacred aspirations: set off from the surrounding profane world, great temples and churches, with their long-lasting and fancy materials, become pocket worlds that shape and mirror the journeys of the spirit. And yet the yearning embodied in these highly structured sacred spaces—for transcendence, for union, for the marvelous—may ultimately reflect our longing for the sort of Paleolithic intimacy that once characterized our relationship to the ordinary natural world. And it is this dream of organic communion that would come to shape and mold California's modern spiritual landscape.

HEMET MAZE, HEMET

CALIFORNIA'S
FIRST MISSION
EL CAMINO REAL
THIS PLAQUE IS PLACED ON THE 250TH ANNIVERSARY
OF THE BIRTH OF CALIFORNIA'S APOSTLE, PADRE
JUNIPERO SERRA, O.F.M. TO MARK THE SOUTHERN
TERMINUS OF EL CAMINO REAL AS PADRE SERRA
KNEW IT AND HELPED TO BLAZE IT
1713 - NOVEMBER 24 - 1963
CALIFORNIA REGISTERED HISTORICAL
LANDMARK NO. 784

MISSION BELL

In 1769, Father Junípero Serra, a child of Mallorca fond of chocolate and self-scourging, raised California's first Christian cross at the site of the future Mission San Diego de Alcalá. Serra had arrived in Alta California from the Spanish colony of New Spain, one of a band of Franciscan brothers given the charge of converting the land's Indians and teaching them the arts of agriculture and construction. The viceroy of New Spain had other practical reasons for sending the friars up the coast from Mexico. Russian trappers and the British fleet were nibbling at the Northern California coast, and Spain needed to get men on the ground. Accompanying Serra were soldiers and settlers, later known as Californios, who were charged with founding military presidios and civilian pueblos in Monterey and San Diego.

Under Serra and his followers, twenty more missions were built, forming a chain of compounds that linked San Diego with Sonoma like vertebrae on a spine. Natives were coaxed to live in the missions, where they became "neophytes," praying to Jesus and Mary and working the rough equivalent of a forty-hour week. They often tried to escape, and occasionally revolted, but many seemed to accept their peculiar new lives. The friars could be brutal, but not as brutal as the soldiers who manned the presidios. Mission San Gabriel Arcángel got off to a particularly nasty start when the wife of a friendly chief was raped by a soldier; after the offended husband fought back and was killed, the soldiers stuck his decapitated head on a pole.

When Americans pushed their way into coastal California in the early nineteenth century, they did not encounter a "virgin land" but a colonial territory already transformed by European power and a European god. By this time, the mission experiment was in decline, its Indians decimated by disease and its political power waning. In the 1830s, the Mexican government dissolved the Franciscan fiefdom. Some of the parish priests soldiered on, but most of the mission buildings were plundered for tile or turned into taverns or left to return to the clay from which they came. By the time the Americans seized California from Mexico in 1848, the mission system was a wreck, the friars dispersed and their Indian charges abandoned. The Americans planted their flag in the clay of a Christian ruin.

Inevitably, these ruins acquired the rosy glow of romance. In the 1880s, Henry Chapman Ford began a series of naturalistic paintings and etchings that presented the missions as lonely, bird-haunted ruins, more peaceful than sublime. In albumen photographs from the same decade, William Henry Jackson framed the shadowy colonnades and crumbling adobe walls the way he had earlier framed Yellowstone's geysers and waterfalls: as picturesque features of an enchanted landscape. For many Californians in the late nineteenth century, the missions served as moody echoes of a lost world, a preindustrial culture of pastoral harmony and earnest faith that was fast going up in factory smoke. The missions also provided Californians with a story of origins that fit the Mediterranean climate. Just as the pagan temples of Greece and Rome had been absorbed into Northern European identity, so did the Catholic husks of Spanish imperialism give Californians—and especially Southern Californians—the raw material to construct an Anglo myth of place.

Along with Ford's and Jackson's images, Helen Hunt Jackson's novel *Ramona* helped transform California's Spanish past into an object of nostalgia. An enormously popular weepy first serialized in 1884, *Ramona* tells the sentimental tale of Indians and Californios attempting to sustain the old ranchero ways in a crude and rapacious America. An East Coast reformer, Jackson was deeply concerned with the plight of Native Americans, and she wanted her novel to be the *Uncle Tom's Cabin* of the West. But it was her romantic evocations of the Moreno Rancho that struck a chord, charming Americans with a vision of Old California as one long languid fiesta of dancing vaqueros and raven-haired beauties. Jackson's romance gave off a distinctly Catholic fragrance as well. Her Franciscans were pure in faith, traveling between missions by foot and devoting themselves wholeheartedly to grateful Indians. At one point in the novel, Father Salvierderra performs Mass with ritual

MISSION SAN DIEGO DE ALCALÁ, SAN DIEGO

ABOVE: "FRAY JUNIPERO SERRA, THE APOSTLE OF CALIFORNIA," MISSION SAN JUAN CAPISTRANO, SAN JUAN CAPISTRANO

RIGHT: MISSION SAN MIGUEL ARCÁNGEL, SAN MIGUEL

implements smuggled out of Mission San Luis Rey after the American conquest; Señora Moreno even erects high wooden crosses on her ranch to remind the newcomers of the core beliefs that first cultivated the land.

Jackson's romance spawned an entire tourist industry, as visitors flocked to the San Diego birthplace of a heroine they didn't even realize was a fiction. But it took the writer Charles Fletcher Lummis, a flamboyant city editor at the *Los Angeles Times* and later editor of the regional magazine *Land of Sunshine,* to fully refashion the Southwest's Spanish and Indian heritage into a source of Southern California identity. A Harvard man who usually sported a sombrero and a Navajo sash, Lummis was something of a poseur. Nonetheless, he had lived with vaqueros and Indians, wrote lovingly and knowledgeably about the region, and fought hard for the rights of its original inhabitants. Lummis also founded the Landmarks Club to preserve and restore the missions, an act of cultural affirmation with definite mystic overtones. In 1916, the club organized Candle Day, a fund-raiser for the ruined Mission San Fernando Rey, which lies in the San Fernando Valley. Six thousand people came, and each bought a candle for a dollar. Lighting the tapers at dusk, the crowd formed a hushed procession through the long arched colonnade of the convento—missionary quarters that had most recently housed a hog farm.

Since the founding of the Landmarks Club, all twenty-one missions have been more or less restored, although the exact distinction between restoration, re-creation, and invention is unclear. Some missions do retain significant chunks of their original structures. The Mission San Miguel Arcángel, near Highway 101 in Central California, remains largely intact. The heavy rafters are the same ones cut from trees the Indians dragged from mountains forty miles away, while many of the frescoes were executed by neophytes, who also apparently scratched Indian graffiti into the earliest levels of the whitewashed church. Unfortunately, San Miguel was damaged during the San Simeon earthquake of 2003 and its buildings condemned. Arguments over who should pay for the restoration of it and other missions reflect the ambiguous spiritual aura of the missions: should public money be used to preserve Catholic monuments that, while visited mostly by tourists, also support active congregations?

The authentic feel of most missions has more to do with simulation than preservation. Like the *Ramona* fans of an earlier era, many of today's mission visitors are unaware that the Moorish fountains and thick whitewashed adobe walls they admire are, in many instances, twentieth-century fabrications. Some restoration efforts went so far as to remove nineteenth-century additions considered "too American," like the wooden New England steeple that a friar erected over Mission San Juan Bautista in the 1860s. A number of missions were rebuilt from scratch; some of these were painstaking historical reconstructions, while others—like Mission Santa Cruz, which is half its original size—are no more authentic than Los Angeles's Union Station or the Stanford University campus. Perhaps the most instructive restoration work graces Mission San Juan Capistrano. In 1812, the mission's great stone church collapsed in an earthquake, killing forty Indians and leaving only the arched sanctuary and portions of the transept standing. An incompetent attempt to rebuild the church in the 1860s brought down more of the masonry, and the ruin was left alone in all its sacred melancholy until 1987, when the Mission Preservation Society began pouring millions of dollars into the stabilization of what it called "the American Acropolis." San Juan Capistrano thus preserves the authentic nostalgic origin of Southern California's mission myth, which is not the glory days of the friars, but their haunting, shattered aftermath.

Much of the charm of the missions is embodied in their simple but strangely comforting construction: the arched colonnades and Moorish windows, the curvy pediments and ripples of red tile. Lacking sophisticated engineers or designers, the Franciscans made honest buildings whose features were as much a function of necessity as of design. The thick walls were built for *tremblores*, and the overhanging eaves for protecting the adobe from rain; the long narrowness of the naves resulted from the paucity of tall trees that might have supported the roof. These functional elements nonetheless inspired Mission Revival, the first in a series of Spanish revivals that have proved the most consistent refrain in California's cacophony of architectural styles. Across the state, town halls, high schools, tract homes, and malls are characterized by a dizzying repetition of eggshell-colored stucco walls, round archways, and red tile roofs. Though California's various Spanish Revivals also drew from fantasies about the sprawling ranchos of the *Ramona* days, the core of the state's most iconic architectural vernacular is, in essence, a religious romance. Behind Taco Bell, the fast food chain spawned in Downey in 1962, lies the mission bell.

Appropriately, one of the earliest expressions of Mission Revival was itself a theme park of sorts. For the 1893 Chicago World's Fair, the architect Arthur Page Brown glommed together a number of different mission facades into a state building widely regarded as the finest of the fair. Brown then spread the style through elite Santa Barbara, while out in Riverside, the hotelier Frank Miller built the Mission Inn: a white-walled wonderland of domes, arches, corridors, and *campanarios*. The inn offered guided tours and held weddings in its Spanish-style chapel—including, in 1940, the Quaker nuptials of Richard and Pat Nixon. But perhaps the most forward-looking expression of Mission Revival was San Luis Obispo's Milestone Motel, whose red tile roof and faux bell tower quote Mission Santa Barbara. Opening in 1925, the Milestone was the world's first motel, or motor hotel, a term and concept that James Vail created to bring together the gypsy freedoms of car travel with the amenities of home. Vail hoped to build a chain of mission-style motels from San Diego to Seattle that could be hopped a day at a time by car—another nod to the original missions, which were connected by a day's horseback ride. For Vail, Mission Revival not only revived a building style but also restored the call of pilgrimage in an age of asphalt.

MISSION SAN JUAN CAPISTRANO,
SAN JUAN CAPISTRANO

HIDDEN VALLEY, JOSHUA TREE NATIONAL PARK

SAINTS COME MARCHING

The seeds of the United States were planted by fed-up pilgrims, and their myth still structures American consciousness: an oppressed religious group lights out for the territories, where it transforms the wilderness into what the early Puritan leader John Winthrop called a "city on a hill." Despite California's Arcadian promise, however, the Anglos who began moving into the state before the gold rush were not, by and large, religious pilgrims. There was one major exception, however, and it belongs to perhaps the most exceptional religious group of nineteenth-century America: the Latter-Day Saints (LDS), more commonly known as the Mormons. Though their impact on California was more of a footprint than a hammer blow, the Mormons were actors in some of the founding dramas of the state. And if one brazen and imperious Saint had gotten his way, California might now host the headquarters of the Mormon kingdom on Earth.

The brazen and imperious Saint in question was a young printer named Samuel Brannan, who found himself head of New York's Mormon enclave in 1845. At that time, Mormons were loathed by many Americans and regularly subject to violence. Their rascal prophet Joseph Smith had been murdered by a mob the year before, and the main body of fifteen thousand Mormons were preparing to flee Nauvoo, the city they had built in Illinois. As far as their new leader, Brigham Young, was concerned, the choice was clear: the church had to abandon the United States and found a new Zion in the western territories. Elder Brannan agreed, and in 1846, he set sail with 238 Mormons and a five-ton printing press, bound for California. The territory was still under Mexican control, and Brannan hatched an audacious plan to storm the garrison at Yerba Buena and stake a claim for the church. But when the Mormons sailed through the Golden Gate, they discovered the Stars and Stripes already flapping above the tiny colony. The Mexican-American War had begun, and Sam Brannan's Mormons became some of the first American settlers of the mission town soon renamed San Francisco.

As much an entrepreneur as a zealot, Elder Brannan immediately started hustling, excommunicating grumblers left and right. He issued California's first newspaper and started to explore the interior, staking out territory in the juicy San Joaquin Delta for a Mormon colony named New Hope. Brannan was convinced that he had found the future home of the Latter-Day Saints and that the Zion Brigham Young sought lay in California. Clambering east over the Sierra to bring Young the news, Brannan and his companions encountered the bedraggled remains of the Donner Party, a group of pioneer families famously trapped in the mountains over winter. The men gave food to Lewis Keseberg, who had survived the ordeal by consuming human flesh and who later partnered with Brannan in a brandy distillery the two ran in Napa Valley. After reuniting with the main body of Mormons, the enthusiastic Brannan was rebuffed by Young, who preferred the inhospitable alkali wastes of the Great Salt Lake. In this battle of wills, Young proved the better prophet: he correctly saw that a land as tantalizing as the one Brannan described would draw the rabble and that the Mormons needed a wilderness of their own to tame. A frustrated Brannan returned to California, where he founded a store near Sutter's Fort in the Sacramento Valley.

About the time Brannan was cruising around Northern California, a far more grueling Mormon journey unfolded to the south. In 1846, at the start of hostilities with Mexico, the Mormons agreed to muster a group of five hundred men for the U.S. Army, a move Brigham Young may have hoped would ease tensions with the government. The Mormon Battalion marched to Fort Leavenworth, in present-day Kansas, and then on to the recently seized city of Santa Fe. Many arrived too ill and exhausted to go on, but the battalion's almost absurd ordeal was only just beginning. Under the command of George Cooke, the Mormons were ordered to open a wagon road across the blazing limbo that lay between Santa Fe and the coast—a task that had the definite air of make-work to it. Hungry, heatstroked, and sick, digging wells in the dust when they ran out of water, the battalion headed west, often dragging the wagons themselves. They fought off wild longhorn bulls and survived on mesquite pods and ox entrails. On January 30, 1847, the battalion finally reached the grubby Mission San Diego. Though the Mormons never engaged the enemy, they had completed the longest and most unpleasant infantry march in U.S. history.

The battalion garrisoned at San Diego and then at the Pueblo de Los Ángeles, where the Mormons raised Old Glory for the first time. After the men were discharged from duty, most headed back to Utah to meet their families. Passing through Sutter's Fort, nine brethren were hired by the rapacious Mr. Sutter to build a sawmill on the south fork of the American River. On January 24, 1848, the mill's contractor, John Marshall, spotted some sparkly yellow flakes floating in the ditch that fed the mill. The flakes were gold, the most sacramental of precious metals, so near in name to God. Soon the word was out, and a fever flashed across the world. Sam Brannan brought a quinine bottle crammed with the stuff to San Francisco, where he paraded through the streets shouting, "Gold! Gold! Gold!" In a week, the place was a ghost town.

The gold rush transformed California irrevocably, establishing an archetype of manic speculation and incandescent greed that Californians would see fit to resurrect on multiple occasions. Although dedicated to Mammon, the gold fields also shaped the curious religious temperament of the territory, which became a state in 1850. For one thing, prospectors were risk takers, unwilling to stay within the comfortable boundaries of custom, and this restlessness would shape later generations, genetically or otherwise. More important, these men came from all over the place, which meant that American Protestants found themselves swimming in a polyglot sea of Italians, Chileans, Irish, blacks, Germans, Jews, mestizos, Indians, Hawaiians, and "Celestials" from Asia. There were no commonly accepted obligations, legal or religious, and the confrontation of so many different customs reframed religious and moral convictions as relative private opinions rather than absolute cosmic laws. Relativism just made more sense than dogmatic absolutes. With random death all around, independent if lonely souls developed a pragmatic tolerance for others, at least when they weren't fighting or killing them.

Mainstream American Protestantism, with its emphasis on rights and obligations, could not explain this world, where Lady Luck undermined the work ethic and divining rods proved more useful than Bibles. Eastern ministers, who understandably saw the gold fields as pagan cesspools of sin, sent the same sort of missionary campaigns that they launched to China or Ceylon. Although local and newfangled Christian sects prospered on the West Coast, these mainline eastern revivals basically failed. By the end of the Civil War, a goodly portion of California residents were indifferent to religion; San Francisco would largely dodge the Puritanism that marked the rest of Anglo America. Despite explosions of racism and intolerance, religion in California was fundamentally diverse and heterodox. In one account from 1883, a mildly religious prospector from Indiana described a day that included getting his head mapped by a phrenologist, hearing a Mormon sermon, and seeing demonstrations of Spiritualism and the magic lantern—all of which he considered of potential benefit to his soul.

Brigham Young was probably right: it is easier to build a theocracy in a parched desert than in a profligate Eden. While Mormons like John Horner made fortunes in midcentury California, most soon moved back to Salt Lake City, taking tens of thousands of dollars' worth of much-needed gold with them. Elder Sam Brannan stayed put, raking in as much as five thousand dollars a day at his Sacramento shop. He refused to send Young a dime, and in 1851, he was kicked out of the community of Latter-Day Saints. Brannan had been there before—back in New York, he had briefly been excommunicated for espousing the theory of "spiritual wives," which basically held that women could sleep with whomever they fancied. Now, with his apostasy complete, Brannan rose to become one of the wealthiest men in California. He founded the first spa in Calistoga and

MORONI, LOS ANGELES TEMPLE, LOS ANGELES

supported the future Mexican president Benito Juárez in his struggles against Emperor Maximilian. But Brannan wasted his fortune and died a penniless if recovering alcoholic, growing figs in the wilds of San Diego County.

In the popular Mormon imagination, Sam Brannan symbolizes the worldly backslider, lured away from Zion by the temptations of Babylon. But Brigham Young, who wanted to establish an immense Mormon kingdom called Deseret across most of the Southwest, did not turn his back on the bounty of California. In 1851, his plans for Deseret sagely crushed by the U.S. government, Young announced plans to form a colony at the western terminus of a trail the Mormons had blazed through the bleak Mojave Desert. To Young's chagrin, nearly five hundred folks jumped at the opportunity to abandon Utah for Southern California, where the Mormons soon established the city of San Bernardino. Tolerated to an unusually high degree by the neighboring "Gentiles," the colony prospered until Young, who was continuing to hemorrhage pilgrims to the West, pulled the plug in 1857. Today, few traces of the Mormon presence mark the area. One exception is the name given to the Joshua tree, a monstrous yucca whose tufted protuberances transform the edges of the Mojave Desert into something out of a Dr. Seuss book. Local lore holds that when emigrating Mormons first saw these trees in 1851, the plant's groping limbs reminded them of the biblical figure Joshua, who, with outstretched arms, led the long-suffering Israelites into the Promised Land.

The Mormons made their home in the West by reimagining it, by laying a prophetic geography on top of territories whose meaning and definition were up for grabs. The Mormons even stretched their divine imagination into Mexico, which the Book of Mormon declares was visited by the risen Christ, known to the later Aztecs as the white god Quetzalcoatl. This sacred history, in turn, shaped the design of the enormous Los Angeles Temple, the first LDS temple built in California. The geometric grilles that decorate the towering stone facing of the building, which was dedicated in 1956, represent a mild example of the Internationalist Mayan style that marked a number of public buildings in midcentury America. But by referencing Mesoamerican architecture in Los Angeles, the Mormons were also making a sacred claim on the region and its Mexican American populace. The entranceway to the Los Angeles Temple is even decorated with John Scott's well-known painting of a white-robed Jesus preaching to crowds of buckskin maidens and feathered shamans in a Mesoamerican plaza. Some California members also regard the temple's 257-foot-high tower, topped with the angel Moroni, as the fulfillment of Brigham Young's prophecy that the Lord's house would one day overlook the shores of the Pacific.

The Los Angeles Temple sits on a hillside once occupied by a movie studio that belonged to Harold Lloyd. Appropriately, this temple was the first in America to replace the live performance of the endowment ritual with a film. (The Mormon endowment is a quasi-Masonic sacred melodrama that teaches Saints of good standing the deep secrets of cosmic history and the future life.) The endowment rooms of the Oakland Temple, dedicated in Northern California in 1962, were specifically designed with widescreen thirty-five-millimeter projection in mind. In part, this turn to film fulfilled an increasingly corporate church's need for efficiency, a need expressed today in the modest scale of many temples. California hosts the largest number of LDS temples after Utah, and recent examples in Redlands, Sacramento, Fresno, and Newport Beach all hew to a more economical design. The Newport Beach Temple makes a particular effort to integrate with the local atmosphere; its dome, archways, and loggia nod to Southern California's endless mutations of Mission Revival and feature the terra cotta hue familiar to mallgoers across the Southland.

Before switching architectural gears, however, the Mormons built one last audacious marvel in California. Dedicated in 1993, the San Diego Temple abuts a freeway, leading some locals to kvetch about the "separation of church and interstate." Though not the most beautiful or well-proportioned of LDS temples, the San Diego building is easily the most fantastic, tantalizing speeding motorists with the same spell of otherworldly invitation that Disney's Matterhorn once brought to the skyline of Anaheim. The Mormon imagination has long possessed a futuristic, space-faring quality—the television show *Battlestar Galactica* was the allegorical brainchild of a Mormon, and the celebrated science fiction writer Orson Scott Card once retold the Book of Mormon as a space opera in his five-part Homecoming Saga. In San Diego the church has crystallized its anticipation of the latter days in a baroque futuristic monument that rockets toward the heavens like two frosted X-wing fighters racing neck and neck. The San Diego Temple is not a city on a hill; it is a line of flight, a concrete reminder that all Earth is just a territory to cross, a waste before the final shore.

SAN DIEGO TEMPLE, SAN DIEGO

FOUNTAINGROVE
ROUND BARN

DIVINE WINERY

In the middle of the nineteenth century, utopian colonies were sprouting up across the United States like mushrooms. Some of the most famous, like Oneida and Brook Farm, broke ground in the Northeast. But California, with its fruitful climate and relatively blank slate, also beckoned those who wanted to build new worlds and new communities. According to the historian Robert Hine, California wound up hosting the largest number of utopian experiments in the nation during its first century as a state. Many of these colonies bonded over secular ideologies, like the communist ideals of Étienne Cabet that inspired the Icaria-Speranza commune in Sonoma County. Other groups clustered around charismatic figures like the Polish actress Helena Modjeska, who attracted a colony of artists to Anaheim, where they tried, and failed, to farm an estate called Arden.

From the beginning, the religious fringe contributed to California's communal experiments. The first English book printed in Los Angeles, for example, was a rant called *Reform of the New Testament Church*. Its author was Reverend William Money, a Protestant roustabout who arrived in the Catholic hamlet in 1840 after Jesus accosted him on a New York street corner and told him to go west. A healer, astrologer, and "weather prophet," Money later moved to the San Gabriel Valley, where he designed and built an octagonal house out of wood and adobe, dubbing the place the Moneyan Institute. Though Money attracted only a few followers, he claimed to have healed thousands suffering from smallpox and other maladies over the years. He died in 1881, supposedly with an image of Mary by his head and an articulated skeleton at his feet.

Like Money, Thomas Lake Harris came to California from New York, although he was born in England. The "best-known American mystic," according to William James, Harris sipped from many religious fonts—Universalism, Spiritualism, the visions of Swedenborg—before setting out on his own unique messianic trip. In 1861, he founded the Brotherhood of the New Life colony in New York's famed Burned-Over District, the site of numerous mass Protestant revivals. Then, hot on the heels of the inner light, Harris relocated the core of the community to the rocky and fragrant foothills north of Santa Rosa in 1875. A number of commanding Victorian structures soon dominated what he called the "Eden of the West," built to house the dozens of people who gave up their private property to join Harris's Theo-Socialist commune, with its goal of igniting a "New Harmonic Civilization." Luckily, some of these followers were rich. Harris and his top-dollar students lived in a magnificent two-story manor replete with Oriental carpets, stained glass images of knights and angels, and one of the most extensive libraries in California. He called the building Aestivossa, which means "the high country of divine joy" in a language known only to Harris and his inner circle. A fountain in the midst of the estate, laid out in the style of an English park, gave the community its name: Fountain Grove.

A slight, pale man with overhanging eyebrows, Harris possessed a resonant voice and, evidently, lots of charisma. He also mainlined the visionary imagination. A series of revelations in 1857 led him to construct his own vast proto-Theosophical cosmology, which included the revelation that Earth's neighboring planets nurtured highly evolved civilizations. Beyond this zone of planetary life lurked "the Boundless Invisible Incomprehensible Eternal One," a plane of reality not dissimilar from the more economical Ain Soph of the Kabbalists. Harris also shared the Kabbalistic obsession with erotic mysticism. He believed that God was a hermaphrodite being that he called "the Twain-One." Jesus

ROUND BARN, FOUNTAIN GROVE, SANTA ROSA

Christ, who took human form in order to save us from an invisible magnetic planet of evil called Oriana, was also a "Divine Man-Woman," although he was unable to show his true form on Earth.

In one way, Harris was a genuine prophet: he foreshadowed some abiding themes of the California consciousness to come. To begin with, Harris put the body and its fluxes at the heart of spiritual practice. He taught his followers a technique called Divine Respiration, which used the lungs to absorb the atmosphere of heaven. This breathing technique also prepared folks to encounter their ethereal counterpart, a heavenly spirit of the opposite sex who could briefly inhabit a physical companion and provide a mystic dimension to conjugal love. Harris, who wrote lots of poetry, some of it pretty decent, captured a taste of this Victorian Tantra in verse:

> . . . when still more I sought to wreathe and press
> Her warm, white shape of gliding loveliness,
> She coyly drew and beckoned to the dance.
> Not much of dead religion I profess,
> But living godliness shone by her glance,
> And in its light I met the Infinite Advance.

Though he made much of his celibacy, Harris was, without a doubt, tuned in and turned on. He saw fairies all the time, but was particularly fond of the sprites that inhabited the female bosom. He also charmed a number of wealthy and attractive women of the day, one of whom, Jane Lee Waring, was known to wander about Fountain Grove in Turkish garb, smoking a pipe.

You can get away with this sort of thing for only so long. Rumors of the colony's excessive friskiness spread among the locals, and when a *San Francisco Chronicle* reporter and Christian Scientist named Alzire Chevalier visited the community, Harris made the mistake of making an Infinite Advance on the woman. In the reporter's subsequent exposé, which relied largely on rumor and innuendo, Harris took on the now familiar guise of the sexually manipulative cult leader, ruling his community with a cruel and sleazy hand. Whatever the truth of this portrait, the revelations were too much for the locals to handle, and in 1892 Harris thought it best to abandon his shot at earthly paradise. Before he left, he married his sixty-four-year-old secretary, and they lived comfortably together until Harris died an old man in 1906.

Breathwork, socialism, and cosmic sexuality were not Fountain Grove's only intimations of the spiritual Californiana to come. The colony also celebrated the sacred powers of intoxication. Harris's group had practiced viticulture in New York, where they attracted vintners like Jacob Moore, originator of the Diamond grape, and John Hyde, an expert on Missouri Riesling. With Hyde at the helm, Fountain Grove started planting vines in Sonoma County's already celebrated sun-baked terroir. Eventually Fountain Grove encompassed seventeen hundred acres of grapes, focusing on Cabernet, Pinot Noir, and Zinfandel, California's home-team favorite. Fountain Grove made some of the best wine in the country, and in the single year of 1886, they pressed seventy thousand gallons of the stuff. For the communards of Fountain Grove, making wine was more than a good living—it was good work. Harris taught that, properly prepared, wine could be a "divine and celestial substance." According to him, all things made by man carry a trace of the energy that motivated their production. Theo-Socialism's devoted and unselfish attitude toward work ensured that the final product was "infused with the divine aura, potentialized in the joy spirit." Lovers of the grape seemed to agree as well; Fountain Grove shipped its wine across the globe.

After Harris left, the property passed into the hands of the guru's most fascinating student. Kanaye Nagasawa was born into a Japanese samurai family during the dying days of the Tokugawa era, when the country was cut off from the rest of the world. According to one story, Nagasawa's clan leader wanted to learn the ways of the West, and so he smuggled Nagasawa and fourteen other boys out of the country in the early 1860s. The young men lopped off their topknots and made their way to London, where Nagasawa met Harris. He followed his teacher to America, becoming one of the first Japanese in the United States. Nagasawa was the guru's right-hand man and one of his head vintners, and he successfully ran the winery for more than forty years after Harris left. An honored citizen of Santa Rosa, Nagasawa became good friends with the city's famous plant shaman, Luther Burbank, who also squeezed value from nature with his amazing hybrids of fruits, vegetables, and flowers. Because of California's Alien Land Laws, however, Nagasawa was unable to pass Fountain Grove on to his heirs, and a subsequent owner stupidly tore out the historic vines.

Nagasawa was responsible for Fountain Grove's one surviving structure, a familiar icon to Santa Rosans: a red, ten-sided circular barn topped with a conical roof and an ornament resembling a gyroscope. Such round barns are the exotic orchids of American farm architecture and are usually traced to the Shakers, a mystic religious community who liked the circular shape because it gave no corners for the Devil to lurk in. The popularity of the round barn peaked in the late nineteenth century, when the form suggested a commitment to efficiency, as well as a progressive, even perfectionist spirit of experiment. In this sense, Nagasawa's barn is of a piece with the octagon that Reverend Money constructed in San Gabriel.

Nagasawa also rebuilt Fountain Grove's winery after it burned down in 1892, which is also, perhaps not coincidentally, the year that Harris left. In contrast to the round barn's plump and cheery profile, the winery is now a spooky ruin, one of those teenage haunts on the edge of suburban communities where wayward energies pool and reckless fetes unfold. Graffiti covers the buildings and casks, and some of these scrawls reflect the dark vibrations that Harris believed emanated from the evil planet Oriana: skulls and satanic sigils, the phrase "You're dead," the perennial motto "Ye who enter here, abandon all hope." But, like cemeteries, such scenes of abandonment and ruin have their own spiritual claim. They are gathering places for desires that reach outside convention and, in that reaching, stumble toward the sacred.

WINERY RUINS, FOUNTAIN GROVE, SANTA ROSA

In the latter half of the nineteenth century, thousands of educated, wealthy, and powerful people across the Western world embraced the cult of Spiritualism. The leaders of the movement, which was spawned by the wily Fox sisters in upstate New York, claimed to communicate with the dead through table rappings, trumpets, automatic writing, and the temporary hand-off of their vocal cords. At a time when industrial machines and electric media were transforming the world outside, Spiritualism provided an apparently modern, experimental framework for facing the inner void uncorked by the loss of friends or family. In an age of growing materialism, the séance gave people a more direct contact with spiritual reality than conventional Christianity could provide.

HOUSES OF THE SPIRITS

One of the many curious characters who tapped Spiritualism's celestial telegraph was Jesse Shepard, a pianist from the Midwest. At the age of twenty-one, without money or letters of introduction but with tremendous confidence in his improvisatory gifts, Shepard left America for the salons of Europe. A magnetic personality, Shepard was soon living the nomadic life of a freeloading dandy, befriending and performing for the likes of the Princess of Wales and Czar Alexander II. While in St. Petersburg, he plunged into Eastern mysticism and transformed his performances into musical séances. Shepard did not materialize spirits or speak with the voices of the dead. Instead he sat behind the keyboard with his enormous hands and channeled music from the beyond. His concerts were literally mesmerizing: haunting programs of operatic songs and witchy Orientalist improvisations performed in a murky half-light. Sometimes he claimed to be in touch with ancient Egyptians; other times the great composers hijacked his fingers.

In 1876, Shepard visited the sleepy village of San Diego and was enchanted by the crumbled charm and "transcendental silence" of the mission ruins. Ten years later he returned to the area to find a rough-and-tumble boomtown. He fell in with a Spiritualist circle that included two wealthy ranchers named William and John High. Likę so many people in Shepard's life, the High brothers rolled out the red carpet, offering to build the pianist a luxurious bachelor pad. This generous promise resulted in the Villa Montezuma, the most exotic and extravagant Queen Anne mansion in San Diego. Impeccably restored in 1972, the two-level home was designed, furnished, and decorated according to Shepard's wishes. He covered the fir floors with Oriental carpets and the upstairs walls with dazzling floral wallpaper. The huge, intricately paneled Music Room includes art-glass images of the poet Sappho as well as allegorical portraits of the Orient and Occident; Shepard's face, appropriately, appears on the figure representing Eastern mystery. The villa holds other mysteries as well. Hidden chambers and crawl spaces behind walls and fireplaces may have helped Shepard produce the mysterious voices often heard during his concerts. Some also wonder whether the elaborate finial over the conservatory was designed to catch lightning—unnecessary in San Diego—or to channel more occult energies. In any case, the villa's air of dark mystery helps explain its pride of place on San Diego haunted house tours; in 2000, a local clairvoyant who claims to channel Jesse Shepard even picked up a mysterious voice on an audiotape she recorded at the villa. "I can't believe we live here," the spirit whispered.

For his part, Shepard seemed to have undergone a metaphysical change of heart once he was ensconced in the villa. He publicly repudiated Spiritualism and denied that his musical salons had anything to do with séances. He also redirected his creative efforts toward writing, scribbling away beneath the arabesque cupola in the villa's south corner tower. Writing under the name Francis Grierson, Shepard penned essays that reflected a mystic and melancholic detachment from the modern world. These went down well in Symbolist France, which may have been why Shepard abandoned the

VILLA MONTEZUMA, SAN DIEGO

ABOVE: STAINED GLASS WINDOW, STANFORD MEMORIAL CHAPEL, STANFORD UNIVERSITY

RIGHT: STANFORD MEMORIAL CHAPEL, STANFORD UNIVERSITY

villa for Paris in 1889, less than two years after moving in. Another factor may have been local grumblings about his relationship with Lawrence Tonner, a younger man who became his secretary and lifelong companion. Decades later, nearly destitute but still working his magic, Shepard wound up in Los Angeles, where he lectured as a "World-Famous Mystic" while Tonner supported him by doing menial work. Shepard's final book, 1921's *Psycho-Phone Messages,* records communications from the illustrious dead; his final piano performance, an Egyptian arabesque, closed with his own demise, right there at the keys.

The 1880s were a restive time for the spirits in California. In 1884, Sarah Winchester began remodeling her now-famous San Jose mansion into an endless labyrinth designed to baffle the vengeful ghosts of those dispatched by the rifle her late husband had manufactured. A year later, Jane and Leland Stanford laid the cornerstone for Stanford University, the research and educational institution that the railroad baron willed into being through the largesse of his pocketbook. The date of the event, which was celebrated with a choir rather than the usual brass band, was May 14, 1885, the anniversary of the birth of the Stanfords' much beloved son, Leland Jr., who had died in Florence three years before at the age of fifteen. Stanford had always claimed that the idea for the university came to him in a dream he had during a mournful doze shortly after the boy's death. But in 1891, a more scandalous explanation was offered by the Spiritualist medium Maud Lord Drake. Drake claimed that, during a séance attended by the Stanfords, she had channeled Leland Jr., who had asked his parents to found the university in his honor. The Stanfords responded to Drake's claim with an official denial, assuring the world that they had no faith in "commercial spiritualism." But the accusation was hardly beyond the pale. Following their son's death, the Stanfords had attended séances in Paris, New York, and San Francisco's Nob Hill, and Jane continued to visit mediums throughout her life. Her enthusiasm was worrisome enough to propel Stanford's first president, David Starr Jordan, to visit a certain Hermann the Magician in order to study the tricks of mediums.

After Leland Stanford died in 1893, Jane honored his memory by directing the construction of the university's architectural jewel, the vibrant Memorial Church. The Stanfords were both deeply believing WASPs, but they were also, for their day and class, open-minded ecumenists, respectful of Catholics and even Jews. As such, the Memorial Church bucked tradition and became a nondenominational—if essentially Protestant—house of worship. This ecumenical spirit motivated the vaguely inspiring maxims carved into the church's sandstone walls, collected by Jane from various sources. The architecture is a mix as well. Like the original campus, the basic structure is Romanesque with a Mission Revival twist, while the exterior mosaics and interior design suggest a Byzantine spin on Arts and Crafts and Pre-Raphaelite styles. Mrs. Stanford's broad vision encompassed gender as well—the mosaics in the west transept feature Rebecca and Rachel rather than their more typical spouses. One stained glass window in the nave also shows Christ resurrecting a dead child before the eyes of her grieving mother, an image that is, in its own way, as haunted as the art-glass portraits of dead composers in Jesse Shepard's Villa Montezuma.

Before her death in 1905, Mrs. Stanford continued to read voraciously about Spiritualism and other spectral matters. Much of the material came from Thomas Welton Stanford, a leading booster of the séance trade and Leland Stanford's youngest and favorite brother. Over the years, Welton Stanford donated many oddities to his brother's university library, including transcripts from séances, spirit slates, and a number of so-called apports—mysteriously

CHARITY

materialized objects that included a Russian kopeck, the remains of a tortoise, and an item labeled "fur bat (implement of death)," which unfortunately seems to have dematerialized back into the ether. In 1911, Welton Stanford also gave the university fifty thousand dollars to create a fellowship for psychical research. At a time when the great psychologist William James still believed in the value of studying psychic powers, the fellowship was not quite the hot potato it would be today. Equipping a lab with crystal balls and Dictaphones, the university established a five-year study of ESP under a hard-headed researcher named John Edgar Coover, who came to ambiguous conclusions. The university has since spent the bulk of Welton Stanford's trust, but only after expediently reclassifying hypnosis, dreams, and other twilight mind-states as psychic phenomena.

Welton Stanford's stab for laboratory evidence is a reminder that, for all its occult spectacle, Spiritualism was a progressive attempt to materialize the soul in an era of industrial science and modern media. Perhaps that's why the spirits had a hand in manifesting the Bradbury Building, the most futuristic of California's nineteenth-century office complexes. Lewis Bradbury had struck it rich in the gold mines of Mazatlán; entering his dotage, he decided to memorialize himself with a factory building in downtown Los Angeles. Bradbury had visited the Bon Marché in Paris, with its frilly ironwork catwalks suspended beneath glass ceilings, and he wanted to create something similarly forward looking. After commissioning the firm of Sumner P. Hunt, Bradbury became dissatisfied with Hunt's conventional designs and instead offered the job to Hunt's draftsman, George Wyman, whose novel sketches Bradbury admired. The thirty-two-year-old Wyman had no formal training in architecture or engineering and was nervous about taking the gig. With his wife, Belle, Wyman turned to a Spiritualist device for automatic writing called the planchette, a flat heart-shaped tripod the size of a Palm Pilot with two casters and a pencil at the tip. Using this mass-produced item, which later evolved into the Ouija board, Wyman asked his dead brother Mark about taking the commission. According to George Wyman's grandson, Hollywood's famous monster-movie überfan Forrest J. Ackerman, the spirit wrote back: "Take the Bradbury building and you will be successful." For some reason, the word *successful* was written upside down.

As the inventor of the term *sci-fi,* Ackerman has taken great pride in pointing out that Wyman based his designs in part on Edward Bellamy's 1887 science fiction novel *Looking Backward,* whose account of the early twenty-first century includes this description of an office building:

> A vast hall full of light, received not alone from the windows on all sides but from the dome, the point of which was a hundred feet above . . . the walls were frescoed with mellow tints, to soften without absorbing the light which flooded the interior.

Wyman brought this vision to life. Although the exterior of the five-story building is rote Romanesque, the foyer ushers the unsuspecting visitor into a narrow courtyard that shoots upward toward a gabled canopy of glass, a lattice of light suspended over delicate wrought-iron trusses that float in the clerestory haze. The atrium's central shaft is defined by a dense Art Nouveau grillework of balusters, columns, and freestanding elevator shafts. The metallic sheen of the ironwork is set against the rose marble and golden stone, the yellow tiles and the gold-grained woodwork, all of which soften the light drifting down from above. During excavations for the building, workmen discovered an artesian spring; turning lemons into lemonade, Wyman used it to power two hydraulic birdcage elevators, whose graceful movements transform the atrium into a clicking crystal machine.

The spirits are fitful, however. Bradbury died months before his building opened in 1893, and Wyman went on to a largely forgettable career. In the 1940s, when the Broadway district became ground zero for Los Angeles's wholesale textile trade, several upper loft spaces of the building were turned into garment factories. Though declared a cultural monument in 1962, the building was not fully restored until 1989, when, in order to maintain the fantastic light, a wire mesh was suspended beneath the vast skylight rather than replace its untempered glass. Ironically, this commercial monument to the utopian aspirations of Los Angeles left its most memorable mark on one of the darkest visions of the city: Ridley Scott's dystopian film *Blade Runner.* In this adaptation of a Philip K. Dick novel, a bleak and dripping Bradbury Building houses the diseased replicant designer JF Sebastian, who alleviates his loneliness with an apartment filled with living dolls. In the foyer, the light of Utopia has been winnowed to the aggressive stab of searchlights from above, probing the shadows for answers: Are the spirits real, and do the androids dream?

BRADBURY BUILDING, LOS ANGELES

THE TABERNACLE OF NATURE

DENSER SUNSHINE

In 1863, America's most famous drug fiend found himself standing on Inspiration Point, gazing slack-jawed at Yosemite Valley. Fitz Hugh Ludlow was a young East Coast journalist and short-story writer best known for his strange autobiographical book *The Hasheesh Eater,* a dreamlike tale of adolescent obsession that did for cannabis what Thomas De Quincey's *Confessions of an Opium Eater* (1821) had already done for the poppy. Ludlow had come to California from New York in the company of his friend Alfred Bierstadt, a German-American landscape painter whose awesome and often enormous canvases brought the CinemaScope romance of the American frontier to a fascinated East Coast public. As a practitioner of the Hudson River school, Bierstadt trumpeted the dramatic scale of the West, the titanic forces implied by its geology, and the spectral plays of light conjured through twilight and storm. Writing dispatches from the road, Ludlow helped promote his friend and his journey, which was sponsored by a railway magnate whose interest in glowing portraits of the western territories presumably involved more than artistic taste.

Ludlow and Bierstadt were both acolytes of the sublime, that shivering sense of awe, at once mystic and aesthetic, that characterizes so much of America's romance with nature in the nineteenth century. Ludlow discovered the mystic sense during college, when he began gobbling hashish balls

INSPIRATION POINT, YOSEMITE NATIONAL PARK

procured from the local apothecary. Following the addiction-and-recovery pattern established by De Quincey, Ludlow eventually came to see hashish as a "witch-plant of hell," but not before it had provided him with a taste for cosmic musings and exotic phantasmagoria—qualities that, while relatively rare in his later work, come to the fore in his description of California's most celebrated valley. Gazing two miles across the floor of Yosemite Valley, Ludlow and Bierstadt were spellbound by a mass of upthrusting rock, which seemed to smile at them "in all the serene radiance of a snow-white granite Boodh." Opposite this Buddha, El Capitan stood like a stupendous citadel hewn by genies having another go at the Tower of Babel. Viewing this scene, Ludlow proclaimed as blasphemous the idea that Half Dome is simply a lifeless rock. For Ludlow, the mountain, which he called by the Ahwaneechee name Tis-sa-ack, suggested nothing less than the life of the cosmos itself. "What if Tis-sa-ack himself were but one of the atoms in a grand organism," Ludlow wrote, "if he and the sun and the sea were but cells or organs of some one small being in the fenceless vivarium of the Universe?"

Ludlow wasn't just having a flashback here. Like other Americans in the middle of the nineteenth century, Ludlow saw California as a landscape of the sublime, at once wild and divine. California was nature writ large and golden, the nation's new horn of plenty, bursting with enormous trees, supersize fruits, and the congealed sunshine of gold. After the collapse of the gold rush, summer lodges and outdoor hikes grew popular in the Sierras, with Yosemite becoming a favored destination for the new nature tourists. A few years after Ludlow and Bierstadt's visit, the San Francisco artist Eadweard Muybridge first toured the valley with a camera. His striking images, which brought fame to both him and Yosemite, sparked a photographic romance between Americans and the valley that transformed the place into a media icon, an almost sacred symbol of what we now call the biosphere.

This frontier strand of nature mysticism had its roots in the Transcendentalist ideas of Ralph Waldo Emerson, who believed that the spiritual world and the organic world were woven together, and that this connection held the potential to radically transform the human heart. Emerson anticipated a good deal of the unchurched spirituality that would arise in California: the embrace of nature mysticism and the deep self, as well as the interest in Eastern thought and impersonal images of deity. Emerson's ideals also influenced the progressive wing of Christianity. Before Ludlow and Bierstadt set off for the Sierra, they stayed in San Francisco with the Reverend Thomas Starr King, a boyish and enormously popular Unitarian minister from Boston who came west in 1860 and died shortly after Ludlow's visit. Though Starr King ferociously supported the doctrine of Anglo-Saxon manifest destiny, he also embodied the very soul of religious liberalism. Preaching to conservative Presbyterians as well as liberal Universalists, Starr King overlooked issues of creed while emphasizing the richness and availability of the sacred forces that inhabit the world.

Traveling and lecturing throughout the state, Starr King became the first prophet of wild California. At a time when many Californians saw nature as nothing more than a vast if recalcitrant store of resources that might become money, Starr King encouraged them to hear the music of the land and to follow those tones back to the source. Starr King loved the Sierra. He logged early tourist time at Lake Tahoe, where he spent hours on the shore listening to the wind stir the firs and sugar pines. Following one Tahoe trip, he wrote a gorgeous sermon that treats the landscape as a hieroglyph of divine forces. The pines recall the cedars of Lebanon, while the lake reflects the Sea of Galilee, the "fountainhead of living water" that courses through creation and in turn reflects the mind of God. By reading the landscape symbolically, King hoped to get at what he called, in his most famous sermon, "the substance beneath the show." But King did not take the next, most radical step, which is to see the show itself *as* cosmic substance. Nature is not just a symbol of something deeper: it is a divine being at once immediate and beyond our categories of thought.

The American who best embodied and communicated this pantheistic vision was John Muir, the most articulate and evangelical poet of the California mountains. Muir came to his love of nature partly through a life-rending physical trial. During the 1860s, the man earned his keep as a machinist and an inventor of automatic gadgetry. While working at a carriage factory in Indianapolis, Muir accidentally pierced his right eye with a sharp file. His other eye conked out in sympathy, and Muir spent a month blind. When he regained his sight, Muir quit work and began a period of drifting, as he called it, through the Sierra. After publishing books about his experiences years later, he became America's most famous apostle of the wild. Fusing Emerson's joyful hymns with a naturalist's gift for crisp and informed detail, Muir's writings galvanized Americans' love of the outdoors, encouraging them to turn to nature as a respite from the "galling harness" of civilization. Horrified by the crass exploitation and ruin of the places he worshipped, Muir used his public profile to achieve concrete gains, founding the Sierra Club in 1892 and battling to preserve Yosemite, the Grand Canyon, and redwood groves across Northern California.

Although Muir abandoned the stern Calvinism he had imbibed as a child, he did not leave his faith behind him as he wandered through the mountains hunting inspired sensation. He lived like a Saint Francis, supping only on bread and tea, and later approached the cause of preservation with the raging zeal of a Jeremiah. But Muir might also be considered the first great California pagan. Revising a famous line of Thoreau's, Muir declared that "in God's wildness lies the hope of the world—the great fresh, unblighted, unredeemed wilderness." The word *unredeemed* tells us that we are outside or before Christianity, in a world perfect just as it is. Muir drank deeply of wildness, and at his most ecstatic, he seemed to melt into the earth. In a 1869 letter, Muir wrote:

> Now we are fairly into the mountains, and they into us. . . . What bright seething white-fire enthusiasm is bred in us—without our help or knowledge. A perfect influx into every pore and cell of us, fusing, vaporizing by its heat until the boundary walls of our heavy flesh tabernacle seem taken down and we flow and diffuse into the very air and trees and streams and rocks, thrilling with them to the touch of the vital sunbeams.

No doubt the most remarkable state of consciousness that Muir ever described occurred during his ascent of

MOUNT RITTER, ANSEL ADAMS WILDERNESS AREA

Mount Ritter. Passing through Yosemite Valley in the fall of 1872, Muir met two artists who he agreed to lead into the mountains. After a few days, they rounded a great projection of rock and came upon what he called a "typical alpine landscape." The artists, one of whom is believed to have been the Scottish landscape painter William Keith, decided to stay put in order to paint the romantic archetype that unfolded before their eyes. Muir was not content with pictures, though. He wanted experience. He pressed on and, reaching a cliff at the side of a massive glacier, began to scale Ritter's peak. Clambering up crumbling battlements of metamorphic rock, hammering off ice with stones, Muir eventually found himself in an impossible spot: spread-eagled against a smooth cliff face, unable to move hand or foot. Convinced he was about to fall to his death, Muir suddenly became "possessed of a new sense," a power that took control of his body, moving it up the rock "with a positiveness and precision with which I seemed to have nothing at all to do."

This is mysticism not as contemplative exercise, but as extreme sport. In his account, Muir scrambles about for the proper religious or scientific metaphor for this "new sense"—instinct, guardian angel, the other self. In the next century, he might have used Buddhist language or the psychologist Abraham Maslow's popular notion of a "peak experience." It doesn't matter. What infused Muir's limbs was life itself, which for Muir meant the wild flux of moonbows and pine pitch and glacial rifts and telescopes—in other words, everything. "When we try to pick out anything by itself," he wrote, "we find it hitched to everything else in the Universe." What he discovered on Mount Ritter was that he was hitched as well, linked not just to some hazy sense of oneness but also to a direct course of action, a knowing spontaneity.

Even before Muir and others reimagined the Sierra Nevada as a zone of spiritual communion, the land had already suffered the violence of modern commercial forces. The gold rush had left vast swaths of ugly and depleted land behind: heaps of slag, poisoned rivers, denuded hillsides. These wounds themselves only dimly reflected the incomprehensible holocaust visited upon the people who originally inhabited the mountains. For these reasons and others, sober historians argue that California's American Eden was always a myth. The sadder but grander truth is that California was (and is) both Eden and the Fall, a genuine Arcadia lacerated by greed, exploitation, and tacky commercialism. The rapid transformation of California into an urbanized, technologically driven consumer economy takes on the character of a mythic tragedy when set against the numinous power, both symbolic and visceral, of her wilderness—a "wilderness" once cultivated by native gardeners who extracted resources with a vastly lighter touch.

The most recognizable icon of California's natural religion is *Sequoiadendron gigantea,* the giant sequoia, which clusters in groves throughout the Sierra Nevada. Relatives of the coastal redwood, these trees are the largest living beings on the planet, and some of the oldest. They astonished the men and women of the nineteenth century as they astonish us today. "I could not stand to look at a bigger tree without taking chloroform," said P. T. Barnum. Americans have always used the image of the Gothic cathedral to describe these groves, so fit a figure is it for the vaulting sense of space, the clerestory light, the pointed arches sometimes naturally traced by the growing bark. But that very sense of the sacred called forth a contrary impulse as well. In 1853, five Americans took nearly a month to chop down a three-hundred-foot-tall sequoia that was alive during the time of the Pharaohs; they then polished the stump into a dance floor and hollowed out the fallen trunk into a bowling alley. Responding to this widely reported news story, Thoreau said that such actions sprang from an anxious hatred of whatever reminded humans of their tiny insignificance. The act was also an augury of sorts, a foreshadowing of all the strip malls to come. And yet the marvelous buildings that some people crafted from these felled giants would also carry a trace of the spiritual wilderness into California's constructed environments, and especially its curious houses of worship.

CATHEDRAL GROVE, MUIR WOODS
NATIONAL MONUMENT

CHURCH OF THE NEW JERUSALEM/
THE SWEDENBORGIAN CHURCH,
SAN FRANCISCO

TEMPLE CRAFT

Near the close of the nineteenth century, the inhabitants of the sleepy university town of Berkeley started referring to the slopes north of campus as "Nut Hill." The term supposedly sprang from the vegetarian diets favored by many of the area's artsy and freethinking residents—though I suspect it may have had something to do with the residents themselves. A key moment in the early history of this leafy bohemia occurred in 1895 when Bernard Maybeck, the Berkeley architect later responsible for San Francisco's moody and marvelous Palace of Fine Arts, designed a home for the poet and naturalist Charles Keeler. Instead of the lacy Victorian confections popular at the time, Keeler wanted an abode that blended in with the hillside, that used local materials and projected an air of simplicity and organic health. Maybeck created an unpainted redwood house that boldly exposed its thick beams and rafters, the latter tucked beneath a sharply slanting roof reminiscent of a Swiss chalet. From his home, Keeler helped spur the Hillside Club, a group of local architects, advocates, and nature lovers who lobbied for a new kind of urban development, one that would respect native flora and follow the folds of the land. The woozy winding roads of the Berkeley Hills are the remnants of their desire to embed architecture in nature rather than master the land through structure.

Maybeck's sparse jewel also helped spur the Arts and Crafts movement in California, where the style would flower

ST. JOHN'S EPISCOPAL CHURCH, PETALUMA

into a distinctly Californian vision of dwelling in organic form. The roots of Arts and Crafts lay in Britain, where the artist and socialist William Morris had reacted to the ugliness of Victorian industrialism by looking back to medieval styles and handicraft methods in order to enable people of modest means to build things and places of natural beauty. As the ideas of Morris, John Ruskin, and their followers trickled into America, architects across the country developed their own language of graceful simplicity, one that emphasized woodwork, earthy tones and materials, and honest forms keyed to the surrounding landscape. In the Los Angeles area, the affordable, low-slung bungalow became perhaps the key American contribution to Arts and Crafts building, while the brothers Charles and Henry Greene took the style into the empyrean with homes built for wealthy folks in Pasadena and Northern California. But unlike their comrades in the East and the Midwest, California architects also applied their regional spin on Arts and Crafts to ecclesiastical buildings. In doing so, they helped to focus the implicit spirituality of the style, whose quest for organic balance and holistic integration resonated with California's own mystic romance with the subtle wizardry of natural form.

The first Arts and Crafts structure in California was built by a man of the spirit. Joseph Worcester was a Swedenborgian minister who moved to California from the East Coast in 1869. As a young man, Worcester had considered becoming an architect but decided his vocation lay in the Christian path outlined by Emmanuel Swedenborg, a brilliant and prolific Swedish polymath who was equal parts natural historian and visionary mystic. Swedenborg believed that nature was the handiwork of God and that human craft should harmonize with God's sacred creation, of which trees, birds, and flowers were special emblems. In the West, Worcester's Swedenborgian sentiments were nourished by his friendship with John Muir and his visits to places like Yosemite, where he admired the rustic miner shanties, with their roofs of shingle or thatch, as well as the sublimities of redwood and rock. In the late 1870s, when Worcester came to build his own one-story dwelling in Oakland's Piedmont neighborhood, he did something at once radical and simple: he covered the exterior with shingles and the interior with unpainted redwood board. Keeler later noted the regional influence cast by Worcester's home and its "quiet, spiritual, reserved type of beauty."

Worcester later moved to San Francisco to assume leadership of a Swedenborgian church. The congregation needed a place of worship, and in the early 1890s, Worcester commissioned and helped design the Church of the New Jerusalem, which still stands at 2107 Lyon Street. The architectural firm that Worcester commissioned also employed Maybeck, who probably influenced the final design. The church exterior is a low-key echo of the California missions, featuring red brick, rough concrete walls, and Spanish tile. But it is the informal interior, with its fireplace and Oregon pine paneling, where the religion of nature flourishes. Worshippers sit in sturdy, rush-seated maple chairs instead of pews, and face an altar that from the beginning has been flush with shrubbery, wildflowers, and twisted chunks of cypress. Gnarled madrone tree trunks lean in from the walls to support the gently sloped ceiling; they still sport the bark they wore when Worcester found them in the mountains above Santa Cruz.

The principal designer of the Church of the New Jerusalem was most likely Albert Schweinfurth, who was trained on the East Coast before moving west. Certainly elements from Worcester's church found their way into the First Unitarian Church that Schweinfurth designed for a Berkeley congregation in 1898. Schweinfurth's church features a long spreading gable roof and a massive shingle facade that, though bare today, was once cloaked with twisting vines of ivy. Two entrance porches flank either side of the facade and its round window, both of which are supported by massive redwood tree trunks covered with bark. Members of the congregation, which included Keeler, Maybeck, and other Hillside Clubbers, contributed homemade articles for interior decoration.

The Unitarians celebrated this rustic scheme in part because they were liberal sectarians who wanted to stand apart from convention, to express their forward-thinking spirit in built space. But Schweinfurth's design also reflected an idealization of nature, at once striking and sentimental, that had marked the liberal wing of Bay Area Christianity since the days of Starr King. This mixture of nature mysticism and organic design was also expressed, to varying degrees, in ecclesiastical buildings created by other regional architects influenced by Arts and Crafts, including Maybeck, Julia Morgan, Irving Gill, and Ernest Coxhead. A High Church Episcopalian, Coxhead served as the semiofficial architect for the Episcopal Church throughout California, dotting the landscape with his eclectic, shingle-mad takes on Gothic Revival, most notably the fanciful St. John's Church in Petaluma.

Another vital element of this spiritual design movement is its often pronounced Japanese flavor. By the turn of the century, the popularity of Japanese art and design, from *ukiyo-e* to lacquer furniture, had firmly established itself across America and Europe. But California's position along the Pacific Rim, as well as its Asian population of farmers and landscape gardeners, embedded the West's aesthetic fascination with Japan in the soil. The power and delight of California's early Asian fusions are particularly noticeable in the work of the state's most famous exponents of Arts and Crafts, the brother team of Charles and Henry Greene. Though the Greenes did important work in Northern California, they were most intimately associated with the dry environs of Pasadena, where they shaped the informal California bungalow into visionary masterpieces like the Gamble House. Ironically, Greene and Greene built many of their fancy homes for just the sort of captains of industry that the reformer William Morris wanted to subvert through his design practices.

Both the spirit and the structural detail of Greene and Greene's homes and gardens—the projecting roof beams, exposed joinery, and overhanging gables—were inspired by the reproduction of a Fujiwara-era Buddhist temple that blew their minds when they visited Chicago's World Expo in 1893. Though the brothers never traveled to Japan, the bungalows and landscapes they crafted tapped the essence of Japanese design more than any other built spaces in America at the time. Wood was their essential material, and their homes and furniture drip with its evocative grains and honeyed colors. In the Gamble House, wood is revealed as a kind of frozen flow, as if something of the tree's life still infuses the banisters and chairs and overhanging eaves. Whether or not this frozen flow tastes like Zen depends on how intimately one links spirituality and design. But it's certainly true that the Western passion for Japanese aesthetics, which infuses the work of the Greenes and many of their peers, helped pave the way for Zen's practice of natural mind to enter American consciousness.

For Charles Greene, at least, the encounter with the Ho-O-Do Temple in Chicago left more than an aesthetic trace. Once World War I had driven clients to more pragmatic and cheaper styles than Greene and Greene offered, the firm dissolved and Charles moved to the genteel bohemian enclave of Carmel-by-the-Sea. He continued to work, principally on the D. L. James House, a moody adobe-inspired structure that hangs over the sea. Built entirely from local stone, the James House seems to emerge directly from the cliff face. But Charles took few other major commissions in Carmel, and devoted most of his time to writing, meditation, and the study of Buddhism and the wily modern mystic George Ivanovitch Gurdjieff. In a 1932 paper called "Symbolism," the architect declared his desire to find "the hidden kernel of the oneness of all that exists." For Charles Greene, at least, the holistic integration of structure and volume had given way to a deeper design.

RIGHT: WINDOW, FIRST UNITARIAN CHURCH OF BERKELEY/UC DANCE STUDIO, BERKELEY

FAR RIGHT: FIRST UNITARIAN CHURCH OF BERKELEY/UC DANCE STUDIO, BERKELEY

ROCK AND HAWK

When the poet Robinson Jeffers and his wife, Una, first visited Carmel-by-the-Sea in 1914, they stumbled across a stone fireplace in a clearing of cypress trees. The crude hearth reminded them of an altar, an impression no doubt enhanced by the animal skulls hanging in the boughs of the surrounding trees. This rough-hewn temple was the work of the poet George Sterling, then San Francisco's most famous literary scion. A handsome bon vivant with the aspect, as one commentator put it, of "Dante in hell," Sterling had first come to Carmel in 1905 to escape the temptations of the city. Like many of his fellow bohemians, Sterling was drawn to the primitive and pagan, and found Carmel a powerful support for his imagination—as well as his hedonism. Attracting literary friends like Jack London, Mary Austin, and Sinclair Lewis, Sterling helped turn Carmel into an artist colony and a haven for unconventional spirits. Sterling's own sojourn there ended disastrously when the poet Nora May French killed herself with cyanide in his home. Twenty-odd years later, Sterling used the same poison to dispatch himself in an apartment above San Francisco's Bohemian Club. A scrap of verse was found in his room: "Deeper into the darkness can I peer / Than most, yet find the darkness still beyond."

Robinson Jeffers also peered deeper than most, but, unlike Sterling, Jeffers continues to be read today. Before the San Francisco Renaissance erupted in the 1950s, unleashing a storm of Beat scribes on the scene, Jeffers was without doubt California's most important and visionary poet. His strongest verse attains a prophetic power at once immediate and remote, its slow, oceanic pulse anchoring an ultimately cosmic reach. Like John Muir, Jeffers submerged himself in the patterns and rhythms of the natural world around him: the wild and surging Big Sur country he and Una fell in love with. But instead of Muir's wild pantheistic glee, Jeffers sought and found in nature a deep, unmoving clarity, an impersonal vantage point that pierced merely human passions. In his poem "Rock and Hawk," the image of a falcon perched atop a massive stone on the headland becomes a symbol of his own spiritual ideal: "Fierce consciousness joined with final / Disinterestedness." Jeffers came to dub his perspective Inhumanism, a term that reflected his sense that man and his much-vaunted civilization were narcissistic traps to overcome.

Jeffers's Inhumanism reflects a critical aspect of California's religion of nature: the fact that mystic insights into the holistic cosmos tend to undermine conventional human values. This theme was articulated with remarkable power in 1911, when the Spanish-American philosopher and poet George Santayana spoke to a packed house at UC Berkeley's Philosophical Union. Santayana argued that nature overwhelms our desire for merely human meanings and that signs of this liberation were beginning to emerge in California:

> When you escape, as you love to do, to your forests and your Sierras, I am sure again that you do not feel you made them, or that they were made for you. . . . In their non-human beauty and peace they stir the sub-human depths and the super-human possibilities of your own spirit. It is no transcendental logic that they teach; and they give no sign of any deliberate morality seated in the world. . . . Everywhere is beauty and nowhere permanence, everywhere an incipient harmony, nowhere an intention, nor a responsibility, nor a plan.

Like many of California's nature mystics, Jeffers was profoundly moved by this wild harmony of impermanence and beauty. He had tasted those superhuman possibilities that the great galaxy seemed to offer. But Jeffers also recognized, with increasing bitterness, that the cosmic perspective only magnifies the absurdity and ignorant waste of ordinary human life. When he looked at people, he focused on their subhuman

UNA'S SITTING ROOM, HAWK TOWER, CARMEL-BY-THE-SEA

PARAPET, HAWK TOWER, CARMEL-BY-THE-SEA

depths. In a number of long narrative poems set along the rural California coast, Jeffers unrolled macabre myths of human perversion, including one about a mad Nietzschean preacher obsessed with violence and incest that earned the poet an almost hip notoriety.

In 1917, Robinson and Una purchased property on Carmel Point, a windswept and barren nub of coastline marked by a jagged outcropping of rock. Here the couple made a home and a family. Una was a remarkable woman, a beautiful Midwesterner who wrote her University of Southern California master's thesis on mysticism. A proto-hippie of sorts, Una favored sandalwood fragrance, wore her long dark hair in braids, and enjoyed cold baths in the morning and whiskey at night. For his part, Jeffers was dark but driven. Over the years, he planted over a thousand trees in the area, and used local granite boulders to build their house, a small and sturdy structure based on a Tudor barn that had captured Una's eye in Surrey, England. The Tor House, as it was known, had four-foot-thick walls and running water but no gas or electricity, and was built over what Jeffers believed had been an old Indian camp.

During the construction of the Tor House, Jeffers worked with the stonemasons, mixing mortar and carrying rock. One day, using his hands, Jeffers was gifted with a deep glimpse of things—what his wife later described as "an awakening such as adolescents and religious converts are said to experience." Jeffers saw his spirit in the stones and realized a kinship with the granite and its hard tranquility. It's not clear if any passages of his poetry directly reflect this experience, but one of his biographers points to the following section of "The Tower beyond Tragedy," Jeffers's reinterpretation of the myth of Orestes:

The knife in the stalk of my humanity; I drew and it broke; I
    entered the life of the brown forest
And the great life of the ancient peaks, the patience of stone,
    I felt the changes in the veins
In the throat of the mountain, a grain in many centuries, we
    have our own time, not yours; and I was the stream
Draining the mountain wood; and I the stag drinking; and I
    was the stars
Boiling with light, wandering alone, each one the lord of his
    own summit; and I was the darkness
Outside the stars, I included them, they were a part of me.

In contrast to Muir's experience on Ritter, Jeffers's fusion with the flows of Earth explodes into an ultimately galactic embrace. Jeffers loved the rootedness of stone, but he also celebrated the awesome and disturbing findings described by modern cosmology. He closely followed the discoveries emerging from the Whitney Observatory in Southern California and took to heart Edwin Hubble's discovery that we live in an expanding universe of myriad galaxies. Indeed, some of Jeffers's poetry approaches science fiction.

Jeffers never lost his spiritual connection to the material Earth, however, an intimacy that was reflected in the amazing citadel he constructed for Una next to the Tor House. Inspired by the towers the couple had seen in Ireland, Hawk Tower is a stone enchantment, a diminutive dream that features turrets, battlements, a sunken dungeon, and a secret staircase. Jeffers built it alone, using a block and tackle to lift stones he dragged from the shore, some as heavy as four hundred pounds. As he did throughout the property, Jeffers included special stones from around the world in the walls and floors of Hawk Tower. In the lower entrance room, he added black lava from Mount Kilauea, an Indian arrowhead from

Michigan, and a polished cube of Italian marble used as a paperweight by his father. The parapets above contain a piece of the Great Wall of China, as well as stones from the grave of the Irish poet George Moore and from Newstead Abbey, Lord Byron's home. Hawk Tower also contains artifacts that reflect female spiritual power, especially in the upper floor, which was paneled with mahogany and known as Una's Room. In the niche near an oriel window Jeffers cemented a Mesopotamian tile inscribed with a cuneiform prayer to the goddess Ishtar. Opposite this he placed a carved stone head of a celestial dancer from the temple of Prah Khan in Cambodia's Angkor Wat. A blackened niche nearby reflects the presence of votive candles, perhaps for an altar of some kind.

With their fused fragments, Tor House and Hawk Tower represent a recurrent theme in California consciousness: the desire to create a sacred mosaic out of bits and pieces of times and places from around the globe, including the time and place of your own life. For Jeffers, this life also meant the life of the land, and Jeffers invited the California coast to seep into him, to become his voice. But he also knew his home lay at the edge of the West, where the restless expanse of technological civilization ran up against the Pacific. Against this civilization, which he compared to a sick microbe, Jeffers inveighed like an Old Testament prophet. He watched as real estate development gobbled up his beloved coast—though tame enough by our standards today, a rash of roads and homes chopped up the old ranches and the remote lifeways of their inhabitants. Jeffers's horror of technological war also led him to adopt an isolationist stance during World War II, a position that turned the tides of taste against him. Bitterness pervades Jeffers's late verse, which waits with misanthropic resignation for what he called "the dance of the / Dream-led masses down the dark mountain."

HAWK TOWER, CARMEL-BY-THE-SEA

WAYFARERS CHAPEL, PALOS VERDES

WAYFARER

Sometime toward the end of the 1940s, the architect Lloyd Wright Jr. stopped for a bite to eat in the redwood-studded hills above Santa Cruz. Though not famous like his father, Frank, Lloyd Wright ran a successful firm in Los Angeles and had recently been commissioned to build a chapel for the Swedenborgian Church on a windswept outcrop in Palos Verdes. From his table, Lloyd Wright gazed through a skylight into towering trees and was struck by the harmony of nature and structure he saw: the clear glass and mosaic sky, the frames and fanning branches. Out of this crystal vision he designed Wayfarers Chapel, perhaps the most intimate ecclesiastical structure in the entire Southland, an adamantine tabernacle of organic design.

Wayfarers Chapel stands on the southern cliffs of Palos Verdes overlooking the sea. When it opened in 1951, the solitary, naked sanctuary stood on a brown and dusty knoll and was called "the Glass Chapel," after Lloyd Wright's dominant material. But as the years passed and the surrounding garden grew, it became clear that the subject of the building is not glass but living things, and that what Lloyd Wright had really built was a tree chapel. Today the sanctuary is flanked on either side by thick stands of coast redwoods, while the window over the altar frames a toyon, which twists with all the bonsai grace of a Craftsman picture frame and blooms with tiny white flowers that give way to red berries. These trees do not just fill in the spaces formed by the angled frames and Y-shaped redwood ribs of the chapel's diamondlike structure. They also create diffuse energetic walls that both contain the sacred space and dissolve the tabernacle into the world outside.

Besides harmonizing structure and environment, Lloyd Wright's chapel also reflects the upbeat nature mysticism of the Swedenborgian Church. Swedenborg believed that God communicates through Earth's beauty, and in one passage of his writings, he compares church architecture to trees. As mentioned earlier, California's first expression of organic sacred architecture was a Swedenborgian sanctuary—San Francisco's Church of the New Jerusalem, headed by the amateur Arts and Crafts architect Joseph Worcester. But while Lloyd Wright belongs in Worcester's lineage of romantic nature mystics, Wayfarers Chapel is a decidedly postwar building: a modern geometric abstraction devoid, for all its berms of naked Palos Verdes stone, of rustic nostalgia. The dominant angles of the chapel, which describe its glass panels as well as the stone flooring and the surrounding grounds, are thirty and sixty degrees—a reflection not of nature's symbolic power but of its underlying design. The chapel is, finally, a work of sacred geometry, a redwood crystal. The only interruption in its angular latticework comes from two circular windows that face each other from atop the entrance and the altar. But these simply serve to round out Lloyd Wright's underlying concept, which he described as "infinite life in infinite space."

Though nothing else matches Wayfarers Chapel, Lloyd Wright built many fine and imaginative homes and gardens, mostly in California; the renderings he left for projects built and unbuilt are particularly gorgeous. Unfortunately, Lloyd Wright was saddled with the name of his father, and the inevitable confusions and comparisons have muffled his sometimes extraordinary work. Though Lloyd Wright's buildings reflected his father's Transcendentalist approach to organic architecture, the son probably surpassed his father in the integration of building and landscape. Lloyd Wright began his career as a landscape architect, working with Olmsted and Olmsted before moving to California around 1913 to take a job with Irving Gill. In 1919, Frank Lloyd Wright gave his son the task of supervising the construction of the fabulous Hollyhock House, an abstract neo-Mayan temple built only blocks away from the enormous Babylonian set that D. W. Griffith had constructed for his film *Intolerance*. On site, Lloyd Wright proved to have inherited some of his father's temper along with his art. After one protracted argument about concrete, a contractor came at Lloyd Wright with an axe, and the architect threw the fellow into an empty pool.

Together with his father, Lloyd Wright developed the system of textile blocks used to such great effect on Frank Lloyd Wright's later homes in the Hollywood Hills. By reinforcing molded concrete blocks with rebar, the Wrights were able to play with mass and abstract pattern on a relatively tight budget. The adobelike earth tones and geometric designs of the four-inch-thick bricks also encouraged both men's self-consciously regional twist on pre-Columbian architecture. Though Frank Lloyd Wright's Ennis House is sometimes characterized as the most exuberant of these Mesoamerican palaces, the home that Lloyd Wright built on Franklin Avenue for John Sowden and his wife in 1926 is easily the wildest of the lot, an Expressionist temple whose primeval exotica makes the visionary aspirations of the Southland's neo-Mayan architecture clear.

The Sowdens were artsy Hollywood folks who liked to party, and Lloyd Wright, who had spent a year or so designing sets for Paramount, indulged their desire for theater. The windowless entranceway lies below a canted cyclopean mass of zigzag rock that hangs like the roof of some antediluvian cave. After climbing a dark stairway, visitors enter the inner sanctum: a long outdoor courtyard lined with concrete columns whose weathered motifs of waves and twining vines deepen the sense that elemental powers are being invoked.

SOWDEN HOUSE, HOLLYWOOD

SPIRIT TO SPIRIT
BOOKS & MUSIC

Two massive freestanding water organs once stood on the far end of the courtyard like murmuring Deco-pagan stelae. Today the courtyard is taken up with a large pool, part of a thorough renovation of the house by designer/owner Xorin Balbes, who enhanced the building's air of almost savage spectacle with an elevated jacuzzi and an altar-like heater. In 2003, Balbes hosted an "interspecies dance ritual" called the Temple of the Cosmic Serpent, which featured fire dancers, stilt walkers, and pas de deux between human beings and boa constrictors.

Lloyd Wright's own brush with the Southland's exotic fringe took place a year or so before he took the Swedenborgian commission, when the architect was approached by a Los Angeles mystic named Ding Le Mei. Ding Le Mei was a remarkable name for a British man to have, but not as remarkable as the fellow's Western moniker, which was Dr. Edwin Dingle. Originally a journalist and publisher, Dr. Dingle had walked across China in 1909 making maps for Sun Yat-sen, and he later claimed to have trekked into Tibet, where he was supposedly recognized as an incarnate lama and schooled by a wonder-working Tibetan sage. In 1927 Dingle moved to Los Angeles, where he founded the Institute of Mentalphysics and began teaching an innovative and vigorous blend of *pranayama,* meditation, and guided visualization. His organization grew, and in 1945, he approached Lloyd Wright with the idea of creating a "City of Mentalphysics" on a high and then-lonesome plateau north of Joshua Tree National Park.

Lloyd Wright wanted to build not an asphalt city but "a city of the Desert—spacious, free sweeping." He envisioned soaring hypermodern monuments set within vast cosmic vistas. Unfortunately, Dingle had trouble getting the money together, and the total design was never realized. Still, the Institute of Mentalphysics remains the largest built complex ever constructed by Lloyd Wright, who designed Dingle's home, an administration building, and various cottages. With their oblique angles, rubble-stone masonry, and long, low lines, these structures settle into the desert like shards of heavy quartz exposed by recent floods. Both Dingle's house and the cafeteria, whose impressively long overhanging eaves resemble honeycombed insect wings, look forward to the jazzy space-faring homes that Lloyd Wright built after Wayfarers Chapel brought him a modicum of fame. Lloyd Wright's largest Mentalphysics building, the deliciously named Caravansery of Joy, induces a pleasant horizontal vertigo with its long diagonal grid.

Lloyd Wright's architecture, so complementary to the high Mojave, has made the Institute of Mentalphysics a favorite retreat center for a handful of spiritual and meditation groups. Unfortunately, Lloyd Wright's most spectacular Mentalphysics designs were confined to his renderings, which the architect continued to work on through the late 1950s, until it became apparent that the manifestation of money was not one of Dingle's esoteric powers. These visionary creations—including the Sanctuary, with its mystic antenna, and the towering Temple of Reverence—were truly cosmic in character. Like some of Lloyd Wright's more flamboyant postwar homes, they arguably shatter the environmental balance so essential to the architect. But they could also be said to express the interstellar essence of the high-desert plateau that cradled the institute, an uncanny land that played a major role in postwar ufology. Lloyd Wright once noted that the region's Joshua trees seemed to stand like sentinels, but he did not say what, exactly, they were on the lookout for.

INSTITUTE OF MENTALPHYSICS,
JOSHUA TREE

PEAK EXPERIENCE

The sight of Mount Shasta lording it over the lesser heights and plains of California's northeast corner can strike a note of cosmic weirdness sounded by few mountains on this earth. Snow-glazed, moonscaped, and often topped with bizarre lenticular clouds, Shasta's near-perfect pyramid appears to have fallen from space or, in one writer's words, to look down on California "like some unblinking, protuberant third eye." For the Shasta, Achumawi, and Wintu tribes, the huge extinct volcano was (and is) a center of sacred power and the site of hosts of legends. In one tale collected from the Shasta, yellowjackets steal salmon from Coyote and hide their booty inside the mountain. Turtle and Coyote try to smoke them out, but the smoke keeps escaping from holes all over the valley—possibly a reference to the volcanic vents, only recently extinct, that line the floor of Shasta Valley to the north.

Unlike many power spots revered by California's first peoples, Shasta never lost its sacred charge, although the vibrations changed considerably as the spiritual imaginations of Californians changed. In the mid-nineteenth century, the peak's mystic imperiousness caught the eye of John Rollin Ridge, a Cherokee journalist and poet who fled to gold rush territory on the heels of a murder rap. Ridge included a poem about Shasta in *The Life and Adventures of Joaquín Murieta,* a popular fictionalized biography of a Californio bandito and the first Native American novel. An educated and assimilated Cherokee, Ridge reframed the aboriginal power spot as a symbol of the Transcendentalist sublime. Comparing the peak to "some mighty unimpassioned mind," Ridge

MOUNT SHASTA, SISKIYOU COUNTY

Shasta Vibrations
Aromatherapy • Bodycare Products
Crystal Essences
400

declared Shasta to be "the great material symbol of eternal / Things!"

Other Americans came to associate the mountain with more fantastic occult forces. In 1883, a disincarnate entity calling himself Phylos the Thibetan took temporary possession of Frederick Spencer Oliver, a Siskiyou County adolescent who began scribbling down Phylos's story. The resulting book, *A Dweller on Two Planets,* describes a jeweled city hidden within Shasta, a hideaway inhabited by a mystical brotherhood from the lost continent of Lemuria. Oliver's vision was the first of many. In 1930, a mining engineer and Theosophy student named Guy Ballard was hiking up the mountainside when, he claimed, he met Count Saint Germain, a mysterious quasi-historical figure who first pops up in the eighteenth-century French court. This "Ascended Master" gave Ballard a sip of a creamy liquid that plugged the engineer into a universal power source, a sort of cosmic battery that Saint Germain claimed could be used to create—or "precipitate"—anything one desired. Saint Germain materialized some gold; then he conjured a sleeping bag. The Master next took Ballard on a whirlwind tour of the West's secret caverns and underground cities, a journey whose most notable feature was treasure: crystal spheres, seven-pointed diamond stars, frosted golden rooms, chests of Spanish bullion covered with hieroglyphs. Through Ballard's visionary eye, the mountain of sacred encounters had fused with the mountain of a miner's greed.

Ballard and his wife, Edna, went on to found the Mighty I AM Religious Activity in Los Angeles. One of the most controversial sects of the day, the movement popularized many of the mystic themes later bandied about by Shirley MacLaine and other New Agers: a color-coded chakra system, a fringe science of electronic vibrations, and an insistence that individuals literally create their own reality. Ballard had spent time in an American Nazi group called the Silver Shirts, and his union-bashing Aryan occultism may have appealed to white Angelenos threatened by the growing racial diversity of the city. But what really struck a chord, especially during the Great Depression, was the Ballards' emphasis on material prosperity. By properly using their prayer batteries, I AM followers could supposedly precipitate cars and iceboxes, not to mention immortal bodies. Unfortunately, Ballard's intimacy with the Mighty I AM Presence did not enable him to dodge death, something he had promised to do. After Ballard succumbed to heart disease in 1939, the lucrative sect came tumbling down, although its remains eventually transmuted into Elizabeth Clare Prophet's apocalyptic Church Universal and Triumphant.

Not all the spiritual masters that Shasta attracted came from the higher planes. Peggy Kennett was a British woman who studied Zen in Japan during the early 1960s. As a Western woman, she was poorly treated by the temple officers but nonetheless experienced *kensho*—an initial awakening—and received formal transmission from the abbot of Sojiji in 1963. Returning to England to teach, Kennett found Buddhists there hankering for a "real" (i.e., Japanese) Zen master. So Kennett moved, like so many religious misfits, to California, founding Shasta Abbey in a former motel that lay at the foot of the mountain. In the mid-1970s, Kennett experienced a powerful series of forty-three visions over a nine-month period. These visions, which the abbess compared to the classic ox-herding pictures of Zen, fused Buddhist and Christian symbolism, and help explain the air of Christian monasticism that permeates the abbey, where Buddhist chants sound like high-church hymns and monks practice mandatory celibacy. This last requirement, which rocked Shasta Abbey when Kennett demanded it in the years following her visions, is very unusual in Western Zen, and may have something to do with the somewhat moribund air of the present abbey.

The Buddhadharma permeates Mount Shasta in even less orthodox ways. Every spring since 1995, Dr. Joshua David Stone, of the Melchizedek Synthesis Light Academy, has sponsored the weeklong holiday of Wesak. Officially Wesak marks the Buddha's birthday, but in the environs of Shasta it has become a great festival of the New Age movement, where a few thousand channelers, UFO devotees, and other graying crystal folk gather to trade tales of magnetic-pole shifts and twelve-stranded DNA. Given the overall waning of the channeling scene, the festival must owe its vitality to the mountain, a Mecca of higher frequencies on a par with Sedona and the Hawaiian island of Kauai. The very contours and weather patterns of the landscape inspire visionary claims about vortex energies and alien civilizations hidden beneath the ground. Particularly uncanny are the saucer-shaped clouds that often crown the mountain, fleecy cones that look like portals to another world. But Shasta's most cosmic aspect remains the simple fact of the mountain, present but beyond itself, a material symbol of something none of us can name.

SHASTA VIBRATIONS, MOUNT SHASTA

OM GATE, RAMAKRISHNA MONASTERY, TRABUCO CANYON

GO EAST

LAND OF THE SETTING SUN

To the white folks pushing westward across the American continent in the nineteenth century, the final encounter with California's shores meant the end of the frontier. But this geographic fact held a different, more expansive lesson as well, because the coastline was also looped into the Pacific Rim, that vast circle of grinding volcanic shore that rings the planet's largest ocean with fire and igneous rock. In the case of California, geography is indeed destiny, for the Golden State would help stage one of the most fascinating cultural confrontations of the modern age: the encounter of East and West, in thought, culture, and spirit. Though this encounter has occured in countless ways and places, Californians have played a major role in the story, especially in their creative commingling of Asian and Western religious impulses.

In Europe, as on the East Coast of the United States, the initial encounter with Far Eastern cultures took place in the context of colonial rule and global trade. Gold rush California provided a very different kind of stage, as tens of thousands of mainland Chinese, mostly young male peasants from the southern province of Guangdong, set their sights on the same shiny nuggets that beckoned Bavarians and Chileans and Turks. Before the completion of the transcontinental railroad, California was easier to reach from China than from most anywhere else, and by the end of the 1850s, roughly one out of ten Californians was Chinese. They brought farming and mining techniques that contributed to the state's growth, and proved quite successful at placer mining throughout the western territories. Despite—or because of—their success, the "Celestials" were not particularly welcome on Gold Mountain, and they faced a rising tide of racist attacks and official discrimination. Amid their suffering and resolve, the Chinese also planted spiritual seeds in California's rootless soil—ideas, practices, and gods that would not only help their communities survive and prosper, but would also mutate into a new dharma that was neither East nor West: a California Tao.

The first waves of Chinese immigrants were mostly Taoists. They practiced a folk religion of divination, ancestral remembrance, and ritual devotion to various life-enhancing gods and immortals. Wherever Chinese communities would form, small "joss houses" would be built—*joss* being a pidgin version of the Portuguese word *deos,* or god. These humble temples sprouted up throughout California, especially in the North, and a handful of them survive today in varying states of repair. The temple in the former Gold Country town of Aurora is hardly more than a weathered shack, while the rustic Won Lim Miu, its ornate wooden exterior restored in the 1950s, forms the nucleus of a state park near the northern town of Weaverville. One of the most venerable halls is the Bok Kai Miu in the Yuba County town of Marysville. Once falling apart, the brick temple and its haunting, pale blue murals have recently been restored—an effort financed in part, it is rumored, by Chinese mobsters from San Francisco. The site of continuous worship since 1880, Bok Kai Miu is also the only remaining Taoist temple in Northern California to host Bomb Day, a winter festival that features a golden dragon and feisty explosives. Bok Kai, the central god of this "Palace of Many Saints," rules over water; his presence here, where the temple directly faces a levee, probably reflects the flooding that frequently threatened Marysville's Chinese community, forced to live, like so many Chinese in California, on floodplains and other unwanted land.

The most popular god among the early Cantonese immigrants was Kuan Yu, a historical figure known for his military valor and fidelity to justice and honor; today his cult remains strong among cops, criminals, and businessmen. One of the old warrior's oldest temples lies in the coastal logging town of Mendocino. Documents date the Kwan Tai Miu to 1882, when a few hundred Chinese lived in and logged the forests along the coast, but the Chinese family that restored and currently maintains the tiny temple traces

KWAN TAI TEMPLE, MENDOCINO

義德同天
廟貌巍巍忠精昭日月
氣塞天地能配天

its origins back to 1854, shortly after their ancestor Lee Sing John arrived from China. Nine red steps, designed to frustrate evil spirits, lead up to a porch attached to a plain green building topped with a gable roof and wrapped in green redwood siding. The Kwan Tai Miu has only two rooms: a priest's room and a simple hall of worship, whose two altar tables hold incense burners, candle holders, oracle books, and divination sticks; here men and women offer prayers to the gods and the gone. Kuan Yu, painted on the back wall, looks out the windows onto the sea, which the Chinese had safely crossed and, according to the wall texts, hoped to pass over again on their return journey.

The folk religion practiced in places like Kwan Tai Miu and Bok Kai Miu was a far cry from the organic mysticism of Lao-tzu or the madcap anarchism of Chuang-tzu, two early Taoist philosophers who would prove tremendously popular among the beatniks and hippies of later days. Nonetheless, through a kind of diasporic geomancy, the early Chinese workers introduced the Tao to the California landscape, establishing channels where very different seekers would later find their own ways to go with the flow. Some of these early Chinese temples also contained idols of an Eastern religion that would have an even stronger impact on California consciousness: Buddhism. A typical joss house might contain statues of Shakyamuni, the historical founder of Buddhism, as well as Amitabha and Maitreya, the future Buddha. Many contained images of Kuan Yin, a goddess known to the original Mahayanists as the many-armed Avalokiteshvara, but whose white and flowing Chinese form remains the most recognizable avatar of this bodhisattva of compassion.

ABOVE: BOK KAI TEMPLE, MARYSVILLE

LEFT: ALTAR HALL, BOK KAI TEMPLE, MARYSVILLE

Before the close of the nineteenth century, California was already sprouting its own homegrown Buddhas. In the hills above Santa Cruz, a Swedenborgian named Herman C. Vetterling started publishing America's first Buddhist magazine, *The Buddhist Ray,* in 1888. A typesetter, homeopathic practitioner, and self-professed pagan who mocked the elite "Aryan Buddhists" of Boston, Vetterling birthed a new tone in the dharma of the West. In the words of historian Rick Fields, Vetterling was ironic, saucy, and self-assured—in other words, "one-hundred-percent American Buddhist." He praised the Buddha's religious individualism because "it does not insult the Human Soul by placing mediators between it and the Divine Spirit." A vegetarian, Vetterling was strongly opposed to vivisection and later in life contributed fifty thousand dollars to an animal shelter in San Jose.

Four years after Vetterling began his chatty dharma almanac, a seventy-foot-tall Buddha was erected south of Marin's Mount Tamalpais, in a shady enclave of coastal redwood now known as Muir Woods. This lath-and-plaster statue, loosely modeled after the enormous seated Daibutsu statue in Kamakura, Japan, was constructed by the Bohemian Club for the ritualistic performances that capped their annual summer gathering. Today the Bohemian Club's yearly convocation takes place fifty miles north in Sonoma County's Bohemian Grove, a camp that lies just south of the Russian River. Here some of the country's richest and most powerful men come to blow off steam, schmooze, and inspire the inevitable conspiracy theories. In the 1890s, the Bohemian Club consisted largely of San Francisco businessmen and a few bona fide bohemians, holdovers from the crew of artists and vagabonds who first founded the group in 1872. Photographs of the Daibutsu in Muir Woods, in a vale also named Bohemian Grove, show these wealthy white men garbed in Orientalist regalia, installed beneath a massive meditating figure whose pale physiognomy betrays a chubby, strangely patrician character.

Following the Bohemian Club's summer fete of 1892, the Daibutsu statue was left to molder, and by the late 1920s it had effectively returned to forest mulch—a fitting end for our planet's great teacher of impermanence. But other big Buddhas would soon find themselves looming over San Francisco. A more faithful Daibutsu was constructed for the 1915 Panama-Pacific Exposition's Japanese Pavilion, which also provided the narrow five-tiered pagoda that presently sits in Golden Gate Park's Japanese Tea Garden, the first public Japanese garden in the New World. Following World War II, San Francisco's S. & G. Gump Company, purveyors of fine domestic design objects, presented this same garden with a massive three-thousand-pound bronze Buddha raising his right hand in a *mudra,* or sacred gesture, spelling "no fear." Originally cast on the Japanese island of Honshu in 1790, the figure is known as Amazarashi-No-Hotoke—"the Buddha who sits through sun and rain without a shelter." One hopes this homeless dharma king embraces fog with equal equanimity.

The still presence of the Gump Buddha, as well as Nagao Sakurai's moderately engaging modern Zen rock garden, signals the spiritual call that draws Asians and Yankees alike to the Japanese garden—a call that would become a long, loud chant during the postwar boom in American Buddhism. But the sacred mazes of the Japanese garden inevitably become garbled and transformed when their organic intricacies are grafted onto new political and cultural terrain. Today's Japanese Tea Garden is almost exclusively a domain for tourists, who traipse about a lovely origami nest of pools and pine that signifies San Francisco as much as it signifies Japan. This bonsai wonderland is also, by some accounts, the origin of the ultimate American artifact of concocted Chinese culture: the fortune cookie. Nor did the garden survive the anti-Japanese fervor of World War II unscathed. During the war, the spot was briefly renamed the Oriental Tea Garden, and its elaborate Shinto shrine was carted off and replaced with the pagoda, which earlier stood sixty feet away. (Baron Makoto Hagiwara, the wealthy Japanese man who created the garden, was carted off as well.) Today's garden therefore features the peculiar sight of a *torii,* or Shinto gate, set before a Buddhist treasure tower—one of many oddball juxtapositions that mark the California Tao.

GUMP BUDDHA, JAPANESE TEA GARDEN, SAN FRANCISCO

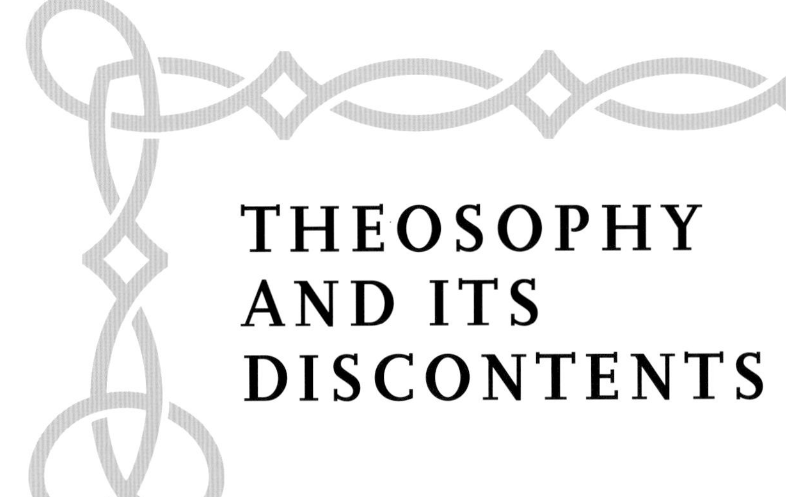

THEOSOPHY AND ITS DISCONTENTS

In 1897, the population of San Diego hovered around seventeen thousand people. In February of that year, nearly a thousand of these souls climbed on their bicycles and buggies and made the dusty trek out to Point Loma, a craggy, windswept finger of rock that thrusts into the Pacific, forming the northern entrance to San Diego Bay. They came to witness Katherine Tingley, a middle-aged woman from the eastern United States, lay the cornerstone for the School for the Revival of the Lost Mysteries of Antiquity. Tingley claimed the school would be "a temple of living light, lighting up the dark places of the earth." Robed in her trademark purple, Tingley anointed the perfectly square cornerstone with oil and wine as her followers read portions of the Bhagavad Gita, the Upanishads, and the Orphic mysteries.

Tingley had recently become head of a major branch of the Theosophical Society, an organization cofounded in New York in 1875 by Colonel Henry Olcott and a cigar-smoking Russian trickster named Madame Blavatsky. Weaving together occult Neoplatonism, parapsychology, and Eastern lore, Theosophy was the most influential mystical organization of the nineteenth century. Theosophy helped introduce Buddhism and yoga to the West, even as Blavatsky's writings attempted to connect the universal truths of mysticism with the latest ideas in science, including Darwin's concept of human evolution. Blavatsky believed that humanity had descended from a series of "root races," including the Lemurians and the residents of Atlantis, and that humanity was beginning to mutate into a new and superior "sixth race." In *The Secret Doctrine,* she argued that this transformation would occur in America. Annie Besant, who later controlled a branch of the society, headquartered in India, believed it would happen in Southern California; Besant claimed that the finest magnetic vibrations in the world were to be found in Pasadena. In some ways both women were right: California would become a major player in the history of Theosophy, and a principal stage in the New Age movement that emerged from its womb.

Despite her mystic trappings, Tingley was essentially a social reformer. She wanted her community to be less an occult brotherhood than an educational center, an example to the world, and to future Californians, that self-development and unselfish service went hand in hand. Tingley liked to cite a passage from Walt Whitman in which the poet describes an imagined community—"say in some pleasant western settlement or town"—where "in every young and old man, after his kind, and in every woman after hers, a true personality developed, exercised proportionately in body, mind, and spirit." Tingley hoped to achieve this through Raja Yoga, a training program that emphasized music, dance, and self-discipline. The first word that young children learned to spell in the community's schools was *attention*—the same word that the mynah bird squawks in Aldous Huxley's 1962 novel *Island,* where the bird serves to remind the inhabitants of Huxley's fictional Utopia to awaken to the moment.

By 1907, Tingley's San Diego community had grown to five hundred people inhabiting nearly as many acres. The area was dominated by the Temple and the Academy, two magnificent buildings whose wooden exteriors were stuccoed to resemble stone facing. Their huge aquamarine and amethyst domes were topped by large glass spheres, which were crowned in turn by pinnacles shaped like flaming hearts, illuminated day and night. The lush surrounding gardens produced half the fruit and vegetables the community consumed, and included new strains of avocados that helped spur the state's growing avo industry. The property also included an Egyptian gate, cliffside residential communities named Camp Karnak and Esotero, and a nine-hole golf course in honor of Tingley's major benefactor, the sporting-goods king Albert Spalding. Spalding's home, with its modest amethyst crown, is one of the few structures from the community that still stands; today it houses administrative offices of the property's current owner, the Point Loma Nazarene University.

SPALDING RESIDENCE/MIERAS HALL, LOMALAND/POINT LOMA NAZARENE UNIVERSITY, SAN DIEGO

Dubbed Lomaland by the locals, Tingley's community became one of sleepy San Diego's main tourist attractions, an early theme park of the spirit. Besides the curious architecture and smartly uniformed inhabitants, visitors were drawn by Lomaland's lovely Greek Theater, the first built in the state. A spare Doric temple that still stands between a large outdoor amphitheater and the Pacific Ocean blue, the theater confirmed a feeling shared by many Californians at the turn of the century: the sense that their state, so Mediterranean in climate, might produce a new Attic culture. Tingley tapped this innocuous pagan current by mounting popular productions of Aeschylus and Shakespeare, along with original productions like *The Conquest of Death* and the peculiarly titled *The Aroma of Athens*—stagy "symposia" heavy on costumes and metaphysics.

Lomaland's good standing with San Diegans did not prevent the *Los Angeles Times,* led by the malfeasant and reactionary Harrison Gray Otis, from claiming that Tingley starved children and forcibly separated families. The *Times* also accused her of organizing "midnight pilgrimages" that led to "gross immoralities," although one of the pilgrimages in question consisted of little more than toga-clad Theosophists eating fruit and listening to Tingley discuss the unusual mental powers of Spot, her cocker spaniel. Otis's accusations aside, many community members became alienated by Tingley's autocratic manners, financial mismanagement, and decisive shift away from occult and psychic powers. Following Tingley's death in 1929, the community declined. When the U.S. Navy took up sustained firing practice off the coast, the remonstrations of Lomaland failed to stop the bad vibrations, which loosened the colored glass of the colony's famous domes and forced it to remove the illuminated heart pinnacles.

Lomaland was not California's only experiment in Theosophical community. The Temple of the People set up its headquarters in Halcyon, near Pismo Beach, while another group of Theosophists, led by Albert Powell Warrington and allied with Tingley's rival Annie Besant, founded the Krotona colony in the Hollywood Hills in the early 1910s. Named after an ancient Pythagorean enclave, Krotona emphasized more esoteric and Hindu lore than Lomaland. Though the buildings were generally less spectacular, many still exude the musky tang of exotica. The Krotona Court, now an apartment complex, housed visitors around a classic Southern California patio courtyard, complete with a lotus pond and an arbor. Topping the building's eastern wing was the Esoteric Room, a

MOORCREST, KROTONA, HOLLYWOOD

ABOVE: FORMER GRAND TEMPLE OF THE ROSY CROSS, KROTONA, HOLLYWOOD

RIGHT: OAK GROVE, OJAI

small dome outfitted with Moorish doors and windows where colony members gathered for group meditations. A few floors below sat the cafeteria, where folks munched on vegetarian fare, including, on one occasion, a Thanksgiving "turkey" composed of lima beans, corn flakes, and eggs. Nearby stood the Grand Temple of the Rosy Cross, a bulky Moorish hall now subdivided into apartments; its western facade still boasts an art-glass window emblazoned with a Rosicrucian seal.

Like countless developments in the greater Los Angeles area, Krotona marketed and sold lots with the promise of a new life bundled in with the usual guarantees of water and electricity. Early ads, which appeared in the group's organ *The Theosophic Messenger,* proclaimed Krotona "the modern Athens" and assured potential buyers that they would suffer neither fog nor dust nor frost. By 1917, the colony had nearly one hundred members, and a number of them began building private homes nearby, some of which were intended for rental or sale. With its Cinderella spires and medieval fenestration, Moorcrest, at 6147 Temple Drive, is the most fanciful of these homes; the building, which has been extensively renovated, was designed by an amateur architect and Theosophist named Marie Russak Hotchener, who rented the home to Charlie Chaplin and later served as the personal astrologer to actor John Barrymore. Hollywood's boom years were good for Krotona's real estate speculators, but urban encroachment threatened the colony's peace and quiet. In 1924, Warrington moved Krotona to the remote Ojai Valley, a dry green oasis whose name is Chumash for *nest* or *moon.* One Theosophist described the valley as "Italy, the Riviera, and the best part of India rolled into one." Ojai was also beloved by Annie Besant, who made it the home of her Happy Valley School—an alternative high school, designed to nurture the coming sixth race, that is still thriving today as an arts-oriented college prep school.

Ojai would play a particularly transformative role in the life of J. Krishnamurti, the most significant teacher to emerge from Theosophy in the twentieth century. In 1909, the fourteen-year-old Krishnamurti was just a kid playing with his brother on a beach in southern India when his aura caught the eye of Charles Leadbeater, a Theosophical leader and probable pederast who had already gotten in trouble for teaching young boys to masturbate. Though Krishnamurti was an indifferent student with a somewhat vacant demeanor, the middle-class Brahmin boy was recognized by Leadbeater and Besant as the human vessel for the coming World Teacher—the Theosophical equivalent of the Messiah. Raised like a raja, Krishnamurti was soon traveling the world with Besant, lecturing as head of the Order of the Star.

In the early 1920s, Krishnamurti and his brother Nitya bought a small ranch house in Ojai, which they dubbed Arya Vihara. Like so many incoming Californians, they were drawn by the promise of health: Nitya had tuberculosis, and they hoped that Ojai's climate, hot and dry, would work wonders on the young man's lungs. The brothers also employed an electrical machine invented by Albert Abrams, a San Francisco doctor who founded the fringe science of radionics; the Oscilloclast was supposed to resonate at the same frequency as disease and destroy it. While in Ojai on retreat with Nitya in the summer of 1922, Krishnamurti underwent a series of convulsive pains and astral journeys that culminated in an overwhelming experience of "God-intoxication" beneath a pepper tree. He encountered Maitreya, and the invisible Master Koot Hoomi. After this psychospiritual crisis—whose considerable physical pain Krishnamurti could alleviate only by resting his head on the lap of his young female nurse—the Messiah became a different sort of fellow, one who often referred to himself and his body in the third person. Leadbeater believed the young man was physically evolving into an example of the sixth root race.

Though continuing to tour as the future World Teacher, Krishnamurti began to question Theosophy, and in 1929, he left the society and publicly dissolved the Order of the Star. He was not just turning his back on Theosophy's esoteric folderol of spiritual grades and invisible astral Masters. He was rejecting the whole notion of mystical schools and proscribed spiritual practices, even the very notion of the guru. He proclaimed that the spiritual search cannot be organized, that "truth is a pathless land." Though liberating to some, Krishnamurti's message of radical freedom and "choiceless awareness" was no warmer than its bearer, a small, thin man who in talks often spat out his words and chopped the air with his hands. His astringent message introduced a powerful existential dimension to modern spirituality; exposure to Krishnamurti convinced many seekers that the Way is made only by walking on it, at which point it disappears.

Despite the paradoxes inherent in following his teachings, Krishnamurti proved a popular anti-guru guru. He hobnobbed with Hollywood celebrities, became close friends with Aldous Huxley and the physicist David Bohm, and helped inspire the spiritual anarchism that lay beneath so much hippie mysticism. Throughout his life, he kept Ojai as his home base, and the area became a mecca for wandering souls, strange sects, and metaphysical centers like the Ojai Institute. By the time he died in 1986, Krishnamurti annually drew thousands of seekers to his spring talks, held outside at Oak Grove. Though too depersonalized to identify with any one place, Krishnamurti nonetheless expressed a deeply Californian sense of spiritual rootlessness, a rootlessness that embraced endless process rather than specific goals. "The journey within oneself must be undertaken not for a result, not to solve conflict and sorrow; for the search itself is devotion."

HARE RAMAKRISHNA

Technically speaking, the Vedanta Society Old Temple that stands on the corner of Webster and Filbert Streets, in San Francisco's Cow Hollow district, is a Queen Anne building. It has bay windows, ornamental brackets, and the standard mix of frilly wall textures. But instead of the cantilevered gables that usually top these painted ladies, the building sprouts a jumble of storybook Orientalist towers that surmount a long enclosed balcony with a lacy Moorish frieze. Certainly the most surreal religious landmark in the city, the temple was designed by Swami Trigunatita, an Indian spiritual leader who arrived in San Francisco in 1903 to run the local chapter of the Vedanta Society. When the temple opened in 1905, Trigunatita advertised it as "the First Hindu Temple in the Whole Western World." But already the building and the spiritual group it represented were almost as American as they were Hindu.

The origins of the Vedanta Society lie with Ramakrishna, one of India's greatest modern saints and an incandescent font of spiritual energy. Born to a peasant family in 1836, Ramakrishna lived almost his entire life in Bengal, where his passionate and unorthodox devotion to the goddess Kali attracted scores of followers. Ramakrishna frequently lapsed into intense states of bliss; one of his disciples once said that "he belongs to the country where there is no night." Ramakrishna embraced elements of Islam and Christianity, welcomed bohemian reprobates from the city into his retinue, and was fond of occasionally donning women's clothes. Ramakrishna's eclectic, ecstatic, and gender-bending style makes him an unofficial California saint, although the Vedanta Society itself came to America through the work of Ramakrishna's main disciple, Swami Vivekananda. A far more accessible figure than Ramakrishna, Vivekananda wowed the crowds at Chicago's epochal Parliament of Religions in 1893 with an eminently reasonable and modern brand of Vedic mind science that emphasized the nondualistic unity of spirit and the world. A handsome, lively, and fiercely intelligent man, Vivekananda traveled across the United States, good-heartedly attacking Christian concepts like sin while planting seeds of Vedanta, including the society in San Francisco.

Like Vivekananda, Trigunatita was a take-charge kind of guy, known for enforcing disciplinary rigor and barking out maxims like "Do it now." In 1904, despite the small numbers of students the society attracted in Gilded Age San Francisco, Trigunatita purchased a sand lot near the bay for eighteen hundred dollars, and started building a temple the following year. Working with a local architect, Trigunatita designed the temple himself. Giving an ecumenical spin to the eclecticism of Victorian architecture, Trigunatita wrote that his building "may be considered as a combination of a Hindu temple, a Christian church, a Mohammedan mosque, a Hindu *math* or monastery, and an American residence." The windows and balcony are Moorish in design, while the towers draw from scattered sacred structures in India, including the Taj Mahal. Trigunatita based the bulbous corner tower on the Shiva lingam, and alludes to the sexual dynamics of Tantra in a pamphlet he wrote about the temple's architecture. Trigunatita also included the crenellated tower of a European castle, which supposedly had something to do with "strength of character." The finished structure was strong enough to weather the 1906 earthquake and fire, and it also survived a bomb attack by one of Trigunatita's former students, a disgruntled and possibly mad young man who died in the explosion that also mortally wounded his former guru.

Trigunatita's crazy quilt of a temple must be seen in the light of the Vedanta Society's universalist philosophy. Like Theosophy, the society presented Eastern ideas and practices as modern, nonsectarian solutions to the sometimes violent conflict between religions, not to mention the growing battle between religion and science. Similarly, his temple attempts to integrate various paths into a harmonized

VEDANTA SOCIETY OLD TEMPLE, SAN FRANCISCO

MOORISH BALCONY, VEDANTA SOCIETY
OLD TEMPLE, SAN FRANCISCO

whole. The thousand-petaled lotus canopy that hangs over the outside entrance to the auditorium refers esoterically to the central psychic channel stimulated by Kundalini yoga, although in this instance the lotus is topped with an American eagle. Trigunatita's eclecticism is thus an early and distinctly Californian affirmation of East-West multiculturalism and spiritual *bricolage*. After all, if you truly believe that there is more than one path to God, then sacred reality is by necessity kaleidoscopic. Some of California's vernacular religious architecture, often written off as kitschy exotica, attempts to manifest this kaleidoscopic perspective. East plants itself in the far West, and what sprouts up is a hybrid flower with a thousand and one petals.

The Vedanta Society's later course in San Francisco was unremarkable. The same cannot be said of its sister center in the Hollywood Hills, which was founded by Swami Prabhavananda in 1930. In those days, Los Angeles was packed with self-proclaimed swamis—mostly turban-wearing hucksters who drew up astrological charts and sold nut burgers and electricity pills. Prabhavananda, on the other hand, was a mild and unpretentious Indian man who largely dropped the trappings of the East. He chain-smoked, wore sweaters and slacks, and enjoyed dragging his monks to the movies on a regular basis. Prabhavananda ran a fairly loose ship, with men and women mingling freely; the swami was also the first leader in the Vedanta Society to bring women into the fold. His temple itself was relatively simple, a whitewashed lecture hall topped with three of the bulbous Mogul domes that have become, through the fame of the Taj Mahal, India's supreme architectural device.

Prabhavananda's laid-back ways attracted Hollywood stars like Tyrone Power and Greta Garbo, one of the most indefatigable seekers in Tinseltown. The swami also intrigued the British expatriate writers Aldous Huxley and Christopher Isherwood, as well as the lesser-known Gerald Heard, all of whom played pivotal roles in Los Angeles's postwar spiritual boom. Heard and Huxley never became Prabhavananda's students; Huxley preferred the less devotional Krishnamurti, while Heard, who consistently meditated six hours a day, rejected Prabhavananda for being too lax. But Isherwood, a penetrating if sometimes narcissistic writer of quasi-autobiographical fictions and later a gay icon, became Prabhavananda's devoted student and an active participant in the Vedanta Society. In the closing years of World War II, Isherwood lived as a monk at the center, and his frank and witty writings about his experience—as well as his decision to return, with guns blazing, to the fleshpots of Los Angeles—reflect a peculiarly Californian tension between asceticism and hedonism.

Like Huxley and Heard, Isherwood was a pacifist who moved to Los Angeles in the 1930s to escape the war; he and Huxley both wrote screenplays for a living. At first, Isherwood mocked the budding spiritual interests of his two friends, but after talking with Heard, he decided to experiment with quiet sitting and grew fascinated with the opportunity to face the unknown inside himself. When he met Prabhavananda, he told the swami that he had always discounted meditation as mumbo jumbo. Prabhavananda just laughed: "And now you have fallen into the trap?" Isherwood went on to write a good deal about Vedanta; he helped Prabhavananda translate the Bhagavad Gita and Patanjali's Yoga Sutras, and he wrote a limpid if tame biography of Ramakrishna. In these texts we hear a strong note of the pragmatism that characterized the hands-on, empirical temperament of much California spirituality. "Religion is, in fact, a severely practical and empirical kind of research," wrote the two men in their commentary on the Yoga Sutras. "You take nothing on trust. You accept nothing but your own experience. You go forward alone, step by step, like an explorer in a virgin jungle, to see what you will find."

Isherwood plunged into this jungle, meditating and praying and practicing hatha yoga with Indra Devi, one of the pioneers of the form in America. But he could never reconcile his religious devotions with his love of alcohol or his attraction to the bronzed Adonises of Santa Monica. Part of what drew Isherwood to Vedanta was its lack of sin-based moral condemnation and its implication that body and soul were ultimately one. He was also attracted to Ramakrishna's own gender play, though he did not believe, as some scholars suggest today, that the master was homosexual. But Isherwood never outed himself to his teacher. For a long spell after he left the monastery, he drank like a fish and cruised Santa Monica's gay bars, eventually settling into a lifelong relationship with the artist Don Bachardy, whom he met at the beach. Isherwood never abandoned his inner devotion to Prabhavananda or the Vedantic spirit of nondualism, and indeed was perhaps most spiritual—or at least most Californian—when he gave up his robes without giving up his search.

Once, walking on Santa Monica Beach with Garbo, Isherwood glimpsed the deep dynamic that runs through desire, the spirit, and the luscious body of the world:

> The sun was brilliant, with a strong wind—the palms waving all along the cliff, and the ocean dazzling with light and foam. The air was full of spray and falling light; it was beautiful beyond all words. The afternoon had an edge of extra-keen, almost intolerable sensation on all its sights and sounds and smells. Seeing a human body in the far distance, you wanted to seize it in your arms and devour it—not for itself, but as a palpable fragment of the whole scene, of the wildness of the wind and foam, of the entire unseizable mystery and delight of the moment. I glimpsed something, for an instant, of the reality behind sex. Something which we reach out toward, as we take the human body in our arms. It is what we really want, and it eludes us in the very act of possession.

For Isherwood, this slippery vision revealed the central gambit of California's spiritual hedonism: that the search for sensation, in its very hunger and evanescence, opens up the unseizable mystery that lies beyond all form, all satisfaction.

VEDANTA TEMPLE, HOLLYWOOD

Self-Realization
Fellowship
Founded by Paramahansa Yogananda

SWAMI'S

At the dawn of the twentieth century, when Mukunda Lal Ghosh was studying at his master Sri Yukteswar's ashram near Calcutta, the young man often had visions of three buildings: a sylvan retreat on a plain, another on a faraway hilltop, and another by a distant sea. One day, Yukteswar's mystic eye picked up these floating images, and the teacher told Mukunda that these were institutions he would one day build. After becoming a monk in the Swami Order in 1915 and taking the name Yogananda, the young seeker—the privileged son of a senior railway executive—did indeed found a boys' yoga school in Ranchi, which lies on a high plateau in the Indian state of Jharkhand. But the rest of Yogananda's vision would not be realized until Yukteswar sent him to the United States, where the charismatic pop Vedantist became America's first superstar guru.

Yogananda did well on the East Coast, packing the halls with accessible lectures about the "science of yoga" and his unique approach to universal religion, which combined cosmic Hindu idealism with liberal Christian morality. After a successful cross-country tour in 1924, Yogananda decided to settle down in Southern California, where he soon founded the Self-Realization Fellowship. When asked why he chose Los Angeles, Yogananda replied that he considered the city to be the most spiritual place in the country, the Benares of America—Benares being the holiest city in India, where pilgrims from across the country go to die. Though Los Angeles lacked the burning ghats and corpse-choked river of the ancient Indian city, the boomtown of the early 1920s did have a surfeit of seekers—for spirituality and real estate alike. Yogananda excelled at both pursuits. On the hunt for a suitable property for the Self-Realization Fellowship, Yogananda drove by Washington Estates, a once trendy hotel that crowned the peak of Highland Park's Mount Washington and had gone to seed. Yogananda recalled his second vision and, discovering that the estate had just been placed on the market, prepared to pay the asking price of sixty-five thousand dollars. But he balked at the last moment, later explaining that God had stayed his hand "because He wanted me to have the property for less money." Yogananda managed to pick up the estate, which still houses the administrative offices of the Self-Realization Fellowship, for forty-five thousand dollars cash.

Yogananda spent the next decade building his institution, traveling, and teaching meditation. Like many neo-Hindu teachers of the time, Yogananda stressed the modernity of the mystic way, proclaiming the global unity of religions and linking scientific invention with spiritual forces. He compared the sound of *om* to a cosmic motor, and the third eye to a broadcasting station. Cinema was, for him, the perfect illustration of the Vedantist claim that the material world was a passing illusion woven from waves of energy. Yogananda also taught "scientific techniques" to attain God consciousness, a practical system of energy work he called Kriya Yoga. Yogananda's gentle showmanship and promise of personal realization proved popular, attracting students like the conductor Leopold Stokowski, the ubiquitous Garbo, and W. Y. Evans-Wentz, the San Diegan who first translated *The Tibetan Book of the Dead* into English.

In 1935, Yukteswar called Yogananda back to India. When the long-haired guru returned to California a year and half later, he found his third vision fulfilled. A disciple named James Lynn, who had racked up millions as a Kansas City railroad man before his spiritual rebirth as Rajarsi Janakananda, gave seventeen acres of gorgeous cliffside property in Encinitas to his master. Located about twenty-five miles north of San Diego, the Self-Realization Fellowship Ashram came to include a large hermitage, sun-flecked groves and arbors, and two solitary meditation caves built into a crumbly bluff that overlooked a dollop of beach. Today this beach is home to surfers plying the point break known as Swami's, while above, in the ashram's mellow meditation gardens, landscaped by Yogananda himself,

SELF-REALIZATION FELLOWSHIP, ENCINITAS

visitors stroll about a succulent refuge of flowers, palms, bent Monterey cypresses, and koi ponds. But the site's most amazing landmark, the Golden Lotus Temple, is long gone. Placed to drink in the view of the vast Pacific, the cliffside temple included an open rooftop, immense windows, and a four-story octagonal glass tower. The temple was topped with the large golden lotuses that serve as the Self-Realization Fellowship's architectural logo; locals compared the landmark to the Taj Mahal. But in California, the call of the cliff is the call of a siren, and in 1942, a landslide caused the temple to slip from its foundation. Yogananda's acolytes managed to save some of the temple, but the main structure eventually tumbled into the sea, leaving little more than the terrazzo steps still visible today.

Hunkered down in his private cottage at the ashram or enjoying his secluded cliffside pool, Yogananda withdrew from his boisterous public life. He puttered about the gardens, fed the fish by the Ming Tree—an old transplanted Monterey pine cultivated as a bonsai—and designed the three squat towers that line the coast highway. Yogananda was living in Encinitas when he wrote *Autobiography of a Yogi,* a classic of pop spirituality that weaves together mystic yarns, homey religious sentiments, and well-placed plugs for Kriya Yoga, whose methods are often mentioned but never described. One of the most popular texts of the mystic counterculture to come, Yogananda's autobiography highlights the author's amazing psychic experiences rather than his philosophical ideas; these cinematic description of "cosmic consciousness" whetted all but the most quotidian of spiritual appetites, helping to reaffirm the central role of personal experience within California consciousness.

Autobiography of a Yogi also includes Yogananda's story of his three early visions, though I suspect he would have told the tale differently had he known that his greatest landscape lay before him. The Lake Shrine in Pacific Palisades opened to the public in 1950 and remains a hidden jewel of west Los Angeles, tucked away in the Santa Ynez Canyon at the sunset end of Sunset Boulevard, a quarter mile from the Malibu coast. Originally a silent-movie site, the area was partially graded for development in the 1920s. The unfinished job left a large depression that filled with water from the local springs, forming a mucky, weedy pond thick with reeds and cattails. The property was purchased in 1940 by Everett McElroy, who cleared weeds and dredged the lake before shaping waterfalls, flower beds, and fern

GOLDEN LOTUS TEMPLE STEPS, SELF-REALIZATION FELLOWSHIP, ENCINITAS

THE GOLDEN LOTUS TEMPLE
This is the site of the Golden
Lotus Temple, built in 1937.
Here thousands came to services
conducted by Paramahansa
Yogananda.
The Guru designed the temple
to take advantage of magnificent
views of sea and sky. At its
dedication he said:
"The Golden Lotus Temple of
all religions is dedicated to the
ideal of brotherhood and non-
sectarian worship of our
One Father."

SELF-REALIZATION FELLOWSHIP LAKE SHRINE, PACIFIC PALISADES

gullies out of the hillsides. A manager of set construction at 20th Century Fox Studios, McElroy introduced more than a few tricks of the trade to his garden wonderland. He added a landing and a diminutive Mississippi houseboat to the lake and built what the present guidebook to the property describes as an "authentic reproduction" of a sixteenth-century Dutch windmill.

McElroy sold the property in the late 1940s to an oil executive. According to Self-Realization Fellowship lore, the oilman awoke one night shortly thereafter, having dreamed of a large group of people gathering at his lake to worship at a "Church of All Religions." The man got out of bed, grabbed a phone book, and came across the Self-Realization Fellowship Church of All Religions in Hollywood. He subsequently sold the property to Yogananda, who added a spiritual—but no less Hollywood—dimension to McElroy's landscape. The hillsides and grottoes became populated with statues of Jesus, Krishna, and Saint Francis of Assisi, along with bougainvillea, bamboo, and a ficus tree descended from the Buddha's original Bo tree. In the small Court of Religions, diminutive monuments affixed with the icons of five world faiths broadcast Yogananda's message of universal religion. The windmill was reborn as a chapel, while Yogananda himself took over the houseboat, where he was often seen idling among the swans and lotus pads before his personal movie ended in 1952. Like many Los Angeles celebrities, he was buried at Forest Lawn.

Despite the loss of their charismatic founder over fifty years ago, the Self-Realization Fellowship soldiers on. In 1998, the institute opened a large octagonal temple on the hillside above the Lake Shrine, its stepped dome flanked on all sides by lovely stone mashrabiya screens. But the holiest spot in the park remains the Gandhi World Peace Memorial, where a handful of the Indian leader's ashes are encased within a stone sarcophagus from China, one thousand years old, and flanked by two statues of the Chinese goddess Kuan Yin. Framing the site, and forming what Yogananda called a "wall-less temple," is a massive triple archway trimmed with blue tile and topped with the trademark golden lotuses. For Yogananda, these flowers symbolized the *sahasrar* chakra, which blooms at the top of the skull during cosmic bliss. But the archway itself—the only major architectural element saved from the ill-fated Golden Lotus Temple in Encinitas—speaks of something else, of the precariousness of all structures of worship in the face of the infinite sea of energy.

BUDDHA TOWNS

In the spring of 1977, two young white Buddhists sporting robes and bald heads set out on foot from the Gold Wheel Temple, the Pasadena outpost of a Buddhist association founded by their Chinese master, the Venerable Hsüan Hua. Dedicating themselves to nonviolence, Heng Sure and Heng Ch'au, originally two Midwestern boys named Christopher Clowery and Marty Verhoeven, had vowed to walk eight hundred miles to Mendocino County. This would have been a healthy stroll even if the monks hadn't paused every third step so that Sure, who was a fully ordained *bhikshu* maintaining a vow of silence, could take a full prostration. The novice Ch'au served as Sure's Man Friday, fielding questions from the curious and dealing with the two-toned '57 Plymouth station wagon that served as their mobile monastic hut. Relying on strangers for food and gas money, the skinny young mendicants bowed their way past bars and broccoli fields, federal prisons and U.S. Air Force bases. Rising early to chant and meditate, then schlepping through the sun and rain on one meal a day, the monks slipped in and out of ordinary mind. Reading the Avatamsaka Sutra at night, they found that its teachings about desire and emptiness came alive in their daylight encounter with California's rolling hills and surfers and taco shops. Even the sudden urge for a Pepsi might boomerang back in the form of a soda-pop bottle hurled at them by passing teens.

TEN THOUSAND BUDDHAS JEWELED HALL,
CITY OF TEN THOUSAND BUDDHAS, TALMAGE

MOUNTAIN GATE, CITY OF TEN THOUSAND BUDDHAS, TALMAGE

After a remarkable thirty-three months of travel, Heng Sure and Heng Ch'au bowed and scraped their way into the City of Ten Thousand Buddhas, which lies nestled in the foothills of a coastal range east of Ukiah. Master Hua had purchased the 488-acre property in 1976 and named it, he sometimes said, after the ten thousand Buddhas he hoped to bring to fruition through the dharma. Hua had lived in the United States since the early 1960s, but he dated his American community, or *sangha,* to 1969, when five of the young Americans who frequented his teachings in San Francisco's Chinatown flew to Taiwan to shave their heads and take traditional monk's vows. Though Hua was a self-consciously modern reformer of Buddhism, he favored a hard-line orthodox stance, particularly on the matter of monastic precepts. Hua's ascetic moral codes and nongroovy Chinese traditionalism dampened his influence on mainstream American Buddhism. Nonetheless, Hua ordained hundreds of monks and founded scores of temples and monasteries, and used his position in the West to revitalize Buddhism among Chinese communities in Malaysia, Taiwan, Hong Kong, and mainland China.

Only America could have engendered the City of Ten Thousand Buddhas. The compound's seventy-odd buildings were originally designed to house the Mendocino State Asylum for the Insane, one of a number of such hellholes decommissioned and put on the market by the state in the early 1970s. Bars still decorate some windows of the drab Tudor-style buildings, while monks live in cells originally reserved for the criminally unhinged. After being taken over by the Buddhists, the institution was not so much renovated as reimagined—dormitories now called Dragon Tree and Horse Whinny remain little changed today. On the other hand, an imposing three-arched Chinese mountain gate now greets visitors, while the interior of the gym has been transformed into a cavernous and resplendent Buddha hall. Here an eighteen-foot-tall statue of Guanshiyin Bodhisattva displays his thousand hands and eyes, while ten thousand identical gold Buddhas line the niches in the walls like a Buddhist version of Warhol's Campbell's soup can paintings. An institutional gloom still lingers about "the Sagely City," although its three hundred monks and nuns seem to embrace the irony of dedicating a former insane asylum to the relief of mental suffering.

When Master Hua and his largely bald followers first moved into their city, they encountered a good deal of hostility from the county board of supervisors. Jim Jones maintained his People's Temple in nearby Redwood Valley, and when the horror show of Jonestown hit the wires in 1978, the deeply creepy spectacle of the Christian sect's mass murder/suicide cooled local enthusiasm for funky religious groups. But today the City of Ten Thousand Buddhas is accepted by the community. Some working-class families especially appreciate the inexpensive private schooling available through the Instilling Goodness Elementary School and the Developing Virtue Secondary School. The city boasts an accredited university as well, although, like the community as a whole, it now caters largely to Chinese from abroad.

The City of Ten Thousand Buddhas proves that the transmission of the dharma between East and West is not a one-way street. That's also the message of the Odiyan Buddhist Retreat Center, a global dharma node that lies on a flat, fog-tickled Sonoma County hilltop right alongside the San Andreas Fault, three miles from the ocean. Odiyan was founded by Tarthang Tulku Rinpoche, one of the last

PRAYER WHEEL, NYINGMA INSTITUTE, BERKELEY

remaining incarnate lamas to receive his full education in Tibet, and one of the first to teach in America. Tarthang Tulku moved to Berkeley in 1968 and, along with founding the first Vajrayana congregation in America, set about preserving the storehouse of Tibetan wisdom and culture. He bought a printing press and kicked off Dharma Publishing, a nonprofit outfit that, in addition to making volumes for Westerners, devotes itself to producing religious books for the Tibetan monastic diaspora. Enlisting a staff of dedicated volunteers, Dharma Publishing set about collecting and preserving the entire Tibetan Buddhist canon, which was no mean feat. In 1981, the press completed 108 sets of 128 atlas-sized volumes designed to last hundreds of years, gorgeously hand-bound in gold-stamped boards and printed on gilt-edged acid-free paper. More recently the nonprofit has compiled and similarly bound more than six hundred volumes of textual treasures belonging to the Nyingma school of Tibetan Buddhism, a collection that includes tantras and works of medicine and astrology. While libraries have purchased some sets, many were distributed free to Tibetan monasteries in the Asian diaspora.

Tarthang Tulku's own books, which read less like Buddhist treatises than visionary exercises in experimental philosophy, are hardly traditional. Nonetheless, the lama is devoted to the preservation of old-school Tibetan culture. Tarthang Tulku has long promoted the efficacy of prayer wheels: traditional devices that contain thin paper strips of sacred mantras that are manually whipped around a spindle, thus generating blessings. Prayer wheels in Tibet are sometimes powered with wind or water, and Tarthang Tulku decided to modernize the process, first by setting prayer wheels on record players and then by directing the design of motorized units that contain mantras printed in the smallest legible typeface. The lama and his followers have built tiny prayer wheels that use microfilm, and two gigantic ones as well; the machine in the backyard of the Nyingma Institute in Berkeley weighs five and a half tons and cranks out billions of mantras a minute.

Tarthang Tulku kept a low profile during the Tibetan Buddhist craze of the 1990s, focusing his energy on what is perhaps his greatest teaching: the visionary landscape of Odiyan itself. The eleven-hundred-acre property is a mandala, not in some hazy metaphoric sense, but literally. The Tibetan mandalas that most of us are familiar with are really two-dimensional blueprints of properly three-dimensional cosmic temples, which are usually reproduced in the meditator's mind's eye, and sometimes in wax or wood. Odiyan is a mandala on the scale of a small theme park, its buildings and gardens designed by Tarthang Tulku as a symbolic blueprint of enlightenment. At the heart of the mandala lies the main temple, a three-tiered palace with an atypical dome and flaring copper roofs that suggest the Copper Mountain paradise of Padmasambhava, the great Tantric sorcerer whose birthplace in the Hindu Kush lends Odiyan its name. The temple is framed by gardens, dormitories, and a huge square moat with stupas set in the four corners, all of which echo the layout at Samye, the oldest monastery in Tibet. To the east stands one of the largest stupas in America, stuffed with relics and covered with gold-leafed copper plates etched with sacred texts. Seaward lies the Vajra Temple, an eight-sided crystal pagoda that houses 108,000 diminutive statues of Padmasambhava. Tarthang Tulku designed the structure with glass-block walls so that the visual blessings from the statues could radiate throughout the countryside.

Although Odiyan includes elements of traditional Tibetan architecture, the center essentially reflects Tarthang Tulku's own deeply innovative Vajrayana vision. The lama's most radical architectural design is also the center's latest and most extravagant monument: the ten-story Cintamani Temple, which is topped with a stupa and completely sheathed in bronze plates and sculptures. Four thirty-five-foot-tall bodhisattva statues, created by Tibetan and Bhutanese artisans to Tarthang Tulku's exacting iconographic specifications, face the four compass directions, while hundreds of smaller life-size bronzes, forged at an on-site foundry, fill the inside of the temple. *Cintamani* means "wish-fulfilling jewel," but outsiders wishing to see Odiyan's jeweled wonders without signing up for the grueling life of a volunteer will remain unfulfilled for the time being. Though the center is developing a nearby retreat center called Ratna Ling, Odiyan is a closed shop—a capsule of sacred space-time that is open to the sea breeze, but not to spiritual tourists.

ODIYAN BUDDHIST RETREAT CENTER, SONOMA COUNTY

THEME PARK OF THE GODS

BABYLON

In 2001, a mall opened at the corner of Hollywood and Highland in Los Angeles. Covering two city blocks, the huge complex features the glitzy Kodak Theatre—now the permanent home of the Academy Awards—along with a dreadful repackaging of Grauman's Chinese Theatre, its classic crimson exterior now rendered a gray shadow of its former self. The mall's most impressive feature is, without a doubt, the Babylonian Court. Atop freestanding columns that soar into the sky, two enormous elephants crouch on their concrete-reinforced haunches, their trunks and forelegs raised in regal glee above the consumers below. A massive gray archway looms behind them to the north, decorated with moderately authentic neo-Assyrian reliefs: a bearded winged divinity holds a bowl that projects from the wall like an oriel window, while an eagle-headed guardian prepares to tend a sacred tree with a little bucket and an implement that Near Eastern scholars alternately identify as a cone, a date-palm spathe, or a sponge. Between the legs of the arch, whose profile resembles the Ishtar gate reconstructed in Berlin's Pergamon Museum, you can see the dilapidated Hollywood sign tooting its horn in the hazy hills beyond.

This Orientalist tableau is a faithful if colorless homage to the immense Babylonian set that D. W. Griffith constructed nearby for his 1916 film *Intolerance.* A visionary reconstruction of the gate of Imgur Bel, Griffith's set featured scores of elephant statues, columns, friezes, platforms, and steps—and, during King Belshazzar's orgiastic feast, scores of lithesome, half-nude revelers as well. In the film, the intolerant priests of the city-god Bel-Marduk attempt to suppress the popular worship of the goddess Ishtar, and, failing that, betray the randy king and his city to the invading Persians. Griffith drew great inspiration for the set from the exotic Tower of Jewels that dominated San Francisco's 1915 Panama-Pacific Exposition, a glamorous ziggurat festooned with colonnades and dangling glass. But Griffith also did his homework, at least to a point, and his fabulation sets authentic Assyrian iconography, like lions from the Ishtar gate, alongside total fantasy—no pachyderms ever stepped foot in ancient Mesopotamia in stone or in flesh.

After *Intolerance* wrapped and flopped, Griffith could not afford to tear down his set, and so great Babylon rotted for years on the corner of Sunset and Virgil, now the location of a Vons supermarket. When the Angeleno filmmaker and occultist Kenneth Anger compiled his scabrous scrapbook *Hollywood Babylon,* he used the image of Griffith's crumbling set to establish the golden age of Tinseltown as a decadent pagan fleshpot. But Griffith's Babylon set also proclaimed Hollywood's power to collapse the barriers between fantasy and reality, not just on the screen, but in the built environment of Los Angeles as well. In subsequent years, the Southland hosted a controlled explosion of exotic architecture that drew from fairy tales and world history alike: Anasazi restaurants, Rhine castle residences, tepee drive-ins, pyramid universities, Mesopotamian tire factories. Even more hallucinatory were the legendary eateries and roadside quick-stops shaped like oranges, or derbies, or barn owls. One diner offering tamales resembled—you guessed it—a giant tamale.

The links between Hollywood and this architectural phantasmagoria were tight. In 1921, the MGM set designer Harry Oliver built a Hansel and Gretel witch cottage for a Culver City production studio, a tumbledown dollhouse later carted over to Beverly Hills for use as a private home. Oliver went on to design portable shingle-covered Dutch windmills for the Van de Kamp's Bakery chain; he also created California's first drive-in restaurant, a lopsided and rambling affair that looked like a backlot set for *Alice in Wonderland.* Some of Southern California's most entrancing pop architecture was reserved for movie houses like Grauman's Chinese, the Egyptian, the Vista, and the Mayan theaters, whose exotic styles beckoned filmgoers into what architectural historian David Gebhard called an "intermediary non-everyday world." Architects like native son Wallace Neff also built storybook mansions for the stars, while backlot-inspired homes like Yamashiro, a historically accurate sixteenth-century Japanese estate built in 1914 for the millionaire silk

HIGHLAND MALL, HOLLYWOOD

LEFT: WITCH HOUSE/SPADENA HOUSE, BEVERLY HILLS

RIGHT: MAYAN THEATER, LOS ANGELES

trader Adolph Bernheimer and his brother, became movie sets in turn.

The Southland's fantasy architecture represented more than the influence of Hollywood or the needs of the region's revolutionary car culture, which demanded an arresting commercial landscape of vivid signage capable of grabbing attention on the fly. These buildings also represented the way that Los Angeles dreamed itself into existence. Long before the movie industry took hold, the developer Abbot Kinney created Venice in the marshlands near the sea, a resort complete with canals, gondolas, and wandering dromedaries. Venice helped set the stage for the canny real estate developers and salesmen who would later package and sell a new shot at life to the hordes of immigrants, many from the Midwest, who were drawn to the Southland by the promise of health, happiness, and home ownership. Fatuous and bewitching hype filled the air, but, as the historian Kenneth Starr argues, the folkloric figure of the California real estate booster—"part preacher, part confidence man"—offered more than humbug. Boosters and developers also helped materialize a built landscape of dreams, testifying to "the notion that imagination and even illusion not only are the premise and primal stuff of art, they play a role in history as well."

In a land without history or tradition, marketing hype and architectural fantasy created a sense of place by grounding built space in the collective (and commercial) imagination. This eclectic raid on the mindscapes of exotic fantasy led Angelenos to build their cafés like wigwams and to name subdivisions like Tarzana after pulp fictions. But this theatrical impulse also lies behind the region's extraordinarily diverse, brazen, and creative spiritual culture. "No other city in the United States possesses so large a

Martin Landau

LEFT: VISTA THEATER, LOS ANGELES

RIGHT: SAMSON TIRE WORKS/THE CITADEL OUTLET MALL, CITY OF COMMERCE

number of metaphysical charlatans in proportion to its population," the writer Willard Huntington Smith sniffed in 1913. "Whole buildings are devoted to occult and outlandish orders—*mazdaznan* clubs, yogi sects, homes of truth, cults of cosmic fluidists, astral planers, Emmanuel movers, Rosicrucians, and other boozy transcendentalists." Fusing mysticism and the market, Los Angeles became a carnival of transcendence, offering esoteric sources of entertainment, transport, and wonder. Many Angelenos had moved west for their health, and many of the fads and sects they encountered offered a mixture of diet, mind-body exercises, and holistic ideas—key elements of the budding California consciousness. Kooky pseudoscience fused with the ancient lore introduced by Theosophists and local occultists like Manly P. Hall, author of the classic omnibus folio *The Secret Teachings of All Ages* and collector of America's greatest publicly accessible library of hermetic and alchemical texts. Even the astral magic bequeathed by the ancient Babylonians was reborn in the Southland's unparalleled obsession with astrology—an apt occult science for the home of the stars.

In Los Angeles, spiritual culture and fantasy architecture went hand in hand, almost as if the area's glut of bizarre buildings prepared the cultural ground for otherworldly creeds and Orientalist practices to grow. After all, the modern spiritual search often begins with fantasy, especially fantasies about the Other—other places, other times, other ways of being. Witch houses and medieval castles tapped a fairy-tale consciousness one step away from mythology, while primitivist pastiches of African grass huts and Southwestern pueblos suggested, in their superficial way, "natural" modes of life antecedent to the rat race. Many of the Southland's fantasy buildings directly sampled sacred architecture, whether Egyptian tombs or sphinxes, Mayan pyramids or Chinese temples. We are certainly in the land of kitsch here—when contemplating Hollywood Boulevard's Calmos #1 Service station, built in 1925 and featuring a mosquelike dome and two minarets, one can only register the absurd. But exotic exteriors can also draw people inside the dream. And if the formal geometry of sacred architecture objectively embodies mystic forces, then even these pop portals offered a trace of genuine transport.

The most concrete evidence for the connection between fantasy architecture and the Southland's peculiar spiritual scene lies in the buildings that fused the two impulses. Angelus Abbey used minarets, palm trees, and other Biblical icons to sell what might be called themed cemetery plots, while the architect Robert Stacy-Judd's neo-Mayan buildings grew out of his mystic speculations about the lost city of Atlantis. Customers eating at Clifton's, a health-food cafeteria that offered nutritious "pay-what-you-wish" meals during the Depression, entered the restaurant by walking beneath waterfalls and jungle vines that signified the naturalness of the fare. But some of the most striking exotic architecture was created by the exotic sects themselves. Looking at the state as a whole, some of California's first major fantasy buildings were designed to express a spiritual vision: Lomaland, San Francisco's Vedanta Society Temple, the Krotona colony in the Hollywood Hills. Indeed, when the amateur architect and Theosophist Marie Russak Hotchener designed a few Moorish homes for Krotona, it is impossible to say whether her buildings represented escapism or faith. The metaphysical creativity of California, and especially the Southland, cannot be understood apart from the state's commitment to exotic commercial spectacle. But neither can it be reduced to it. When you set foot in Rosicrucian Park or a Self-Realization Fellowship temple, you have left mere kitsch behind: otherworldly fantasy transforms into something else, something more like promise.

AZTEC
HOTEL
AZTEC
HOTEL
311
AZTEC
BARBER
SHOP

MAYALAND

When the wacky English architect Robert Stacy-Judd emigrated to Los Angeles in 1922, he definitely moved to the right place. Scores of British expatriates had already made Los Angeles a sort of London-on-Pacific, but what must have really appealed to Stacy-Judd was the city's embrace of colorful and fantastic architecture. With Egyptian picture palaces and Tudor mansions already under his belt, Stacy-Judd was hot to plunge into the wilderness of exotic revivalism. But the fantasies behind his most distinctive buildings did more than add a few roadside attractions to Southern California's carscape—instead, they attempted to bring the architecture of the Southland into accord with an ancient and esoteric source of regional power.

Sometime in 1923, a vendor of architectural books visited Stacy-Judd, insisting that he take a look at what was then an obscure two-volume travelogue published eighty years before. The book was John Stephens's *Incidents of Travel in Central America, Chiapas, and Yucatan,* and the woodcut plates by Frederick Catherwood—gothic documents of crumbled monuments and friezes of unknown gods—blew Stacy-Judd's mind. The architect became an idiosyncratic devotee of Maya Revival, convinced that the temples of Mesoamerica were the key to the development of an authentic American architecture. In 1925, Stacy-Judd built his masterpiece, the Aztec Hotel in Monrovia, a terraced chunk of whimsy plopped along Route 66, then the main westward road into town. The name of the hotel itself shows how commercial concerns like name recognition shaped Stacy-Judd's folly, which freely mixed and matched Catherwood's images into a dream temple of cast concrete appliqué that includes, among its pre-Columbian bas-reliefs, a life mask of the architect himself. The building was praised in publications ranging from the *New York Times* to *American Architect,* and it launched Stacy-Judd's career. Soon he was applying his pre-Columbian imaginings to private homes, clubhouses, and ecclesiastical buildings. Recognizing the Southland's surreal opportunities for self-promotion, Stacy-Judd also styled himself as an archaeological expert on the Maya. He distributed pictures of himself in pith helmets and Mesoamerican garb, wrote books and published codexes, and even patented and sold the Hul-Che Atlatl Throwing Stick.

Though Stacy-Judd claimed that the Aztec Hotel was the first building in the U.S. that was "100 percent American," other architects were already exploring the idea that pre-Columbian architecture might provide the seeds of an authentically regional style. I have already discussed the early Southland homes of Frank Lloyd Wright and his son Lloyd Wright, who used patterned blocks, stepped walls, and other Mesoamerican elements lifted from the Yucatan and the Zapotec ruins at Mitla. Like many artistic modernists, the Wrights wanted to forge links between indigenous art and contemporary abstraction, but Stacy-Judd had mystic reasons for embracing the Maya. Stealing more than a few pages from febrile crypto-archaeologists like Ignatius Donnelly and Lewis Spence, Stacy-Judd argued that the Maya descended directly from colonists who had fled the destruction of the fabled island of Atlantis, which the Maya apparently called "Aztlan." In his hefty and stunningly illustrated *Atlantis: Mother of Empires,* Stacy-Judd claimed that Mayan ruins represent our only link to that ancient civilization; he also asserted that Jesus was a master of esoteric lore whose last words were pure Maya. Stacy-Judd was supported in these beliefs by his friend Manly P. Hall, whose Philosophical Research Society published Stacy-Judd's titles alongside books like *The Freemasonry of the Ancient Egyptians* and *The Road to Inner Light.*

For Stacy-Judd, the impulse toward fantasy architecture became perfectly fused with an esoteric sensibility shaped by Los Angeles's metaphysical scene. The architect's striking

AZTEC HOTEL, MONROVIA

designs for the Philosophical Research Society complex in the mid-1930s bear this out, though the plans themselves were only slightly realized. Other examples of sacred architecture that remained on Stacy-Judd's drawing board included a Mormon temple for Mexico City that would have been even more marvelous than the Mesoamerican mélange the church eventually constructed. Stacy-Judd based his plans for the Mexico temple on an actual building: the First Baptist Church that he designed and built for a Ventura congregation in the late 1920s. Now an outpost of the Church of Religious Science, a group that bases itself in the Science of Mind teachings of Earnest Holmes, Stacy-Judd's antediluvian marvel is dominated by a steep tower that suggests both a stepped pyramid and a pipe organ. Visitors pass through a sharp V-shaped opening into the sanctuary, which is decorated with richly patterned cast-grille work, more Mayan arches, and a pulpit that looks suspiciously like a sacrificial altar. High above the altar, Stacy-Judd set a beautiful baptismal tub that was later cloaked by the Religious Scientists with stained glass.

When the Krotona Institute abandoned Hollywood for Ojai, Stacy-Judd designed their new digs, opting for a minimalist Spanish Revival charm that recalls Irving Gill more than the bloody sanctuaries of Quetzalcoatl. On the other hand, the 1951 temple that Stacy-Judd concocted for a Masonic lodge in the San Fernando Valley is another grand Mayan fiction, although a terribly dull paint job in 2004 basically destroyed the hall's air of mystic charm. Freemasons take their temples very seriously; the order's elaborate ritual mythology is, after all, built on the lore of stonemasonry and the principles of sacred architecture embodied in Solomon's temple. As the artist and media critic Jesse Lerner points out, some Masons also found these principles reflected in pre-Columbian architecture. Augustus Le Plongeon, an early Mayanist and Freemason, found evidence of Masonic lore in the corbelled arches of Uxmal in the 1880s; he also argued that the Maya were the source of all great past civilizations. The Masons of the San Fernando Valley thus had deeper reasons for turning to Mesoamerican architecture than the desire to look cool. This hidden link

FAR LEFT: LOBBY, AZTEC HOTEL, MONROVIA

LEFT: NORTH HOLLYWOOD MASONIC TEMPLE, NORTH HOLLYWOOD

RIGHT: FIRST BAPTIST CHURCH/ CHURCH OF RELIGIOUS SCIENCE, VENTURA

between the Maya and the Masons may also explain the formal similarity between the V-shaped angle of the Mayan arch above the entrance of the San Fernando temple and the angle of the compass in the famous Masonic emblem etched on the glass.

By creating a regional architecture based on Mayan designs, Stacy-Judd may have hoped to tap powerful Atlantean energies and so bless the Southland. Unfortunately, the history of the Aztec Hotel, Stacy-Judd's masterpiece, does not seem to bear out such occult beneficence. The hotel became a brothel and speakeasy during Prohibition, and went utterly to seed with the downfall of Route 66. During its decades as a sleazy flophouse, the Aztec Hotel witnessed drug overdoses and suicides and at least one violent death, which occurred when the head of a woman having sex in Room 120 collided with a radiator. The ghosts in its halls are lost souls, wandering far from the City of Angels. But perhaps Stacy-Judd was more in tune with the nefarious powers than he let on. Today the freshly repainted lobby of the revitalized Aztec Hotel displays a yellowed newspaper interview with the architect. In it he explains that one of the murals still visible in the vestibule depicts the Kingdom of Darkness, presided over on either side by the god and goddess of death. The central panel shows a man "falling into the nether regions" beneath the moon, harassed by demonic turkeys. These images remind us that the primitivist kitsch so often celebrated in the Southland's tiki scene derives some of its power from the dark side of the force, and that powerful exotica always toys with savagery.

THE ROSY CROSS PARADE

In the early seventeenth century, so the story goes, two European explorers sailing off the coast of Carmel came ashore with a stash of esoteric documents, which they buried with an eye toward future generations of California mystics. According to the West Coast occultist who claimed to have discovered these texts, the two men were Rosicrucians, initiates in a mystery tradition that some trace back to the wisdom schools of ancient Egypt but that conventional historians date to a series of popular pamphlets that appeared in Europe in the early 1600s. These manifestoes proclaimed the existence of a secret order of Christian alchemists working for the enlightenment of the world. The chapbooks were most likely esoteric fictions, the Carlos Castañeda books of their day. But so many men wanted to join up that actual fraternal orders emerged, each taking as its central icon the rose blooming at the heart of the cross—a symbol of, among other things, the spiritual life blossoming forth from the material body.

The man who claimed to have disinterred Rosicrucian documents from California's soil was H. Spencer Lewis, an energetic Egyptophile and adman who founded the Ancient Mystical Order Rosae Crucis in New York in 1915. Lewis was initiated by a Rosicrucian master in Toulouse and spent time as well in the Ordo Templi Orientis, an occult order led by the notorious Aleister Crowley; Spence took AMORC's Rosicrucian emblem from the pages of Crowley's journal, *The Equinox*. In 1927, Lewis purchased a modest plot of land amid the luscious apricot and peach orchards that once thronged San Jose. The Grand Imperator dubbed the property Rosicrucian Park, which would become home base for the largest and most famous Rosicrucian group in America.

Today Rosicrucian Park is one of the crown jewels of California's visionary landscape. An inviting maze of temples, fountains, statues, plants, and bas-relief gods, the site is part Egyptian Revival, part Deco, and part Disney. (Walt Disney, it should be mentioned, was once a member of AMORC, as was *Star Trek* creator Gene Roddenberry.) Though Lewis saved his heaviest sacred designs for the interior of the windowless main temple, the park's grounds and exteriors stand as a public monument to the esoteric imagination. Rosicrucian Park also includes the largest Egyptian museum in the western United States, a collection of coffins, mummified baboons, and stelae—as well as a few items of dodgy provenance—housed inside a massive mock-up of the Temple of Amon at Karnak. A goofy statue of a pregnant hippopotamus goddess greets visitors, who pass through a dramatic peristyle and huge bronze doors before entering the museum. The theatrical deployment of sacred space carries on inside the building, where hordes of schoolchildren are regularly hustled through a full-scale reproduction of a Middle Kingdom tomb.

Outside the museum, Rosicrucian Park continues to work its magic through exotic stage sets and symbolically coded environments—a kind of mythic theming that extends even to the flora, which includes papyrus, lilies-of-the-Nile, and scores of roses. Entering the park from the northwest corner, one passes through a small pylon gate with a painted relief of a scene from the Egyptian afterlife: the baboon of Thoth preparing to weigh the hearts of the dead against the feather of Ma'at. Passing through this threshold of judgment, one enters a landscape that lies, in a sense, between the worlds. The diminutive scale of the gateway and the rosy obelisk that stands nearby—the first in America—recalls the toylike dimension of the eclectic period villages at Disneyland or Epcot Center. One is therefore hardly surprised to see a Moorish building break up the Egyptian theme. Designed and somehow built during the Depression, this recently restored planetarium—a green dome with an octagonal base, tri-lobed archways, and a zigzag facade flanked by narrow corner towers—honors the Islamic scholars

FOUNTAIN OF THE LIVING WATERS, ROSICRUCIAN PARK, SAN JOSE

SCHEDULED FOR
RESTORATION

who kept ancient Greek science alive. Near this temple to the stars stands a bronze replica of a famous Roman statue of Augustus Caesar. Behind this cheerily incongruous mixture of times and places lies a deeper claim—that an unbroken stream of wisdom has passed through the ages, from Egypt's Middle Kingdom through Greco-Roman civilization and medieval Islam all the way to contemporary San Jose.

In the sunken patio at the heart of the park stands the Fountain of the Living Waters, an energetic focal point whose colored mosaic tiles and lion's-head reliefs encode alchemical secrets. Two stone sphinxes nearby guard the entrance to the Rose-Croix University International, whose classical Egyptian facade includes columns that resemble bundles of papyrus. The university, which is now closed, once contained chemistry labs, darkrooms, and classrooms, and reflected the modern mystic dream of embedding science in the cosmic context of ancient harmonies. Lewis was himself an inventor and engineer. In addition to building the projector for the planetarium—the first such device made by an American—the Imperator also constructed a color organ, which represented the frequencies of different musical tones as colored lights that danced across the sort of triangular screen you might expect to see in a 1950s flying saucer movie.

Across the patio from the university stands one of the park's earliest and most lovely spots, a small shrine to Pharaoh Akhnaton that is reserved for those who pony up $215 a year for an AMORC membership. Built in honor of initiations that Lewis conducted in Luxor, Egypt, in 1929, this simple colonnade, fringed with papyrus plants and dark green elephant ears, now houses the Imperator's ashes, stored beneath a small pyramid inscribed with the single word *Lux;* a nearby ankh reflects the hope for immortality that ties together ancient kings and modern mystagogues. It is a sign of AMORC's health that, unlike so many esoteric orders of the early twentieth century, it has survived the death of its charismatic founder. Long after the passing of Lewis and his son Ralph, who served as Grand Imperator until 1987, AMORC's incarnation of the Rosicrucian dream shuffles along. And much of the reason lies with the park itself, an open secret that satisfies needs as civic as they are mystic.

One sacred stream that runs thin at the AMORC headquarters is the Christian revelation, a somewhat odd scenario given the allegorical connotations of the rose and cross. Other modern Rosicrucian groups pay far more attention to Jesus than to Akhnaton, and one of these orders also built a large and intriguing compound in California. Like Lewis, Max Heindel met a mysterious Rosicrucian master while visiting Europe; afterward, he returned to the United States to found his own order in Seattle in 1909. Heindel soon moved his Rosicrucian Fellowship to Southern California, where, the Elder Brothers informed him, the electrical currents were best attuned to the approaching Aquarian age. Heindel settled in Oceanside, on a high southern overlook of the broad San Luis Rey Valley, close to what is now the boundary of the U.S. Marine Corps base Camp Pendleton. Here on Mount Ecclesia, Heindel built a small mission-style chapel to hold healing services based on his Aquarian blend of astrology and Christian mysticism.

The community grew, and Mount Ecclesia today includes a cafeteria, a print shop, small homes, and a large guesthouse that services Rosicrucians who trickle in from South America, Africa, and Europe. At the center of the property lies a voluptuous rose garden and a fanciful lotus pond surrounded by calla lilies, lavender, papyrus, and datura. The Healing Department takes up a small cruciform bungalow nearby; here secretaries handle the correspondence of fellowship members seeking the healing balm of the Invisible Helpers. A hushed if somewhat claustrophobic twelve-sided chapel nestles in the crux of the building, its placement corresponding to the location of the rose in the Rosicrucian emblem. Diffuse light filters into the chapel through a small art-glass dome on the ceiling, while the room's pastel colors seem to dissolve the solid walls into the diaphanous vibrations of the higher planes. Besides a rosy cross, the main icons in the chapel are zodiac symbols and a great big Bible—a fitting juxtaposition for folks who hold that the Son of God corresponds more or less directly with the sun in the heavens.

The finest building in the compound is the Healing Temple, which tops Mount Ecclesia. A large white concrete rotunda, the temple was Heindel's last major project on the property before he died in 1920. The twelve sides of the building correspond to the twelve signs of the zodiac; this division is carried on inside, where students sit in sections according to their natal sun signs. The building has an air of secret rites; students must study as probationers for a few years before gaining access to the round hall, hidden from outside eyes by marblesque windowpanes in opalescent green and blue. Two squat palm trees echo the two pillars that frame the entrance to the building, whose hardwood doors are carved with Art Nouveau images of Leo and Aquarius. The most curious element of the building is the nine-pointed star-shaped doohicky that tops the rotunda; it looks like the model of an atom from a 1960s filmstrip. Even in its somewhat dilapidated state, Mount Ecclesia still traces the lineaments of the visionary. According to one resident, "Some probationers in Africa think the Elder Brothers actually live here."

LEFT: ROSICRUCIAN PARK ADMINISTRATION BUILDING, ROSICRUCIAN PARK, SAN JOSE

RIGHT: HEALING TEMPLE, MOUNT ECCLESIA, OCEANSIDE

SMALL WORLD AFTER ALL

Before California's Indians were decimated by incoming Europeans, they spoke some one hundred and four languages classified into twenty-one major language groups—the densest diversity of tongues found in the New World, and probably the entire planet. What was true of the premodern era, it seems, is also true of the postmodern one. Everywhere is a linguistic mix today, but California stands out as a polyglot stew, whether in the Bay Area, the Central Valley, or, especially, the megalopolis of Los Angeles. Even New York City, long considered America's melting pot, cannot match the jarring juxtapositions of the Southland. The residents of Artesia, for example, fill two and a half square miles of low-rent sprawl with nearly forty languages. Los Angeles County is not a melting pot—it is a multiverse.

The dizzying and sometimes difficult diversity of Los Angeles reflects the fact that the city has long been a major nexus of immigration—a global border town where one out of three people claims a foreign birth. Los Angeles now hosts the highest concentration of Mexicans outside of Mexico City, of Koreans outside Korea, of Samoans outside Polynesia. There is a Little Ethiopia and a Little Saigon, a Filipino Town and a Little Phnom Penh. There is even a Little Oaxaca snugged inside of Koreatown, a booming enclave whose residents represent Los Angeles's largest Asian population. This diversity is not just an ornament of Los Angeles; it is fundamental to the spirit of California, and certainly all

WAT THAI OF LOS ANGELES, NORTH HOLLYWOOD

VENKATESWARA TEMPLE, MALIBU CANYON

its metro areas. Though Anglos have played out the usual tawdry drama of exclusionary policies and racist violence over the last century and a half, it remains the case that the state, compared to most, anyway, was born a polyglot collage of multiple cultures. This is a birthright that should be claimed, not a chaos to be feared. Besides, the dynamics of population in the state, which have already sunk the Anglo population permanently below the 50 percent mark, assure that Californians will find themselves dreaming in creole whether they want to or not.

The diversity of Los Angeles has turned the Southland's religious marketplace into a clamoring bazaar. Even Christianity, which is often, if wrongly, considered to be a homogenizing agent, wears a many-colored coat in Los Angeles. Churches routinely post two or three languages on their marquees, while both Catholic institutions and mainline Protestant denominations have been forced to split their services, and sometimes their governance structures, to serve their multicultural flocks. Korean Angelenos, who are predominantly Christian and boast a rate of church attendance far above the national norm, have founded hundreds of exuberant congregations of first-generation believers. Contrast this with the Armenians clustered in Glendale and Montebello, who make up the largest such community outside the Caucasus. While many Armenians attend Protestant houses of worship, the orthodox Armenian Apostolic churches in the area, some of them quite lovely, perform some of the oldest continuously practiced rites in Christendom.

Many recent immigrants find themselves embracing their native cultures more intensely in America than they did in the homeland. This is especially true in the matter of religion. For one thing, immigrant religious institutions often double as community centers, hosting music performances or job fairs or language lessons for kids. They also provide safety nets, ministering to the lonely or to those struggling to shake off the nightmares that often motivated their flight in the first place. Priests ministering to the huge and rather traumatized Cambodian community in Long Beach—again, the largest outside Southeast Asia—face troubles that call out equally for medical referrals and healing incantations. Immigrant religious organizations also provide a framework for managing a mutating identity. For those attempting to navigate postmodern America, the familiar matrix of native faith—once simply part of the background—can pop out like a shining pole star, offering a communal counterweight to assimilation and American anomie.

Traditional religious architecture plays a vital role in shaping these parallel identities, especially for Asian and Middle Eastern believers who worship outside the overhang of Christianity. Familiar icons and ground plans, some rooted in sacred geometries centuries old, can transform vacant lots into spiritual transporters. While such "exotic" religious structures are found across America, they take on a peculiar resonance in California, where local Orientalism and fantasy architecture have already transformed the region into a patchwork of pocket worlds. Within their iconic walls, the Asian and Middle Eastern religious institutions that continue to sprout up across the state are encouraging newer Americans to walk in two worlds. At the same time, these structures, with their domes and minarets and flaming filigree, are continuing California's ongoing production of otherworldly spaces—even if the otherworlds in question are the old worlds of origin.

The importance of sacred architecture to immigrant identity may help explain the monumental nature of so many Asian and Middle Eastern religious structures in California. One of the earliest large-scale compounds was the Wat Thai of Los Angeles, a San Fernando Valley monastery built in 1978 to serve a community that has been expanding since a change in U.S. immigration laws opened the doors to Asians in the mid-1960s. Still the largest Thai temple in North America, Wat Thai was constructed along strongly traditional lines. Though lacking the extreme flamboyance of many wats in Thailand, the main temple still features a multitiered roof with red tiles, tapering hornlike finials called *chofa,* and abstract golden snakes slithering down to the cornices. Particularly striking are the two towering Yak statues that guard the front of the temple—two fanged brocade giants clutching bejeweled but thankfully sheathed swords. As in Thailand, the wat includes a number of additional buildings as well, including a small *vihara* housing Buddha images (and floral wallpaper) and a *kuti* where the saffron-sporting monks reside. But California creeps in as well. Nontraditional columnar cacti stand near the traditional banyan tree, while the state and national flags flutter over the grounds. On weekends, when the temple grounds host a boisterous food fair, hipster chowhounds prowl among the crowd of devotees, scarfing up satay and the monastery's legendary pad thai.

The Wat Thai of Los Angeles is only one of around 150 Buddhist centers in the county. With sanghas representing all parts of Asia, and a fistful of white dharma groups to boot, Los Angeles now qualifies as the most complex Buddhist city in the world. The largest Buddhist temple in the Western hemisphere lies in the San Gabriel Valley: fifteen acres of temples, courtyards, gardens, and pagodas packed into a triangular lot on a green rise in Hacienda Heights. Venerable Master Hsing Yun, who established the largest monastery in Taiwan and promotes something he calls Humanistic Buddhism, built Hsi Lai Temple in 1988, essentially to serve the Taiwanese community. About thirty monks and nuns live on site. Hsi Lai, which means "coming to the West," draws from Ming- and Ching-dynasty architecture and reproduces a ground plan familiar to habitués of Chinese Buddhist temples. After passing through a freestanding gateway and the bodhisattva hall, pilgrims cross a huge courtyard to a flight of steps leading to the large main shrine. The strips of grass that frame the rectangular flagstones of the courtyard are said to represent the weeds of desire that must be pruned to practice the Buddha Way. Alongside these symbolic pathways, the temple grounds serve more functional needs as well, providing dharma practitioners with a conference room, an auditorium, a museum, and, of course, a gift shop.

The Hsi Lai Temple grew out of a Buddhist order founded abroad. The most magnificent Hindu temple in Los Angeles, on the other hand, was willed into being by a nonprofit group of local volunteers who wanted to build a place of worship for "the Hindu community of America." Designed and sculpted largely by traditional artisans brought over from the motherland, Malibu's enchanting Sri Venkateswara Temple reflects a style of south Indian architecture a millennium old. Venkateswara is an avatar of Vishnu who makes his abode at a famous temple amid the seven hills of Tirumala in Andhra Pradesh; Malibu's Conejo Valley features a similar cluster of surrounding hills. Visitors enter the temple from the east, through an elaborate *gopuram,* or entrance tower, decorated with intricate carvings of dragons, lions, and lotus blossoms. The temple grounds include a number of smaller shrines devoted to most major deities, including Krishna, Shiva, Rama, Ganesh, and Lakshmi. Such a wide range of deities is common to Indian temples, whose grounds almost seem to foreshadow the diversity of today's religious climate. A more unusual inclusiveness marks the grand Shiva-Vishnu Temple in Northern California's Contra Costa County, which opened in 1986 to a sky full of rose petals dropped from a helicopter. Within a common wall lie two central sanctums: a northern-style shrine housing a Shiva lingam, and a southern-style temple sheltering the god Venkateswara.

Hindu teachers have been visiting California for over a century, but today's gurus are less likely to be charismatic mavericks than mainstream priests hired by a board of directors to serve settled and increasingly affluent South Asian communities. Indeed, one of the paradoxes of today's monumental temples is that their architectural authenticity and high-dollar style depend on the deepening assimilation of Indians into corporate America. Nonetheless, the relatively high status of South Asians in the California economy—especially in Silicon Valley—can still generate familiar patterns of backlash. In the early 1990s, the Sikhs of San Jose,

SIKH GURDWARA - SAN JOSE

having outgrown their old *gurdwara,* set out to build a ten-million-dollar temple—the largest and most expensive in the country—in the quiet hillside community of Evergreen. Unlike the Hindus, the Sikhs have had a strong presence in California since the early decades of the twentieth century, when thousands of Punjabi workers, most of them Sikh, migrated to the West Coast. Still, the San Jose Sikhs faced some crude opposition when they began building their grandiose palace of golden Mogul domes and scalloped archways. Though Evergreen residents were understandably peeved about a heavily trafficked Costco-sized compound appearing on the site of a former apricot orchard, such concerns hardly warrant the signs some brandished in protest: "No Sikh Jose."

The passions stirred up by other large California immigrant temples reflect deeper conflicts than zoning wars or local prejudice. There are a few hundred thousand Muslims in the Los Angeles area, and one of the largest congregations gathers at the huge King Fahd Mosque in Culver City. The $8.1 million building, with gleaming marble walls and a seventy-two-foot-tall minaret, is not only named after the former ruler of Saudi Arabia, it was also built entirely with money from the coffers of the king and his son, then Crown Prince Abdullah ibn Abdulaziz. These potentates were and are deeply imbricated with Saudi Arabia's Wahabi religious establishment, which preaches a rigid and sometimes paranoid brand of Islam that is almost as nasty toward Shi'ites and other non-Wahabi Muslims as it is toward Christians and Jews. The Saudi family supports this ideology, at least indirectly, through the funding of schools, educational materials, and religious institutions across the globe, including the King Fahd Mosque and other centers in California and the United States.

King Fahd is only one of over fifty mosques in the Los Angeles area, and these institutions reflect the fitful diversity of American Islam. In some mosques, Sunnis and Shi'ites have managed to table their differences; Friday prayers at the mainstream Masjid Omar ibn Al-Khattab mosque near the University of Southern California are attended by so many ethnic groups—African Americans, Persians, Egyptians, Lebanese, Saudis, Thais, Somalis, even some Latino converts—that some members call Friday prayers "the United Nations on its knees." The King Fahd Mosque, with its Wahabi intransigence, is a different kettle of fish. Fahad al Thumairy, a former chief imam who also served as a Saudi diplomat, held incendiary views that troubled some congregants; in 2003, the U.S. State Department refused to allow him to reenter the country because of suspected ties to terrorism. Two of the hijackers who flew planes into the World Trade Center also most likely spent time at the mosque after entering the country through LAX. Even before these developments were made public, the mosque had already become a lightning rod for global religious conflict. Shortly after the fall of the Twin Towers in 2001, the FBI confiscated bomb-making equipment and five pounds of powder from two Angeleno members of the Jewish Defense League who planned to blow up the "filthy" mosque to teach the Arabs a lesson. Such ugliness reminds us that a small world can be a claustrophobic and violent one. But even the singing multicultural robots at Disneyland warned us what was coming: "a world of hopes, and a world of fears."

LEFT: SIKH GURDWARA, SAN JOSE

BELOW: KING FAHD MOSQUE, CULVER CITY

THE SMILING CHRIST

SACRED SCIENTISTS

For all its eccentric paganism, California's landscape of religious belief has been principally shaped by American Christianity. But there are many different Christianities in America, and the sects and styles of practice that took hold on the West Coast in the late nineteenth century often followed a different drummer than the faiths that dominated the East. In California's rootless and mixed environment, where fidelity to traditional Anglo-Protestant churches was relatively weak, unorthodox brands of Christianity found easy purchase. While groups that promised practical benefits like healing and personal power were often successful, a number of sects also catered to a growing interest in paths that targeted the inner life. The historian Susan Frankel argues that one of the main alternatives to conventional Anglo-Protestant churches in California were these so-called metaphysical religions. While still inhabiting the margins of Christianity, these sects focused on the spiritual growth of the individual, whose progress through deepening states of mind led to an ever greater intimacy with God—a God who was often stripped of the usual beard and sandals and envisioned as a more abstract force of light and life.

The most popular of these metaphysical sects was the First Church of Christ, Scientist, more popularly known as Christian Science. The sect was founded in Boston in 1879 by Mary Baker Eddy, a former homeopath who wrote the book that, along with the Bible, serves as the group's central source of guidance and revelation: *Science and Health with Key to the Scriptures*. Following the miraculous disappearance of a serious back injury, Eddy came to the conclusion that pain, disease, and death were, like the whole of material reality, illusions fostered by our lack of spiritual understanding. In this belief she resembled the Gnostics of old, who held that we are immortal spiritual sparks imprisoned in the false dream of matter. Health was the outward sign of spiritual progress; positive thinking and contemplative prayer, not the medicines she considered snake oil, were the remedy for our ills. While this doctrine would later draw Christian Scientists into a number of legal battles, Eddy's church of spiritual healing scored big in California, a state that attracted many an immigrant with the sunny promise of health. By 1890, California had the third-highest number of Christian Scientists in the country; by 1906, Frankel estimates, Los Angeles alone had twelve to fifteen hundred members. And it was during this period, when Christian Science's fortunes were waxing, that Church members commissioned two of the state's most marvelous architects to build what would become two of its most marvelous sacred structures.

In 1909, five women who attended Berkeley's First Church of Christ, Scientist, approached Bernard Maybeck, the eccentric king of Bay Area Arts and Crafts architects. They told him they wanted a "a church that would look like a church"; what he gave them was one of America's most magnificent houses of worship, an organic modern expression of medieval religious romance that resembles nothing so much as a Rohirrim temple hall from the set of Peter Jackson's *Lord of the Rings*. Maybeck wrote of being moved by the faith of these women, which reminded him of the sincerity and conviction that he felt was embodied in the Romanesque churches he visited in southern France while a student at Paris's Ecole des Beaux-Arts. But despite Maybeck's taste for medieval forms and simple faith, his Christian Science church sucked the marrow from tradition in a very contemporary fashion: by sampling and synthesizing a variety of past styles. Like Maybeck's private homes, his church echoes a number of historical genres—in this case, Gothic cathedrals and Byzantine churches, Japanese temples and Viking halls. To his old Beaux-Arts buddies, such eclecticism would have seemed barbaric; to Maybeck, as to many Californians, it simply reflected the freshness and availability of the past. By opening up a space for wholeness at the

AUDITORIUM, FIRST CHURCH OF CHRIST, SCIENTIST, BERKELEY

EXIT
51
257
406
51
257
406
EXIT

LEFT: READER'S DESK, FIRST CHURCH OF CHRIST, SCIENTIST, BERKELEY

RIGHT: FIRST CHURCH OF CHRIST, SCIENTIST, SAN DIEGO

crossroads of different traditions, Maybeck birthed a building as fabulous as it was orthodox.

When Maybeck designed his Romanesque homage, he tried to "put [myself] in the boots of a fellow in the twelfth century." At the same time, the architect gleefully experimented with some of the latest industrial materials, including asbestos panels—whose toxicity was then unknown—and steel casement windows whose factory frames the architect inlaid with leaded Belgian art glass. Maybeck's most noticeable nod to the Romanesque is a series of freestanding columns that lie to the right of the main portico, their molded capitals each topped with an exposed, vaguely Japanese trellis now overrun with wisteria vines. This playful and charming exterior does not entirely prepare you for the sweet sublimity of the main auditorium, which slopes down from the entrance like a theater, drawing you in. California timber here becomes an illuminated manuscript, rendered with extensive Gothic tracery and patches of Byzantine stencilwork executed in gold, red, and blue. Maybeck used poured concrete for the reader's desk, which replaces the altar in Christian Science churches; when the concrete set poorly, the architect improvised with the results, painting the creases to form a frieze of irises. But the real drama of the sanctuary lies in Maybeck's characteristically forthright expression of structure and mass. Looking up from their pews, worshippers confront the cruciform truss that supports the redwood-paneled ceiling, a powerful Greek cross, its beams as thick as sequoia trunks, that manages to hold the space with lightness and ease. Resting in the auditorium, which continues to host Christian Scientist meetings, one can

FIRST CHURCH OF CHRIST, SCIENTI
FIRST CHURCH OF
CHRIST, SCIENTIST,
SAN DIEGO
THE CITY OF SAN DIEGO

appreciate Maybeck's visionary belief that the artist's true goal is to express "a particle of life behind the visible."

A year before Maybeck began his Berkeley church, a Christian Science congregation at the other end of the state decided they needed a new building to house their expanding numbers. With half the money pledged by a candy baron from Philadelphia whose ailing wife had been cured by Christian Science, a San Diego church approached Irving Gill, a New York architect who had also moved to Southern California for his health. In contrast to their Bay Area brethren, the San Diegans wanted a thoroughly modern church, with none of the ornate Victorian bric-a-brac that dominated the Banker's Hill neighborhood where the church would be built. Once again, the Christian Scientists had picked the right guy. A high school graduate who learned architecture from mentors rather than schools, Gill thought of the West as "the newest white page," a place to write things afresh. Like Maybeck, he had a romantic respect for the past; he loved Southern California's adobes and missions, with their stucco walls and tile roofs and graceful arcades. In his greatest buildings, like this Christian Science church, Gill winnowed the romance of the missions down to its abstract essence: long, low lines, minimal decoration, and the graceful repetition of the arch and other simple forms. Gill's lyric austerity can make some of his white blocks appear especially modernist today. But Gill did not reject decoration—he just wanted nature to do it, with sunlight and shade, flower and vine.

Gill seemed to resonate with Christian Science. While working on an earlier Christian Science church for a San Diego architectural firm, Gill donated some of his own money to finish the platform, which is the central area of the auditorium where the reader's desk resides and the laymen who replace the preachers in the sect stand as they intone set passages from the Bible and *Science and Health*. More than Maybeck's creation, Gill's church reflects the spirit of Christian Science, whose sanctuaries tend to be plain and whose ritual style almost defines the term *understated*. Gill's building communicates the clear calm that comes with balance and proportion, and here his characteristic repetition of simple shapes has the effect of sacred geometry, of suggesting forms that exist more in mind than in matter. Both light and volume seem to pass gracefully between interior and exterior, another Gill trait that takes on deeper resonance in this sacred space. One of the architect's more interesting moves was to lay the building long, so that the auditorium is wider than it is deep, the platform hugged up close to the curved pews. The one odd note in the scheme is the stained-glass dome, which Gill did not design and which may have reflected the congregation's desire to tip their hat to the mother church in Boston.

During World War II, the U.S. War Department ordered the dome tarred over, but this was nothing compared to the aesthetic horror delivered in 1953, when an extreme makeover transformed Gill's luminous mission into a jumbled brick box. In the 1980s, an overloaded truss forced the congregants to stop holding services. One of the engineers who investigated the problem was an Irving Gill fan who suggested to the congregation that they restore the church. With synchronistic luck and much "prayerful work," they raised the millions needed and hired the architect Jim Kelley-Markham, who wrapped up his stellar restoration job in 1998. (Today Berkeley's Friends of First Church are hoping to lavish a similar level of care on Maybeck's leaking marvel.) Only a few changes from Gill's original design were made. Given the dwindling numbers of Christians Scientists in the area, the auditorium was downsized in order to create a library and a Sunday school. Not all the stained glass was restored, which allowed the sanctuary to be bathed in even more natural light. When the jacarandas bloom, the interior explodes with color, although the flowers often play to an empty house.

AUDITORIUM, FIRST CHURCH OF CHRIST, SCIENTIST, SAN DIEGO

216

UNITY FIRE

The fastest-growing brand of Christianity across the globe today is Pentecostalism, a vibrant, dizzying, often ecstatic mode of worship whose followers soak up the sanctifying influx of the Holy Spirit like an intoxicating wine. The planet now boasts something like half a billion Pentecostals, but at the start of the twentieth century, the movement as such did not exist. Though sparks of the Pentecostal fire flared up in Kansas and Texas, the conflagration did not begin until 1906, when Julia Hutchins, who pastored a Holiness mission in Los Angeles, invited a black minister from the South named William Seymour to come and preach. Seymour had some powerful new ideas about sanctification, the purifying force of the Holy Spirit. Most notably, he believed in the central importance of speaking in tongues—the inspired babble, in foreign or unearthly languages, that first seized the apostles during the feast of Pentecost, when the Holy Spirit allowed them to communicate to men "out of every nation under heaven."

Seymour proved too enthusiastic for Hutchins, however, so she padlocked the church door against him. The minister soon found himself holding Bible study in the home of a couple who lived in a clapboard Victorian cottage on North Bonnie Brae, just southwest of Echo Park. On April 9, 1906, the Holy Spirit arrived. Jennie Evans Moore, who later became Mrs. Seymour, miraculously acquired the skill of piano playing and began belting out tunes in strange languages. Some people began to yell and prophesy, while others landed the gift of interpreting the angelic lingo. All this hullabaloo attracted attention, and soon Seymour was preaching to a roiling, shaking crowd from his modest pulpit, a small porch that conveniently loomed over the street. Seymour spoke of a cleansing fire to come, and when, on April 18, the San Francisco earthquake leveled California's own Sodom, the Last Days seemed at hand.

Needless to say, the end did not come. The porch broke, however, and the meetings were moved to a ramshackle barn on nearby Azusa Street, which lent its name to the revival that would last for another three and a half years. It was a wild scene. "In that old building," wrote one participant, "God took strong men and women to pieces, and put them together again, for His glory." Journalists, generally appalled at the democratic sea of shaking and babbling, helped transform the revival into a global phenomenon. Many missionaries came, hoping for a sanctified (and convenient) acquisition of the language skills they needed to spread the good news across the world.

Though Azusa Street's whitewashed barn is long gone, the Bonnie Brae house still stands. The building was slated for demolition in the early 1980s, when God apparently called a Holy Ghost warrior named Dr. Art Glass to found Pentecostal Heritage Inc., which bought and preserved the structure. After surviving fire, earthquake, and Glass's shoestring budget, 216 Bonnie Brae is now a small museum run by the Southern California Jurisdiction of the Church of God in Christ. Though the recessed porch that briefly served as Seymour's pulpit is gone, Jennie Moore's piano stands proud, an icon of inspired sacred flow.

Despite the enormous doctrinal differences between Pentecostalism and the unchurched spirituality of the West Coast, the Azusa Street Revival reflects the core California faith in the ennobling power of intense spiritual experience. The revival also proved that such boundary-dissolving ecstasy has the potential to eliminate racial barriers. At the time, scores of white pastors and parishioners were slain in the spirit alongside blacks and Catholic Latinos. The multicultural implications of Pentecostalism, with its polyglot glossolalia, became manifest in a sanctified gathering of the tribes. But the party could not last. Many observers, including future Pentecostal leaders, were shocked by what one journalist dubbed "a disgraceful intermingling of the races." After the Azusa Street Revival died down, Pentecostalism

216 BONNIE BRAE HOUSE, LOS ANGELES

almost immediately divided along racial lines, and for all the future splits and branchings the movement would take, this fundamental cleft stayed true.

The radical dream of Christian multiculturalism did not return to California until the end of World War II, when Dr. Howard Thurman opened the Church of the Fellowship of All Peoples in San Francisco. A black Baptist minister from Florida, Thurman focused his considerable intellectual and rhetorical skills on transforming American Christianity from a tool of segregation into a force of liberation. The idea for a radically inclusive church came to him on, of all places, the Khyber Pass in India, shortly after he had met with Mahatma Gandhi, then knee deep in his nonviolent struggles against the British. At the time, Thurman was deeply troubled by Christianity's legacy of violence and hate. Partly with Gandhi's encouragement, he recommitted to his faith and dedicated himself to a Jesus who brought everyone into the fold.

Thurman's writings and ideas would later influence Martin Luther King Jr., but the minister did not put America's social ills ahead of the need for individual spiritual transformation. An everyday mystic, Thurman believed that a personal encounter with the inner truth of unity would inevitably manifest that unity in society. Proclaiming dogma to be "the rationalization of somebody else's personal religious

ABOVE: SANCTUARY, GLIDE MEMORIAL CHURCH, SAN FRANCISCO

LEFT: PIANO, 216 BONNIE BRAE HOUSE, LOS ANGELES

experience," Thurman made his San Francisco church the first nondenominational, fully integrated church in America, and its doings prophesied the liberal multiculturalism to come. Besides the ethnic and religious mix in the pews, which were stocked with Jews and Catholics and the barely religious, the organization staged Egyptian harp concerts and programs of Jewish folklore, while children's workshops focused on Native American and African culture. It all helped hammer home Thurman's basic theme: "We are one at any level."

One of the highlights of the fellowship church service was its mixed-race choir, a concept that was later taken through the rafters by Cecil Williams, San Francisco's next visionary preacher of unity. An immense personality, Williams was born in West Texas and became one of the first blacks to study for the ministry at Southern Methodist University in Dallas. In 1964, he was invited to minister at Glide Memorial Methodist Church, then a small, somewhat paternalistic congregation that gathered in the pit of San Francisco's grungy Tenderloin district. Along with a team of other pastors, Williams transformed Glide into America's most radical Christian experiment in inclusion. Besides drawing a multiethnic crowd, Williams opened the doors to the Tenderloin's prostitutes and speed freaks. He welcomed gays and lesbians and transsexuals, and started performing same-sex commitment ceremonies in 1965. He took down the cross and removed the hymnals. Thousands came to participate in Glide's psychedelic celebration of diversity, fueled by Williams's radiant oratory, and by the many-hued choir and its blaring gospel jazz.

Glide pushed the envelope about as far as it could go. In 1967, Williams turned the church over to the Diggers, a group of freak activists and artists who staged a seventy-two-hour "Invisible Circus" that reached such heights of exuberant blasphemy that church officials closed it down in the ninth hour. In 1974, Williams riled up many local Methodists by allowing the prostitute organization COYOTE, led by Margot St. James, to hold the first National Hookers' Convention in the church. Meanwhile, Williams became San Francisco's religious superstar, a kente-cloth-wearing reverend who hobnobbed with Angela Davis and the Black Panthers, shuffled taped messages from the Symbionese Liberation Army to the family of Patty Hearst, and even defended the Reverend Jim Jones a year before Jones doled out the famous Kool-Aid to his largely African-American followers in the dank jungle of Guyana.

By boldly embracing the marginalized in one of America's most progressive towns, Williams also built the nonprofit Glide Foundation into a heavyweight local charity flush with government grants. The foundation today runs scores of programs, offering recovery services to drug addicts, health care to AIDS sufferers, and free meals to the city's vast homeless population. Such good works define the place where the spiritual revelation of essential unity meets the cold hard concrete. But the revelation wavers as well. Today, as Williams's generation retreats and a conservative and unforgiving tide sweeps through America's mainline denominations—not to mention the country's fraying network of social services—Glide appears, at times, like an anachronism, a ragged dream of nearly heretic communion.

WALK-IN CENTER, GLIDE MEMORIAL CHURCH, SAN FRANCISCO

hope
PLEASE BE ADVISED THAT GLIDE IS NOT RESPONSIBLE FOR YOUR PERSONAL PROPERTY
Welcome
Teach a man to fish and

SAINT ANGELUS

The Pentecostal fireball that shot out of Azusa Street changed the face of American religion and world Christianity alike. As the Holy Ghost power percolated through the land, many observers, including many Christians, condemned the holy rollers as outrageous opportunists—and never more so than when the roller in question was Aimee Semple McPherson. The wife of a fierce Pentecostal preacher who died of malaria while the couple were evangelizing abroad, McPherson broke the gender ranks when she hit the revival circuit on her own in 1916. A bold and buxom powerhouse, the evangelist attracted thousands to the tents whose stakes she hammered down herself. Though McPherson was more focused on saving souls than in mending bodies, it was her famed healing powers—attested to by many skeptical reporters—that drew the crowds. Sister Aimee was the biggest show in town—bigger than Houdini or Barnum or Billy Sunday.

After her daughter nearly died during the 1918 influenza pandemic, McPherson decided she needed to settle down. God gave her a vision of a golden bungalow out west, and so she packed up her mom and kids in an Oldsmobile seven-seater and headed to Los Angeles. She may have been the first woman to make the drive without a man around, and certainly the first to do so in a vehicle plastered with the admonition "Jesus Is Coming Soon—Get Ready." Using Los Angeles as a home base, the increasingly flamboyant McPherson mounted massive revivals across the West. In the summer of 1921, she packed San Diego's Dreamland Boxing Arena with some rope-a-dope evangelism, and as the weeks passed and the streets clogged with her fans, she moved the revival up the hill to Balboa Park, where the U.S. Marines were called in to control a thirty-thousand-person crowd that still managed to rush the stage.

McPherson then decided to sink her funds into a Los Angeles tabernacle that would serve as both temple and headquarters for her International Church of the Foursquare Gospel. It took three years and well over a million dollars to build the Angelus Temple, which lies on the northern shore of Echo Park Lake like a beached whale, just a few miles from the site of the Azusa Street Revival. When the church opened in 1923, it boasted the largest dome in America, a massive unsupported concrete vault whose exterior was topped with a rotating neon cross and glazed with ground abalone shells that twinkled in the sunlight. The space inside boasted excellent acoustics, over five thousand fold-up cinema-style seats, and multiple doors for crowd control. It was the first American megachurch.

Today McPherson's International Church of the Foursquare Gospel has grown to include over three million members. Success has brought the usual tomfoolery: in 2004, two top church officials were forced to resign after investing fourteen million dollars of church funds in a Ponzi scheme. But the Foursquare Gospel continues to thrive in today's hot global market for Pentecostal worship. In 1992, the Angelus Temple was designated as a national landmark; ten years later, the sanctuary underwent major renovations. Parishioners now confront the sort of sound and video technology that major rock stars utilize on tour.

McPherson herself would definitely have approved of the gear, because when it came to staging her own "illustrated sermons," the evangelist pulled out all the stops. Actually, Sister Aimee dispensed with the stops altogether, replacing the usual church organ with an all-brass jazz band and mashing up popular tunes with Christian lyrics. Fleshed out with costumes and props and acrobatics, her Bible Belt lessons bloomed into vaudevillian shtick. On one Sunday, she dressed up as a motorcycle cop to illustrate how God will someday pull us over on the road of life; on another occasion, she brought a live camel onstage, burdening the beast with crates labeled Worldly Pleasure and Love of Riches, and then tried, in vain, to lead it through the eye of a giant needle. For a sermon entitled "The Way of the Cross Leads Home," her set designer, Thompson Eade, outfitted a tilted wooden cross with an electric conveyor belt, so that little cardboard souls could be shown being ferried into the Promised Land.

These skits reflected McPherson's desire to channel Pentecostalism's chaotic manifestations into more manageable entertainments, and to thereby sustain a revival that neither traveled nor dissipated. Small "tarrying rooms" were reserved

NEON CROSS, ANGELUS TEMPLE, LOS ANGELES

off the main auditorium for those taken by glossolalia and other voluble gifts of the spirit, but in general Sister Aimee shifted the attention to herself. In this sense, McPherson tapped into the almost pagan power that would make the images manufactured in her adopted city some of the most influential in the world: the glamour of spectacle. The earliest movie studios had opened in her Echo Park neighborhood before moving west to Hollywood; when McPherson put a Trojan horse or a gold rush town onstage, the lineage was clear. She was also sexy, her dark-eyed charisma and sensual swoons enveloping her fundamentalist message with Babylon glitz. For her audience—largely Midwesterners who were both enticed and appalled by flapper Los Angeles—McPherson's erotic ambivalence made her a bona fide star, the Mary Pickford of Pentecostalism.

As a young woman, McPherson described her first experience of divine healing power as "a shock of electricity." When it came to her visionary use of media, the metaphor clearly worked both ways. In the Angelus Temple's "prayer tower," which looked forward to a similar tower built by Robert Schuller in Garden Grove, volunteers manned a bank of telephones, fielding prayer requests, talking to the troubled, even giving the time. In 1925, McPherson made her radio station, KFSG, the first major source of religious broadcasting in the country. Her morning "Sunshine Hour" was heard as far away as Canada and New Zealand, and some claimed to have been healed directly through the loudspeaker. McPherson set up tents with radios around the city, and at one point created a sort of etheric group mind by networking eight simultaneous revival meetings through two-way radios. When regulators hassled her for various spectrum shenanigans, she sent Herbert Hoover, then the U.S. Secretary of Commerce, a telegram: PLEASE ORDER YOUR MINIONS OF SATAN TO LEAVE MY STATION ALONE. YOU CANNOT EXPECT THE ALMIGHTY TO ABIDE BY YOUR WAVELENGTH NONSENSE.

McPherson discovered that modern media can also be a tool of the Devil—especially in Los Angeles, where the business of celebrity gossip was just kicking into high gear. Kenneth Ormiston, KFSG's radio engineer, was a married man and an avowed agnostic who used to rib McPherson on a telephone intercom during her broadcast performances. Apparently, these playful chats could be heard from the second balcony of the tabernacle, and rumors about the twosome began to fly. In 1926, Ormiston quit his job. A few months later, McPherson disappeared while vacationing at Venice Beach and was presumed drowned. After a month of rumor and scores of proto-Elvis sightings, McPherson showed up near the Mexican border, claiming she had been abducted by three mysterious figures named Steve, Jake, and Mexicali Rose. Reports soon emerged that the evangelist had actually been holed up in a Carmel "love nest" with Ormiston. The case was never resolved in court, although the press made up its mind pretty quickly.

SANCTUARY, ANGELUS TEMPLE, LOS ANGELES

Despite the scandal, McPherson kept her fans happy, in part by presenting herself as a repentant sinner without actually admitting anything. She also started sporting short skirts and a dyed blond bob. Pressures on the woman rose, and in 1930, she suffered a nervous breakdown from which she never really recovered. Though McPherson helped scores of folks during the Depression, both materially and spiritually, she also weathered various lawsuits and a fight with her mother that involved a broken maternal nose. Barbiturates wormed their way into her life, and she overdosed in an Oakland hotel room in 1944. She was buried alongside the stars at Glendale's Forest Lawn cemetery. The rumor that she was interred with a live telephone is almost certainly an urban legend, although an undeniably potent one for a being so wired with God.

COLVMBARIVM
PUSH

LOVED ONES

One of religion's biggest selling points is its capacity to dull the sting of death. For those staring down that long, dark tunnel, faith can bring both courage and acceptance; for those left behind, religion provides a framework for making meaning out of what can seem like an incomprehensible rip in the fabric of reality. On a more mundane level, religion also provides answers for the rather messy question of what to do with the mortal remains. After all, besides creating a host of practical problems, the rituals of preparing, disposing of, and honoring dead humans almost inevitably raise and reflect ultimate concerns. Even for secular people, the business of death is shadowed by God.

California's eccentric spirituality, which both reshaped and escaped the boundaries of American Christianity, is reflected in how Californians have handled and memorialized corpses. Most notable in this regard is the state's early and relatively exuberant embrace of cremation. In the late nineteenth century, most Americans considered cremation—which had not been practiced in the West since Roman times—a disgusting and heathen practice. But then some genteel elites started touting cremation as an efficient, sane, and healthy alternative to burial, which they condemned as a source of miasma and disease. Beneath the modern rhetoric of reform lurked the conflict between different religious models of the soul. Catholics feared for the cremated body come Resurrection Day, while some cremation advocates countered with the more mystic notion that we are actually pure spirits temporarily locked in a disposable vessel. The first widely publicized American cremation, which took place in 1876, was of Baron De Palm, a freethinker and Theosophist whose last rites were likened by the papers to a "pagan funeral." Colonel Henry Olcott, cofounder of the Theosophical Society and orchestrator of the funeral, stored De Palm's ashes in a Hindu-style urn, a nod to the burning ghats of India and the Vedic conception of the soul they reflected.

At the dawn of the twentieth century, while most Americans still rejected cremation, Californians embraced the practice. Four of the nation's twenty-four facilities were in the Golden State at the turn of the century; by the 1920s, seven of the ten leading crematories in the country stood on Californian soil. One reason for the boom was California's relatively large Asian population, especially of Sikhs. More important, though, was the fact that many West Coast crematories were attached to columbaria, where cremated remains could be stored—and, more importantly, memorialized. The term *columbaria* comes from the Latin word for *dovecote,* but instead of housing pigeons, columbaria provide niches for urns, which serve the function of headstones. Besides proving popular with clients, columbaria were good for business. After the Odd Fellows fraternal order opened its magnificent neoclassical columbarium in San Francisco in 1895, its crematory became the busiest in the country, performing nearly a quarter of the nation's cremations in the first five years of the twentieth century. Shortly thereafter, San Francisco banned cemeteries inside city limits; mortal remains were eventually moved, for the most part, to Colma. (Many of the city's current inhabitants, however, still live over the dead.) The Odd Fellows Cemetery gave way to residential blocks, and though the columbarium was not torn down, the building was abandoned to fungus and rodents. In 1979, the grand rotunda was acquired by the Neptune Society, smartly restored, and reopened. Today, the columbarium's holdings reflect the full diversity of San Francisco's population, and a number of its niches host innovative and deeply moving personal shrines: nuanced collections of photos, mementos, and paper decorations that recall Mexican-American altars and radiate the melancholic charm of Cornell boxes.

SAN FRANCISCO COLUMBARIUM, SAN FRANCISCO

The most remarkable California columbarium began life as a facility established in Oakland in 1902 by a group of East Bay undertakers. Business was good, and in 1926, the director, Lawrence Moore, commissioned Julia Morgan, one of California's most intriguing native architects, to restore the space and design new additions. A tiny workaholic who shied away from the limelight, Morgan grew up in Oakland and studied at Berkeley. She became the first woman in California to earn an architect's license, and the first woman anywhere to win acceptance into the architecture school at the Ecole des Beaux-Arts in Paris. In Berkeley, Morgan befriended the Craftsman oddball Bernard Maybeck, whose expressive deployment of structural elements like beams and trusses influenced Morgan's most extraordinary sacred space, the hushed redwood sanctuary of Berkeley's St. John's Presbyterian Church. Morgan's most famous commission was San Simeon, the gaudy and glorious villa that William Randolph Hearst built in the coast range of Central California. Stuffed with objets d'art that Hearst obsessively collected in Europe, including sizable chunks of convents and palaces, this surreal estate represents an arguably Californian collage of high and low culture—or, rather, of high culture rendered both tacky and marvelous through recombination and hedonistic display. Here, the facade of an actual Greek temple overlooks a swimming pool where Hollywood stars gathered, with classical statues of the sea god and his Nereids added to the pediment to set the proper theme.

Morgan brought a bit of San Simeon's theatricality to the Oakland columbarium, as well as the estate's rich Spanish blend of Romanesque and Gothic styles. But she designed something far more satisfying to the soul. Aiming for a cheerful tranquillity rather than gloom and doom, Morgan crafted a mazy Mediterranean dream that came to be called the Chapel of the Chimes. Narrow passageways and stairwells link a nest of rooms, trickling fountains, terraced gardens, and spaces for reflection. A long cloister with ribbed vaulting and concrete Gothic tracery leads to the main chapel, whose carillons in the square bell tower above lend the columbarium its name. Clerestory light animates the vaulted ceilings of the columbarium proper, a diffuse and shifting glow aided by stained-glass windows and electrically controlled skylights that were a first when they were installed. The drifting light, as well as the lush interior gardens and the strong rhythm of alcoves and archways, plays with the boundary between interior and exterior, creating an almost Moorish balance of openness and containment, a tempered joy before the ineluctable labyrinth of life. Even when the columbarium continued to expand following Morgan's retirement in 1951, the new rooms, though monumental and sparing on craft, seemed to grow organically from her earlier designs.

The Chapel of the Chimes avoids morbid atmosphere through grace; elsewhere in the state, the shadow of death would be banished with manic Christian optimism and entrepreneurial glee. Glendale's Forest Lawn is certainly the most famous cemetery in California, the final resting place of many a Hollywood star and the object of derision in *The Loved One,* an acerbic Evelyn Waugh novel and later a funny 1960s cult film. Eight miles of roads wind among over three hundred acres of rolling green hillsides, dotted with fountains, gleaming statues, and stone chapels. Trees and flowers abound, and the absence of conventional headstones allows the green slopes to flow and beckon. Forest Lawn is a pleasant place, the happy hunting grounds of the San Fernando Valley, not so much a cemetery as a park. Indeed, the mastermind who designed it, a Christian cowboy and failed mining engineer from Missouri named Hubert Eaton, invented a new term to describe his revolutionary concept: the memorial park.

According to Forest Lawn lore, the young Eaton was struck by a vision in 1917, when he stood atop the parched hills of the cemetery he had come to manage and took in the shabby scene of crooked headstones and devil grass below. If the dead are going to a happy place, he wondered, why are cemeteries so depressing? That night, he scribbled out "The Builder's Creed," which begins with his essential faith: "I believe in a happy Eternal life," he wrote, "in a Christ that smiles." To manifest this vision at Forest Lawn, Eaton decided to replace the headstones and chaparral with a park fit for strolling lovers and landscape painters, a place "devoid of misshapen monuments and other customary signs of earthly death." Today the creed is etched into an enormous slab of marble outside Forest Lawn's mausoleum. Alabaster statues of two little kids, one clutching a doll and the other standing next to a toy puppy, stare up at Eaton's now immortal words.

For all its beauty and curious charm, Forest Lawn remains haunted—not by the gloomy ghosts of the traditional cemetery, but by the Californian specter of the theme park. There are swans in the entrance fountain, replicas of Tudor homes and English parish churches, and a "wishing chair" built with Scottish stones supposedly blessed by fairies. "Lands" abound, including Vesperland, Borderland, and Slumberland. Near Babyland, designed for the youngest set, lies Lullabyland, an area demarcated by a heart-shaped path and overlooked by a storybook monument shaded by pines. The monument is a wonder: bounded by cavorting cherubs, a Cinderella castle, and bas-reliefs of little bears,

LEFT: GARDEN OF PROMISE, CHAPEL OF CHIMES, OAKLAND

BELOW: "BUILDER'S CREED," FOREST LAWN, GLENDALE

a poem promises bereaved mothers that they will one day once again embrace "dimpled, loving baby hands." Just as Disneyland could be seen as a memorial park for the American dream, so could Forest Lawn stand as a theme park of heavenly reward.

Like Walt Disney, Eaton combined visionary sentiment with commercial instinct. Before implementing the Builder's Creed, Eaton had already revolutionized his industry by selling cemetery plots and services "before need"—that is, before you actually die. Potential customers had practical reasons to buy before need, but for Eaton's troops of salesmen to truly succeed, he needed to sell something beyond the assurance of a hole in the ground. Like the Southland's real estate boosters, Eaton needed to sell a dream. In particular, he wanted to satisfy the "memorial impulse" he believed was reflected in places like the Taj Mahal and Westminster Abbey. Besides landscaping Forest Lawn and removing the headstones—which also helped with maintenance—Eaton filled the cemetery with charismatic architecture and well-known works of art. He was especially drawn to statuary, which took the iconic place of the upright grave markers he had banished.

Eaton's first purchase was the Duck Baby, a bronze statue of an infant cuddling ducklings that was apparently a big hit at San Francisco's Panama-Pacific expo in 1915. Like Julia Morgan, Eaton also went shopping in Italy, although he was primarily focused on procuring reproductions of Michelangelo's most famous statues. Whatever cultural capital Eaton believed these copies of David and Moses would bring to the Southland, he also knew that famous sculpture served as what he once called "a silent salesman." But the most remarkable statues at Forest Lawn are the nubile women scattered about, reclining in couches or fondling roses, many with perky nipples and flapper hairstyles. In his novel *After the Summer Dies the Swan,* which satirizes Forest Lawn, Aldous Huxley notes how, with these statues, the park had reinterpreted the Biblical promise that "Death is swallowed up in victory." Instead of depicting the victory of the soul, Forest Lawn trumpeted the body, the athletic and sexy figure of youth that had already become a primary archetype of California consciousness.

More than anything, Eaton wanted to procure a statue of the smiling Christ he saw in his vision. Though Eaton never really satisfied this quest, he did manage to memorialize what he believed was the "Sacred Trilogy" of Jesus' biography: the Last Supper, the Crucifixion, and the Resurrection. For the first act, Eaton commissioned an Italian craftswoman to develop a version of da Vinci's *Last Supper* in stained-glass—"not a copy, but a stained glass re-creation," as the gravelly-voiced narrator proclaims at the hourly shows that present the piece inside the mausoleum. For the Crucifixion, Eaton procured one of the largest paintings in the history of the planet—an insanely detailed panoramic canvas wider than two basketball courts set end to end. To house and display this behemoth, painted by the Polish artist Jan Styka and languishing at the time in a warehouse in Chicago, Eaton spent over a million and a half dollars to build the Hall of Crucifixion, an eight-hundred-seat theater that opened in 1951. Every hour, a twenty-minute show uses spotlights, music, and voice actors to unfold the tale of Golgotha using Styka's painting as a storyboard. After this multimedia extravaganza, the two-ton curtain closes and the third portion of the Sacred Trilogy—a smaller painting of the Resurrection commissioned by Eaton—mechanically rolls into view. It shows a glowing Christ looking up at the kingdom of heaven. And the kingdom of heaven looks rather like Forest Lawn.

The spirit of Forest Lawn continues to inspire both the landscape and the spectacle of the California cemetery. In 1998, Tyler Cassity, scion of a St. Louis funeral magnate, purchased the bankrupt Hollywood Memorial Park, which contained the graves of classic movie stars like Rudolph Valentino and Douglas Fairbanks. Redubbing the place Hollywood Forever, Cassity spruced up the grounds with peacocks and jasmine trees, and began projecting films on the mausoleum walls. He also provides multimedia A&E-style "LifeStories" for clients; after being screened at the memorial service, these digital mixes of old photos, Super 8s, and audio recordings are made available online. Following Hollywood Forever's success, Cassity decided to create the most ambitious "green" cemetery in the United States. Forever Fernwood is located in Marin County, where the "death-midwifery" movement was born and an astounding 80 percent of folks opt for cremation. In designated areas of Fernwood, ashes or unembalmed bodies are buried in shrouds, biodegradable urns, or simple bamboo caskets, their location marked by nothing more than oaks and stones and GPS signals. Fernwood markets itself as an Edenic ecological preserve: the memorial park as memorial wilderness, where all signs of human passage have been carefully dusted away.

BABYLAND, FOREST LAWN, GLENDALE

PATRICIA HAYWARD
APRIL 2, 1930 NOV 8, 1939

OC SUPERSTAR

"THE SMILING JESUS," CRYSTAL CATHEDRAL, GARDEN GROVE

In 1955, a young minister and his wife took Route 66 from Chicago to California, cruising through the Cajon Pass and finally landing in Garden Grove. The man was Robert Schuller, and he came to Orange County to start a ministry under the auspices of the Dutch Reformed Church, one of the oldest Protestant denominations in America. With prophetic insight into the changing mindscape of the Southland, Schuller did not found a conventional church. Instead, he started preaching from the roof of a snack bar at the Orange Drive-In movie theater. By allowing parishioners to worship in their cars, Schuller honored their twin desires for religious community and the convenience of mediated isolation. His first sermon—or "message," as he called it—focused on "Power for Successful Living." It was the sort of upbeat motivational topic that Schuller honed throughout his career, and that helped him create a megabucks ministry as devoted to positive thinking as it is to Jesus.

For his first sermon, Schuller asked the members of the choir to drive separately, so the lot would look full. Two years later, when he invited fellow positive-thinker Norman Vincent Peale to speak, he caused a traffic jam on Interstate 5. Soon a larger space was needed, but when it came time to build the Garden Grove Community Church, Schuller did not want to abandon his drive-in congregants. So Schuller hired the great Angeleno architect Richard Neutra to build a chimera: a walk-in/drive-in church. Rejecting the usual stained glass, Neutra used glass windows, huge and clear, to invite nature into the auditorium—nature in this case being mowed grass lawns and fountains spitting from a long rectangular pool. For all of Neutra's "biorealism," though, the church's real inspiration was the car. As the architectural critic Reyner Banham points out, the church's design, and especially the hockey-stick pylons that thrust the carillon into the sky, resemble vernacular monuments to "Autopia" like quickie car washes and coffee shops. From the pulpit, Schuller could press a button and cause a glass wall to open up like the Red Sea, allowing him to step out onto a balcony and directly face a parking lot full of souls.

Schuller kept building. In 1968, Neutra overshadowed the carillon with a thirteen-story administrative building topped by a ninety-foot tapered cross. The Tower of Power housed New Hope Telephone Counseling, the first twenty-four-hour church-sponsored crisis hotline. Schuller continued to expand into media, launching his enormously successful *Hour of Power* television show, which included interviews with Southland heroes like Charlton Heston, Mickey Rooney, and Ray Kroc, the founder of McDonald's. Unlike most popular TV preachers, Schuller was neither a fundamentalist nor a Pentecostal. Instead, he preached an entrepreneurial gospel of prosperity and self-esteem, dropping mantras like "The Cross sanctifies the ego trip" and "If you can dream it, you can do it." Schuller understood that, while Orange County residents were conservative, they were also Californian. Their desire for success was driven by a vision of the redeemed and happy self, and they were unmoved by strict tradition.

Schuller's prosperity gospel served him well in his next, most audacious quest: to build an enormous, eye-grabbing church on his Garden Grove campus. After seeing a picture of the Fort Worth Water Gardens in a magazine, Schuller approached the park's architects, Philip Johnson and John Burgee. Johnson was already dean of American modernism, an unbeliever who did not need commissions from beaming Californian preachers who discussed financing by invoking the Lord's will. But as American showmen, Johnson and Schuller were cut from the same cloth, and after watching Schuller grin his way through the *Hour of Power,* Johnson decided he was a fan. Schuller, on the other hand, was not pleased with Johnson's initial design, a somewhat traditional scheme in the form of a Greek cross. "I'm not traditional," the minister was reported to have said. "This is California. People here don't come to church to be closed up in a box."

What Johnson designed instead of a box was a four-pointed crystal star, an immense tabernacle of glass. Reflective coating on the windowpanes gives the exterior the icy, mirror-shades gleam of many a 1980s office complex, but the inside is a joyous geometric wonder. Nearly three thousand seats fill an auditorium eight stories tall at its highest point, a space framed by a dazzling three-dimensional lattice of welded steel trusses painted white. This structural arabesque suggests an offworld biosphere or a sunbelt remake of the Fortress of Solitude from the first *Superman* movie. The clear glass is open to the land and sky, and a complex array of louvered windows provides the cross-ventilation that replaces air-conditioning, further evaporating the difference between inside and out. An enormous pipe organ, and an equally enormous Sony Jumbotron video monitor, ensures the temporary abeyance of all attention deficit disorders. Perhaps in homage to Neutra's earlier church, two motorized ninety-foot-tall doorways open beside the granite pulpit, allowing Schuller access, again, to the parking lot.

GARDEN GROVE COMMUNITY CHURCH/THE ARBORETUM, CRYSTAL CATHEDRAL, GARDEN GROVE

Johnson's building is awe inspiring, but no more awe inspiring than Schuller's ability to pay for the thing, which wound up costing over twice its initial bid of ten million dollars. After Schuller's prayer for an initial million-dollar commitment was answered by one of his many wealthy followers, the minister came up with the idea of selling memorial inscriptions on each of the building's 10,600 windows for five hundred dollars a pop. In June 1978, desperately needing a major infusion of cash, Schuller held a Million Dollar Sunday; by the end of the day, 1.4 million dollars in cash and pledges had been gathered in wheelbarrows pushed by hard-hat-wearing ushers. Whenever Schuller faced financial hurdles, he recited his Possibility Thinker's Creed and pushed on, and when he dedicated the cathedral in 1980, the building was free of debt. The Crystal Cathedral thus represented a sort of spiritual pyramid scheme: Schuller's extraordinary ability to raise the money confirmed the truth of his prosperity gospel, and this success in turn drew more funders to identify their dreams with his will—or God's, as the case may be.

In 1990, Johnson accented the cathedral with a twenty-three-story bell tower, a densely faceted campanile that moved the acerbic atheist so much when he saw it completed that he gushed that a higher force had guided his hand. Twelve years later, Schuller's campus was rounded out with the International Center for Possibility Thinking, a cubist cupcake with stainless steel frames and plaster skin designed by Richard Meier, who also created the high and mighty Getty Center in the Santa Monica hills. But these modernist monuments do not exhaust the aesthetic surprises of the Crystal Cathedral. A handful of life-size bronzes are scattered throughout the campus, their garish sentimentality seemingly designed to compensate for whatever aesthetic demands the high-brow architects have made. Moses brandishes the Ten Commandments with Hestonian fury, while a moppet in modern garb tugs on the Savior's beard. The inspiration here is not Le Corbusier, but Hubert Eaton and the happy religious sculpture he brought to Forest Lawn. These statues are emblems of a world-affirming, nearly hedonistic Christianity. Two particularly toothy bronzes even embody Eaton's most cherished image of redemption: the Christ who smiles.

The Crystal Cathedral looms over Orange County as a glass-and-steel symbol of Robert Schuller's prosperity gospel. But many conservative Christians consider Schuller to be a New Age apostate and reject his self-help Christianity. Despite Schuller's mediagenic profile, the minister and his monument have influenced American Christianity far less than the boisterous nondenominational evangelical churches that burst out of Orange County onto the national scene in the 1970s and '80s. For the most part, these churches hold the conservative center and reflect little of California consciousness beyond their informality. But the fire behind this nondenominational revival can be traced back to a deeply freaky local, a longhair prophet of God with the extraordinarily groovy name of Lonnie Frisbee.

A child of Costa Mesa, Frisbee dropped out as a teenager. He spent a lot of time in the canyons near Palm Springs, where legendary proto-hippies like Gypsy Boots, eden ahbez, and other Nature Boys had lived raw and wild as early as the 1940s. Shortly before the Summer of Love, Frisbee made his way to Tahquitz Canyon, bringing along a Bible, paints, and some LSD to drop with other skinny-dipping freaks. Tripping hard, Frisbee asked God to reveal himself, and He did. Frisbee was granted a vision of the Pacific Ocean drying up and filling with hordes of people, who raised their hands to heaven and cried out to be saved. Not long afterward, Frisbee made his way up to the Haight, where he took more drugs, polished his occult powers, and slept with tons of people. Hanging out one day in the Living Room, a coffee shop run by street Christians set on evangelizing hippies, Frisbee handed his soul over to Jesus. But though his heart had changed, his clothes and hairstyle had not.

A year later Frisbee was back in Costa Mesa, standing at the doorway of a pastor who wanted to meet a bona fide hippie. The minister was Chuck Smith, who headed a small nondenominational church called Calvary Chapel. Smith wanted to minister to the surfers and potheads of the coastal town, and so he hooked up with Frisbee, who was a spitting Anglo image of the Savior. Frisbee proved infectiously charismatic, his extraordinary success with young people helping turn the Jesus movement from a California eccentricity into a mass phenomenon. Christ became a long-haired revolutionary of love, and his followers used countercultural media like underground newspapers and folk rock to turn on others to the convulsive power of the Holy Spirit. The movement crackled with apocalyptic intensity, sometimes devolving into creepy cults like David Berg's Children of God, whose followers brought converts into the fold by having sex with them. In general, however, Jesus freaks achieved a strange *hieros gamos,* wedding idealistic hippie mysticism with Bible Belt beliefs.

In 1971, Frisbee parted ways with Smith, who became wary of the magnetic evangelist's Pentecostal emphasis on intense conversion experiences rather than working line-by-line with Scripture. Smith nonetheless honed Calvary Chapel's informal, rock-solid style into an immensely successful international movement that, in its quest to restore the atmosphere of the early Church, was morally conservative but lively and antiestablishment in tone. Frisbee himself plunged even deeper into signs and wonders. On Mother's Day, 1980, he preached at a Calvary Chapel church in Yorba Linda. Frisbee exclaimed, "Come Holy Spirit," and the hall erupted in tongues and healings and prophecy. The power unleashed by this event eventually caused a split between Calvary and John Wimber, the church's pastor. Wimber went on to spearhead the Vineyard Christian Fellowship, which would in turn spark one of the most influential and controversial charismatic movements of the last twenty-five years.

Though Wimber's "power evangelism" set him at odds with Smith, the two sister churches revitalized American Christianity with their decentralized, lay-oriented emphasis on the workings of the Holy Spirit inside people's lives. Suburban megachurches across the land, including Rick Warren's 22,000-member Saddleback Church, can trace their roots to this movement. But as this boomer great awakening settles into middle age, Lonnie Frisbee's catalytic role has been quietly covered up. Frisbee was a spiritual live wire, and like many live wires, he burned too hot. He also struggled mightily with the flesh—and man-flesh, to boot. In 1993, the onetime Jesus-freak coverboy died of AIDS, raising issues that most people in the evangelical community would rather ignore. Frisbee was eulogized at his funeral as a Samson, a spiritual hero brought down by moral drift. His body lies beneath swaying palm trees at the Crystal Cathedral cemetery. Frisbee himself never attended Schuller's church, which did not reflect his gutsy experience of the Holy Spirit. Frisbee chose it to be his final resting place because the cathedral is about as flamboyant as it comes.

CRYSTAL CATHEDRAL MEMORIAL GARDENS, GARDEN GROVE

MEDITATION HUT, DRUID HEIGHTS, MARIN COUNTY

CALIFORNIA CONSCIOUSNESS

CLEANSING THE DOORS

The grand old man of California consciousness was not even American. When Aldous Huxley docked in New York City with his family in 1937, he was about as brilliant a mind as Britain had produced, an acerbic novelist, wide-ranging essayist, and biting social critic responsible for the prescient dystopia *Brave New World.* As he puttered through the dust to reach California, there was little indication that this spindly, half-blind polymath would come to lay the groundwork for the spiritual counterculture to come. Like many European artists and writers in the 1930s and '40s, Huxley moved to Los Angeles to escape the war, although in his case he was also fleeing the opprobrium heaped upon him because of his public commitment to pacifism. Once in Hollywood, Huxley wrote screenplays and lived the life of a bohemian brainiac, hobnobbing with celebrities like Harpo Marx, Charlie Chaplin, and the astronomer Edwin Hubble. He shared an open marriage with his wife, Maria, who procured lovers for him and frequented the lesbian "sewing circles" of Hollywood with the certifiably divine Greta Garbo. But in 1942, Huxley grew weary of the Southland's great "Metrollopis" and, in a prophetic move, headed back to the land in search of a simpler and more natural life.

Huxley remodeled a humble ranch on the edge of the Mojave Desert, in the scrubby Antelope Valley, which hugs the northern foothills of the San Gabriel Mountains, about forty miles north of Los Angeles. The writer lived very near the ruins of the Llano del Rio Cooperative Colony, a farming collective founded in 1914 by Job Harriman after his nearly successful bid to become the first socialist mayor of Los Angeles. Embittered by conventional politics, Harriman and a few hundred followers launched an experimental Utopia. Like nearly all socialist projects of the time, Llano was a secular

LLANO DEL RIO COOPERATIVE COLONY
RUINS, LLANO, ANTELOPE VALLEY

VIVEKANANDA STATUE, TRABUCO COLLEGE/RAMAKRISHNA MONASTERY, TRABUCO CANYON

enterprise, as well as a reflection of the dropout culture that has long fringed California society. Word about Llano spread through socialist newspapers, and soon the community had attracted nearly a thousand refugees from capitalism. Llano's agricultural and publishing activities briefly kicked into high gear, but local water conflicts and the inevitable financial and power struggles sent the colony plunging toward bankruptcy. In 1917, Harriman dissolved the colony and led two hundred of his original followers to Louisiana, where they established another community that lasted for an impressive twenty-two years.

Living near these utopian ruins, Huxley plunged into the studies that made him a mystic, albeit a cantankerous and critical one. In his earlier novels and essays, Huxley had cast a cold and sometimes jaundiced eye on the foibles and delusions of the human personality. As a social critic, he had concluded that people needed to change on an individual psychological level if civilization was going to avoid the disasters he glimpsed on the horizon: overpopulation, high-tech war, ecological catastrophe, and the sort of narcotized totalitarian propaganda depicted with such lasting power in *Brave New World*. Inspired by his friend and fellow pacifist Gerald Heard, Huxley came to suspect that only mystical experience could give people direct access to states of consciousness capable of eroding their mean and selfish egotism. Even as Huxley settled into his desert asceticism, the brilliant and impish Heard was building the Trabuco College of Prayer in a remote canyon in the Santa Ana Mountains. A loose-limbed spiritual training center, Trabuco College was designed to creatively and collaboratively explore Eastern and Western mysticism without hewing to any specific tradition. Heard's spa for the soul was two decades before its time, however, and the experiment lasted only a few years, after which Heard passed on the property, with its Italianate monastic brick structures, to the Vedanta Society.

In Llano, Huxley embarked on a massive cross-cultural study of experiential religion. The resulting book, *The Perennial Philosophy,* argued that the writings of mystics across the world revealed the same ultimate reality—a oneness that transcends the ordinary personality while affirming the essential "suchness" of things as they are. Huxley found evidence for this nondualistic view by amassing a huge collage of quotations from various traditions—a graceful and fiercely intelligent expression of the spiritual sampling that characterizes California consciousness. This notion of a shared core of religious experience was later taken up by the influential Berkeley scholar Huston Smith, who, like Huxley, experimented with and praised psychedelics. Despite his deep familiarity with Christian mysticism, however, Huxley interpreted ultimate reality in nontheistic and distinctly Vedantist terms. The Christian or Sufi emphasis on sacred personality did not receive equal billing—a reflection, perhaps, of Huxley's misanthropic tendencies.

Huxley's impersonal vision of Being, of the one substance behind the show, would come to dominate the spiritual counterculture. But the most Californian note sounded by *The Perennial Philosophy* was its pragmatic insistence that knowledge of ultimate reality could come only through spiritual practice, rather than dogmatic belief or rote ritual. Spirituality was a matter of mind-body techniques, individual discovery, and an open-ended embrace of transformation. Inspired, perhaps, by his friendship with Hubble, Huxley compared his "empirical theology" to the technology that undergirds astronomy. While a faint smudge glimpsed with the naked eye might allow us to theorize about extragalactic nebulae, such theories can never tell us as much about the cosmos "as can direct acquaintance by means of a good telescope, camera and spectroscope." So too does spiritual reality transcend theory, only to be "directly apprehended by a mind in a state of detachment, charity and humility."

We don't know if Huxley's turn to the spirit was inspired by a personal encounter with some *mysterium tremendum,* although a decade or so later the writer would embrace mescaline and LSD as handy catalysts of the mystic vision. In Llano, where he lived and worked in a hexagonal apartment the couple added to the main building, Huxley adopted an ad hoc spiritual regimen based on paring down his quotidian routine. Keeping distractions to a minimum, he grew carrots, pumped water, and devoted himself to his studies of mysticism. Instead of their usual flings, he and Maria practiced celibacy. They adopted a "natural" diet that apparently had something to do with making beans and legumes as bland as possible. Huxley, who was nearly blind, also deepened his practice of various eye exercises proposed by the New York ophthalmologist W. H. Bates, who argued that poor eyesight should be approached as a holistic mind-body imbalance. Huxley transformed these practical techniques into a Buddhist meditation on attention that not only improved his poor visual acuity—for a time, at least—but also allowed the self who desired so anxiously to see to relax a bit into the process of simply being.

Huxley's understanding of the One within and behind all things was certainly nurtured by the spare landscape of the Mojave. In his brief time there, before terrible allergies drove him back to the Hollywood Hills, Huxley came to understand why so many mystics resonated with the silence and emptiness of the desert. "God seemed nearer there than in the world of men," he wrote. In one essay about his Antelope Valley sojourn, Huxley described a vision of a Joshua tree in which the hairy yucca became a living icon of absolute spirit: "There is a coolness against the cheek, and from overhead comes the scaly rattling of the wind in the dead dry leaves of the Joshua tree. And suddenly the symbol is essentially the same as what it symbolizes; the monstrous yucca in the desert is at once a botanical specimen and the essential Suchness."

Most of the essay concerns the old Llano del Rio Cooperative Colony. For Huxley, the colony symbolized not the divine ground but the folly of even noble men, struggling with perennial ignorance and greed. Harriman's failed Utopia reminded Huxley of the fatalistic theme of Shelley's poem "Ozymandias," which describes a monument proclaiming the greatness of a long-forgotten king, a memorial statue slowly collapsing into the "lone and level" sands of a desert. Like Robinson Jeffers, Huxley held a rather pessimistic

HUXLEY STREET, LOS ANGELES

assessment of human development, even as he came to believe in the individual potential for extraordinary psychospiritual transformation. Huxley's embrace of mystical techniques and social experimentation arose from a deep conviction that twentieth-century humanity was going to hell in a handbasket, and the colony's failure was only more proof. But even Huxley could not resist constructing a Utopia, if only in words. His novel *Island* was published in 1962, a year before his LSD-laced death, and it describes an island community that fuses the best of Eastern wisdom and Western know-how. Constantly called to attention by the cries of mynah birds, the people of Pala embrace herbal medicine, Tantric sex, and the judicious use of psychedelics in adolescence; they also have recourse to credit unions, hydro power, and birth control. As a narrative, *Island* is not much more successful than Harriman's original community, but the visionary society it depicts provided a far more compelling road map for the spiritual radicals of the coming decades.

DRUIDS AND FERRIES

When her longtime companion died on the eve of World War II, the poet Elsa Gidlow decided to abandon the bohemian enclave of Greenwich Village and hitchhike to California. This was an unusual thing for a woman to do in 1940, but Gidlow was an unusual woman. Fiercely independent and largely self-educated, Gidlow had been raised in poverty before moving to New York to edit a poetry journal. She was both an anarchist and a lesbian, and in 1923, she published *On a Grey Thread,* the first unabashedly Sapphic book of poetry issued in the United States. She could handle hitching across the States.

Arriving in Marin County, Gidlow holed up in a derelict house in rural Fairfax. She was forty years old. Facing winter solstice alone and unsettled, she decided to perform what she later described as a "transforming ritual." As a storm raged outside the leaky house, she built up a roaring blaze of madrone logs. Slowly, Gidlow sensed the room fill with the spirits of all the mothers and grandmothers who have ever tended fire, all the way back to the Paleolithic. "I knew myself linked by chains of fire," she wrote, "to every woman who has kept a hearth." In the morning, Gidlow honored this vision—simultaneously sacred and domestic—by wrapping some of the cold coals in foil and red ribbon, and keeping them for the next year's solstice fire.

In 1954, Gidlow brought one of these solstice coals to her new home, a junky five-acre patch of hillside on the edge of Muir Woods, lying at the end of a precarious road more clay than dirt. Shadowed by a looming wall of eucalyptus to the southwest, a few tumbledown frame houses and barns were already returning to earth, and there was no plumbing to speak of. Gidlow dubbed the place Druid Heights, and it would soon blaze into a hidden hearth of bohemian culture, a beatnik enclave before the term was coined or needed. Scores of sculptors, sex rebels, freaks, and seekers lived or visited the spot over the decades, including Gary Snyder, Dizzy Gillespie, Alan Watts, Neil Young, Tom Robbins, and the colorful prostitute activist Margot St. James. Too anarchic and happenstance to count as a commune, Druid Heights became what Gidlow jokingly called "an unintentional community"—a vortex of social and artistic energy that bloomed out of nowhere, did its thing, and, for the most part, moved on. Although the U.S. Interior Department now owns the land, the hamlet lingers on, a liminal zone that still does not appear on many maps.

Gidlow initially shared the property with a man named Roger Somers and his wife, Mary. A house builder and jazz musician, Somers moved to Marin County in 1950 and was one of the more breathtaking bon vivants of the era. In his woodwork and design, Somers developed a flamboyant, organic, deeply Californian style influenced by Frank Lloyd Wright, Japanese architecture, and the twists and turns of living things. (He once met Wright after impersonating a busboy and bringing the master his breakfast.) Somers's most outlandish commission was a tour bus he built for Neil Young in the mid-1970s, a massive elven dream machine with teak siding, a roof deck, and Art Nouveau interiors of syrupy wood.

Many of the homes and structures in Druid Heights were built or converted by Somers and Ed Stiles, a custom furniture maker from the East Coast who tracked down Somers after seeing a photograph of him in an article about California beatniks in *Esquire.* Like Somers, Stiles enjoyed working with salvaged materials as well as good hardwoods. He also built Marin County's first filtered, self-regulating redwood hot tub, an icon of laid-back California hedonism that Stiles believed was an important social equalizer; its prototype is now a crenellated ruin crumbling into the hillside. Stiles also built the bare bones of the wildest house at the Heights, a home for Gidlow's sister that was heavily modified by Somers once Alan Watts commandeered the place in the early 1970s. The blobular, radial structure was called the Mandala, although from the hillside above it looks a bit like

THE MANDALA, DRUID HEIGHTS, MARIN COUNTY

RIGHT: ALAN WATTS LIBRARY/ MOON TEMPLE, DRUID HEIGHTS, MARIN COUNTY

BELOW: ZENDO, DRUID HEIGHTS, MARIN COUNTY

a clown—a resemblance Somers claimed was intentional. Somers tricked out the interior with ingeniously embedded lights, art glass, and a dining area sunk into the plush carpet floor for maximum comfiness. Outside lies a deck where San Francisco's legendary Mitchell Brothers once shot a porno film.

Sexual experimentation was only one of the colony's means of exploring the boundaries of consciousness. One of the most charming structures on the land is a simple meditation shack that juts out from the hillside. Irregular clapboard shingles resemble geological strata, while the hut's mitered windows pop out like quartz crystals or eyes agog with vision. The interior features Japanese wallpaper and a ceiling covered with bamboo slats, and the whole space invites quiet contemplation. The shack was built by a couple of the community's constantly rotating inhabitants, but its Pacific Rim vibe was first established by Somers with the amazing shoji room he built inside the modified farmhouse that served as his first home. A raised platform surrounded by paneled screens that Somers made out of cheap fiberglass material rather than rice paper, the graceful Japanese room—dubbed the "zendo"—once featured a Buddha and a *kamidana*, or ancestral shrine. In summer, light pierces a large telescoping round window crossed by two thin wooden shelves that resemble wispy clouds. Here Alan Watts gave lectures on Zen aesthetics; here Tom Robbins cavorted with groupies for all to see.

If there was a guiding spiritual force behind the hedonism of Druid Heights, it came from the East, from the sly immediacy of Zen and the earthy anarchism of the Tao. Already by the mid-1950s, Gidlow was studying Chinese and calligraphy at San Francisco's American Academy of Asian Studies, a groundbreaking center of East-West exchange and a seedbed for the hybrid hippie forms of Zen, Taoism, and Hindu Vedanta to come. In the 1960s, the Beat poet and Zen practitioner Gary Snyder briefly lived at the Heights with his Japanese wife, Masa Uehara; later, barefoot monks from the San Francisco Zen Center's nearby Green Gulch Farm would occasionally tramp over for a visit. Even the land seemed unrolled from some Chinese scroll, with its gnarled cypresses and the craggy rock in the distance called Cloud Hidden.

The rock got its name from Alan Watts, the most illustrious spiritual hedonist associated with Druid Heights. An ordained Episcopal priest, Watts moved to the Bay Area in 1951 to teach at the American Academy, where he probably met Gidlow. With his seminars, KPFA radio shows, and books, beginning with 1957's *The Way of Zen,* Watts coaxed countless hip and literate Americans into the deep stream of East Asian art and mysticism. Emphasizing perception and spontaneity rather than formal practice, Watts painted a picture of the Tao that was fresh, resonant, and countercultural *avant la lettre.* By experiencing the Way or the suchness of things, Watts claimed, we can temporarily shed our "skin-encapsulated ego." This expansion of consciousness gives us a glimpse of the larger ecological reality of which we are always a part. It also throws a monkey wrench into the social programming we take to be our personalities.

Today Watts's writings and recorded talks still shimmer with a profound and galvanizing lucidity. At the same time, and even as Watts took the beatniks to task for their druggy rebel Zen, the man himself hardly cut the figure of a wisdom teacher. A womanizer and hardcore alcoholic, the middle-aged Watts died at Druid Heights in 1973, for reasons related, more or less directly, to the demon drink. Although Watts wrote frankly about the need to balance mysticism and sensuality—to be "both angel and animal with equal devotion"—his hymns to spontaneity can seem like justifications for license and his own lax engagement with meditation or other formal spiritual practices. In this, he truly served as an avatar for California consciousness, in all its wayward confusions.

Druid Heights was Watts's home turf, and you can sense its presence in *The Way of Zen,* where he characterizes the essential aimlessness of the Tao as a kind of organic freedom:

> the freedom of clouds and mountain streams, wandering nowhere, of flowers in impenetrable canyons, beautiful for no one to see, and of the ocean surf forever washing the sand, to no end.

Watts dedicated his autobiography to Gidlow, and 1962's *The Joyous Cosmology* to the people of Druid Heights. The latter book, a slim volume subtitled *Adventures in the Chemistry of Consciousness,* was Watts's *Doors of Perception,* a limpid and inspiring description of a group of friends—including "Ella" and "Robert"—all exploring the "goal-less play" of an LSD trip. The same year, Watts holed up with Somers and some other hepcats and recorded an astounding tribal freak-out LP called *This Is IT,* which includes Somers and Watts performing spontaneous voodoo scat over bongos. The album is the first aural document of psychedelia.

Working with a bit more discipline, Stiles and Somers later built Watts his own pad at Druid Heights. Looking like a large redwood hot tub crowned by a sylvan UFO, the snug little retreat sits on a redwood platform regularly pelted with sticky eucalyptus droppings. Watts mostly used the space as a library, and it was later dubbed the Moon Temple when Gidlow began inviting lesbian writers to the property and the Goddess currents intensified. Sinewy posts on an interior balustrade show Somers's continued devotion to the Tao of wood, while a single weathered marker sunk in the clay outside marks the spot where a handful of Watts's ashes were scattered.

Though Watts spent a good deal of time living and partying at Druid Heights, the main center of his operations lay elsewhere in Marin County. The SS *Vallejo* began life as a steam-powered paddle-wheel ferry that shuttled passengers between Vallejo and Mare Island before the Bay Area's bridges snuffed out the great era of ferry travel. After completing its final run in 1948, the *Vallejo* was abandoned in a Sausalito shipyard built by the Bechtel Corporation during World War II. An exuberant Greek artist named Jean Varda

VALLEJO

found the vessel shortly thereafter, and purchased it with some fellow artists, including the Surrealist Gordon Onslow Ford. The *Vallejo* became the nucleus of Sausalito's hardscrabble houseboat hipster scene, which attracted scores of Beats and bohemians to the mud flats north of town, where folks had been vacationing in their "arks" since the 1880s. Kerouac himself stayed on the boat, supposedly building a fence around the landing during one of his famous alcoholic tears. Well into the 1990s, the *Vallejo* continued to house trippy characters and host outrageous parties; its current owner, an old friend of Timothy Leary's, played a leading role in the Bay Area's visionary virtual reality scene.

While he lived, Varda was the soul of the *Vallejo*. When he wasn't sailing, cooking, or enjoying the company of beautiful young women, he made colorful cubist collages and mosaics out of textiles, wood, and other found materials. Varda's embrace of collage—a frugal art of scavenging and juxtaposition that attracted many postwar California artists—also remade the *Vallejo*. Varda painted its flanks with suns and pennants, hung colored bottles in the windows, and embedded shards of glass around the fireplace to catch the light. In 1961, Watts and his wife, Jano, moved onto the *Vallejo*, taking over all but Varda's portion of the boat. Under the auspices of the Society for Comparative Philosophy, which helped the writer hide his money from his ex-wives, Watts held Zen teachings and seminars in the loftlike space, including a combative 1967 dialogue among Leary, Gary Snyder, and Allen Ginsberg that was published in a peacock-hued Haight Street rag called *The Oracle*. At the time, much was made about the difference between Varda's exuberant décor and Watts's austere Zen interior, with its white walls, dark wood, and large bronze Buddha. But eventually the two epicureans sawed a doorway between their two sides, just to facilitate the flow between sense and spirit.

LEFT: THE **VALLEJO**, SAUSALITO

RIGHT: GANESHA SHRINE, THE **VALLEJO**, SAUSALITO

SILENCE

LIFE SPRINGS

No wonder California is an unstable place. An enormous fault line, one of the world's longest, runs roughly parallel to the coastline like a giant zipper, the result of two continental plates grinding past each other at the rate of five centimeters a year. Occasionally, the grind goes giddy and lets fly one of the massive earthquakes that have become, even more than wildfires, mud slides, and drought, California's signature natural disaster. Ever since 1906, when San Francisco shook and burned, the threat of the Big One has shadowed the California psyche, feeding a fascination with risk and apocalypse. But the land's vast network of fault lines, cracks, and stresses also makes the region a geothermal wonderland. Like much of the West, California is pockmarked with vents, geysers, and bubbling vats of stinky mud—as well as copious hot springs. These mineral-rich pools of tension-melting bliss, which bring ancient water bubbling up from cavities miles below the surface, have shaped California's culture of healing as much as the land's looming seismic threat has shaped its culture of disaster.

California's original inhabitants treated hot springs as sites of healing and telluric power. Some springs were set aside as neutral ground, where different tribelets could meet without fear of conflict. In the late nineteenth century, when Yankee medicine was awash with homeopathic remedies and naturopathic cures, spas and resorts developed around many springs, helping to deepen the California equation of pleasure and healing. Saratoga Springs and Calistoga, today an entire township of spas, catered to the sanitarium crowd, while more rough-and-tumble sites served miners and lumberjacks across the state. A century later, when the counterculture's spiritual hedonists were grooving to naked flesh and the great outdoors, hot springs transformed into power spots yet again. Hippies and nudists made pilgrimages to undeveloped springs like Sykes or Deep Creek, while other spots bloomed into sustained communities. A riverside spring resort deep in the Ventana Wilderness became the Zen monastery of Tassajara, where the hot waters alleviate the suffering of cramped legs during long winter retreats. Orr Hot Springs, once the site of a rowdy logger bathhouse, became a commune in 1975 and still retains a laid-back, cannabinoid air.

One of California's most celebrated hot spots is Harbin Hot Springs, whose seven springs pump out fifty thousand gallons of pure mineral water a day, supplying the baths and the water needs of an entire community. Fringed by the forests of the Mayacamas Range, just over the mountains from Calistoga, Harbin presents a palimpsest of California healing. The community occupies a steep valley the Lake Miwoks referred to as *'eetawyomi*—the hot place. A wall beside the current cold plunge was built just after the Civil War, when the Harbin Hot Springs Health and Pleasure Resort invited folks with dyspepsia, rheumatism, or other ailments to take the waters. In the early 1970s, the area was purchased by Ishvara, a mellow guru of something called Heart Consciousness, although a contemporary visitor to Harbin could be forgiven for feeling that other organs of the body are most on people's minds. Under Ishvara's leadership, Harbin has become a subdued center of New Age culture, with its own healing modality—*watsu,* a sort of aquatic Shiatsu—and an annual Neopagan gathering called Ancient Ways. A natural builder named SunRay Kelley has recently constructed a graceful hobbit-worthy temple using strawbale and cob. Perhaps the most sacred spot, though, remains the hot pool, which at nearly 115 degrees seems to threaten tissue damage, and is housed inside a hushed, candlelit structure where a prayerful silence reigns.

Ishvara's Heart Consciousness grew out of the human-potential movement, a revolutionary philosophy of healing

HARBIN HOT SPRINGS, LAKE COUNTY

and human psychology that sprang from yet another California hot springs community. The waters in question bubble out of the cliffs near a low and impossibly gorgeous tuft of land that juts into the Pacific from the coastline of Big Sur, where the Santa Lucia Mountains plunge into the inky depths with a disturbing cant. The area has attracted spiritual hedonists since the writer Henry Miller moved there in the 1940s, riling up locals with his anarchist sentiments. In 1961, when the springs served as a rough-and-ready gay bathhouse, the property came into the hands of two Stanford graduate students named Michael Murphy and Richard Price. A sporty but monkish sort from the Salinas Valley, Murphy had spent sixteen months at Sri Aurobindo's ashram in Pondicherry, India, an experience that left him with a profound love of meditation—which he practiced as much as eight hours a day—but serious reservations about the guru model of spiritual training. Price was a more bohemian character, a denizen of North Beach who practiced Zen and had done time in a U.S. Air Force mental ward undergoing past-life flashbacks and electroshock therapy in equal measure. Together, the two intellectuals were committed to radical psychological development. Inspired by Gerald Heard's Trabuco College experiment, they decided to form an example of what Heard called "gymnasia of the mind." They named it Esalen, after the Esselen Indians, a small and pacific network of tribelets who inhabited Big Sur and are often considered, wrongly, to have been the first of California's native cultures consigned to oblivion.

The Esalen Institute spawned and nurtured the human-potential movement, an eclectic and influential blend of psychological therapies and secularized spiritual practices that transformed the American image of the self. Initially, Esalen was a scholarly place, where folks would gather to hear talks by thinkers and writers like Arnold Toynbee, Aldous Huxley, and especially Abraham Maslow. In Maslow's view, the psychology of the day erred in its fixation on the broken or neurotic individual. Maslow spoke instead of peak experiences, those godlike flashes of joy, insight, and self-empowerment that seem to spring from some deeper source than the mundane personalities that constipate our ordinary days. Maslow's conception of self-actualization was crucial to the idea of human potential, but within a few years, people wanted to do the do rather than talk about it. Soon an enormous number of techniques, new and old, were piled on the Esalen table: Gestalt therapy, meditation, tai chi chuan, psychedelics, Rolphing, primal scream therapy, holotropic breathwork, hatha yoga, biofeedback, Tantra, massage. Esalen participants felt like they were surfing the frothing edge of human evolution, as if a new kind of person were being birthed—or, more properly, rebirthed. Even madness, bouts of which Price continued to experience from time to time, was seen by some as an organic initiation rather than a malady to be squelched. As Esalen's legendary Gestalt therapist Fritz Perls said, "Lose your mind and come to your senses."

Esalen's most dangerous game was the encounter group, a spontaneous collective psychodrama that encouraged catharsis and the sometimes forceful dismantling of what the radical psychologist William Reich called our "personality armor." Murphy was amazed by the explosive dynamics of group therapy, which he considered a better deconditioning agent than LSD. The maestro of the form was William Schutz, who developed a macho "open encounter" style that worked toward joy but could also bubble over into anger and hostility. Encounter was scary, a kind of emotional Outward Bound, and no doubt shook up a freewheeling scene already awash with psychoactive and sexual opportunities. In this environment, Esalen's earlier emphasis on integration took a backseat to the process of letting it all hang out.

By the end of the 1970s, Esalen's practical therapies and holistic ideas had spread around the world, even as the institute became the butt of jokes and the flashpoint for attacks on the Me Generation. Some of the digs were deserved, as were some of the jokes: at one point in the mid-1970s, the list of staff members included "the Nine," a group of disincarnate entities channeled from the star system Sirius. But Esalen's essentially secular engagement with human transformation was, in its way, as revolutionary as anything launched in those epochal days. Esalen's leading thinkers and researchers, especially Murphy and the aikido master George Leonard, mapped and morphed

BATH WITH BUDDHA, ESALEN, BIG SUR

our understanding of the extraordinary capacities latent within the individual—prescient work given the radical augmentation therapies, pharmaceutical drugs, and technologies that are now transforming our definition of the human being. Esalen also explored the social and psychological implications of cybernetics and ecology, developing a more integral approach to mind, body, and nature. Esalen's best facilitators nudged people toward a more embodied and less hypocritical engagement with the tangled realities of the self. And they did this while largely dodging the authoritarian traps that swallowed up so many other avatars of California consciousness.

Today's Esalen is less an institute or a gymnasium of the mind than a genteel New Age resort that keeps the flame of the human potential movement alive by catering to aging baby boomers. Ketamine workouts and scary encounter groups are long gone, replaced with well-rounded weekends featuring organic food, art workshops, and massage. In 2004, six years after storms destroyed the old cliffside hot tubs, a new high-profile bathhouse and massage room opened. Designed by Mickey Muennig, an organic architect who has lived and worked in Big Sur since 1971, the high-dollar compound graces visitors with spare archways, cannily crafted views of the Pacific, and a mosaic fountain with a design drawn from a Hokusai painting. It's a reserved temple of sensation, and though it lacks the funky character of the early spa, bathers are still suspended above the infinite sea. Indeed, Esalen's most abiding California teaching may reside in the land itself. The property's cliffs, gardens, streams, and vantages not only possess an implacable beauty but also seem to incarnate the crux of transformation itself—that precipitous point of exaltation and threat that Robinson Jeffers, the great poet of the region, called "the verge extreme."

ESALEN, BIG SUR

RING OF BONE ZENDO, NEVADA COUNTY

BEAT ZEN, GREEN ZEN

In the late 1960s, Gary Snyder settled with his family on a remote farmstead among the pines of the San Juan Ridge, which lies in the Yuba River watershed of the northern Sierra Nevada. Snyder, one of America's most celebrated Beat poets, dubbed the place Kitkitdizze, the Indian name for a hardy native shrub. A few hundred yards from Snyder's house—a low-slung Japanese log affair he designed and built with the help of friends—lies a *zendo:* a long wooden meditation hall encircled by a raised porch whose eaves are supported by naked logs. There are Japanese bells and racks for shoes and a tiny kitchen attached by a sheltered bridge. Snyder and part of his tribe built this place in 1982, at the edge of an open pasture, and soon a lay Buddhist sangha crystallized out of the area's rural seekers and entheogenic poets.

Snyder never received dharma transmission from his Zen master Robert Aitken Roshi, but the presence of a formal zendo so near his mountain fastness should counter the persistent belief that the Beat fascination with Eastern religion, and especially with Zen, was just a hipster flirt. A native of San Francisco, Snyder studied East Asian languages at UC Berkeley in the 1950s after logging and climbing up and down the craggy ranges of the West Coast. Reading Chinese mountain poets and writing verse that embodied Native American and Buddhist lore, Snyder nurtured his peers Jack Kerouac and Allen Ginsberg in their deepening engagement with Asian mysticism. In Kerouac's 1958 novel *The Dharma Bums,* Snyder, as Japhy Ryder, plays the authentic West Coast hedonistic seer, drinking wine and having Tantric sex and famously prophesying the "rucksack revolution" to come. During the 1960s, Snyder helped lead that revolution, staging antiwar Zen blockades of the Oakland Harbor and helping organize the 1967 Human Be-In in Golden Gate Park. But the poet still spent the bulk of the decade studying and practicing Zen in a Kyoto monastery.

The name of Kitkitdizze's zendo, Ring of Bone, exposes another vein of California's Zen ore. The phrase comes from a group of earthy, wine-fired hermit poems written by Lew Welch, a relatively unsung Beat poet who grew up in California and attended Reed College in Oregon in the late 1940s. There Welch befriended Snyder and Philip Whalen, who would go on to write some great frisky poems of his own and to serve as abbot of the Hartford Street Zen Center in San Francisco. Welch suffered a nervous breakdown in the 1950s and retreated to a corporate job in Chicago, but he soon found himself back on the West Coast, driving a cab in San Francisco and sitting *zazen* with Snyder. In 1962, Welch took to the woods like an American Han Shan, living alone at the Beat poet Lawrence Ferlinghetti's cabin in Big Sur before moving on to an abandoned shack up in Trinity Alps country. Here he "kicked the habit, finally, of Self, of / man-hooked Man." Unfortunately, the habits of Man, which in Welch's case included heavy drinking and despair, are often hard to kick. In 1971, while camping near Kitkitdizze, he left a suicide note in his truck and wandered into the mountains. His body was never found.

In a gnomic poem called "Geography," Welch explains why so many Californian seekers were attracted to Asian ways rather than Abrahamic traditions:

> The Far East is west of us,
> nearer by far
> than the Near East,
> and mysteriouser.

Snyder recognized this geographic connection as well, for his is a poetry of the Pacific Rim, bubbling up from the Ring of Fire that binds the West Coast to the Aleutians, Mount Fuji, and the South China seas. As a teenager in Washington, Snyder recognized the kinship between the Cascades he had climbed and the Chinese landscape paintings he saw in the Seattle Art Museum. This insight eventually led to his epic poem *Mountains and Rivers without End,* which recasts America's western lands as a craggy Tantric mindscape whose peaks and valleys teach a hardscrabble earth dharma.

In Snyder's poetry one is rarely far from ordinary physical experience. The vision that the thirteenth-century Zen master Eihei Dogen describes as "mountains walking" can also be realized by walking around mountains, which is just what Snyder did when he brought the Asian practice of ritual circumambulation to Marin's Mount Tamalpais in 1965. He and his buddies Ginsberg and Whalen marched around the mountain, recited sutra, and closed their rite with a conch blow in the parking lot at Redwood Creek. There is nothing particularly mystical about the poem Snyder wrote about the event. "The Circumambulation of Mount Tamalpais" is basically a recipe, a liturgical map that allows others to follow in their footsteps—which others most certainly have. But Snyder would probably remind such folks of his own sharp gloss on the first line of the *Tao Te Ching:* "A path that can be followed is not a spiritual path."

The path that Redwood Creek takes as it runs off Mount Tam is easy to follow: it rolls southwest through the redwoods, eventually spilling into the Big Lagoon estuary, which hugs the snug strand of Muir Beach. Big Lagoon also accepts the flows from a more southerly gulch that snakes a mile or so inland like a languid dragon and that nestles another important outpost of California Zen. Green Gulch Farm is one of a handful of properties that belong to the San Francisco Zen Center, the largest and arguably most influential Zen institution in the United States. Besides serving as a residential monastery and retreat center, Green Gulch is a working farm and garden where many budding organic growers train. Here Zen meets the biosphere. One of the architects of the farm was Alan Chadwick, a visionary gardener from England who single-handedly influenced a generation of American growers in the 1970s with his organic methods. A radiantly spiritual earthling, Chadwick introduced the Zen gardeners and his students at UC Santa Cruz to biodynamic farming, a method and philosophy of horticulture developed by the Austrian mystic Rudolph Steiner. Biodynamic farming—whose holistic methods are both productive and profoundly, if subtly, occult—is now widely practiced by organic growers in Northern California and across the United States.

Shunryu Suzuki, the Japanese founder of the San Francisco Zen Center, died in 1971, just a year before Green Gulch was purchased. Suzuki would have loved the place, because he was a passionate gardener. Suzuki also had a green thumb when it came to seeding California with Soto Zen, a tradition whose gradual, unhurried cultivation of

"SHADOW INSTALLATION," SAN FRANCISCO ZEN CENTER, CITY CENTER, SAN FRANCISCO

EXIT

still meditation resembles a sort of spiritual photosynthesis. Though neither Suzuki nor his flavor of Zen were very razzle-dazzle, his Way, which encouraged a simple but full engagement with everyday practice, continues to resound. Suzuki's book *Zen Mind, Beginner's Mind* is a masterpiece of American spiritual literature—American not just because of its pragmatism but also because Suzuki's limpid prose reflects the hand of his American editor Trudy Dixon, who had studied Heidegger and Wittgenstein before committing to the Zen Center, and was dying with fierce grace at the time of the book's creation.

Suzuki came to San Francisco in 1959 to serve at a Japanese temple in the Fillmore. He had barely unpacked his bags before Western seekers tanked up on Alan Watts and the book *Zen Flesh, Zen Bones* started showing up. With his understated charm, Suzuki hardly resembled the hard-assed tricksters of Zen literature, but the Caucasians stuck around. By 1969, so many renegades and acid veterans were sticking around that Suzuki was forced to leave the temple. The Zen teacher had not planned to stay in America forever, but the sincerity and hunger of his idealistic white disciples moved him. "For them I will become American soil," he said. He moved his city sangha into a large red brick building in the Lower Haight that had originally served as a Jewish women's residence. Designed by Julia Morgan with her usual attention to detail, the place was perfect: a large dining room and kitchen, a serene interior courtyard, and beautifully crafted ironwork and wooden trim. In addition, the building had a religious heritage. A small mezuzah still hangs by the heavy doors that open onto Page Street, and the Star of David recurs throughout the ironwork. But the most remarkable sacred trace in the building now is a 1986 installation by the San Francisco artist Al Wong: a screen that hangs in a stairwell, outlining Suzuki's diminutive shadow.

There was no real garden at Page Street, however. Suzuki's full transformation into American soil would occur elsewhere, in the remote Ventana Wilderness, which blankets the coastal range above Big Sur. Tassajara Hot Springs, which formally became the Zenshinji temple in 1967, is not only the first Zen monastery in the Western world but also the most beautiful and isolated. The compound lies at the end of a steep and windy fourteen-mile-long dirt road, in a narrow valley surrounded by the dense and protected woodlands of the Los Padres National Forest. For centuries, the sulphur hot springs had been frequented by Esselen Indians who killed and dried their deer meat there. A bear hunter built a cabin in the 1850s, and by the end of the century the site had grown into a frontier resort. Today Tassajara remains a resort of sorts, with summer guests paying handsome fees that support the operation during the fall and winter months, when the monastery closes to outsiders and fifty or sixty men and women bear down on themselves, and their no-selves, through the cold and shadowy damp.

ZENDO, TASSAJARA MONASTERY, VENTANA WILDERNESS

Suzuki was first taken to Tassajara by his disciple Richard Baker, who headed the San Francisco Zen Center after Suzuki's demise and later caused one of the most notorious and divisive sex scandals in the history of American Buddhism. At first Suzuki thought the place was too remote, but when he finally saw the valley, he hopped out of the car and danced down the road in glee. The sulphur springs and live oaks, the birds and waterfall, the sycamores and boulders lining the creek—Tassajara was already the pure land. In a Pacific Rim flash, Suzuki said that the spot reminded him of China—not, that is, of his own island home, but of the ancestral landscape of original Zen. Here Suzuki was also able to garden again. During work periods, the frail older man spent time carefully selecting and lugging the local stones used throughout the property. He said that some rocks were inert, while others were somehow alive.

The Tassajara community represented something of a paradox for the 1960s: a tribe of nonconformists and freethinkers signing up for a life that possessed more than a superficial resemblance to boot camp. The Zennies rose at 4:30 A.M. to light their kerosene lamps and begin their day of zazen, manual labor, and ritualized meals eaten in silence; most males chopped their hair off. Dogen, the founder of Soto Zen, had written an entire book on the practice of monastic cooking, and Tassajara's kitchen staff worked hard to perfect their vegetarian fare; recipes coming out of Tassajara would find their way into the hands of health nuts across the land. Although Tassajara's routine would have been familiar to monks in Japan, the monastery also revolutionized Zen by having male and female students practice together. Suzuki drew the line at the baths, however, and insisted that men and women frequent different pools.

Since those pioneer days, Tassajara has minted many a Zen priest and practitioner. It has also developed into a modest Shangri-la of Asian fusion architecture, although the beauty of the monastery's buildings is as much about handicraft and function as design. Tassajara's first great builder was Paul Discoe, a blue-collar California carpenter who worked on many of the monastery's early buildings. After Discoe was ordained a Zen priest, Suzuki sent him to Japan for five years, where he studied traditional joinery and temple design before returning to the Bay Area to build lovely structures for Tassajara and Green Gulch. Another canny woodworker was Gene DeSmidt, a native East Bay carpenter who was hot-spring hopping in the early 1970s when he first visited Tassajara. He burst into the office ranting about the dangers of the temporary arched bridge that led to the baths; when DeSmidt finally paused, Suzuki simply asked if he could fix it. Over the next thirty years, DeSmidt and his work crew not only built a new bridge but also worked on bathhouses, steam rooms, gates, trellises, and a Japanese-style cabin complex—all while living alongside the monks and priests during the off season. When DeSmidt's company restored the resort's original dining room in the 1990s, they emulated its unique stonework, done by the same Chinese laborers who had used hand tools to build the road a century before.

FOUNDER'S HALL, TASSAJARA MONASTERY, VENTANA WILDERNESS

Tassajara's buildings not only honor their wild surroundings, but also reflect the interface between traditional Japanese aesthetics and California consciousness. The classic Japanese approach to materials, detail, and design embodies an organic receptivity, a suggestion that humans can follow the flow of natural forces while remaining upright and fully engaged. For a master builder like Discoe, the art is also a practice, in the spiritual sense of the term that Suzuki's style of Zen helped elucidate. Such rarified and esoteric craftsmanship is also expensive, but Discoe has had the good fortune of working for the Oracle Corporation CEO Larry Ellison, an obsessive Japanophile who recently built a 150-million-dollar home and garden complex on the Peninsula. Designed by Discoe, the twenty-three-acre property features a moon pavilion, landscaped waterfalls, a ceremonial cedar gate, a koi pond the size of a small baseball field, and a made-in-Japan replica of a sixteenth-century teahouse. Ellison imported two hundred mature trees from Japan for the gardens, which were built with nearly four thousand tons of hand-chiseled Chinese granite and five thousand tons of Yuba River boulders, a single one of which forms the hot tub.

The symbolic resonance between Ellison's estate and Hearst Castle is impossible to miss, especially given the fact that, in order to execute his ambitious vision, the CEO was forced to dismantle and preserve a 1912 house built on the property by Julia Morgan, the lead architect of San Simeon. Although some workers did take to calling Ellison's estate Larryland, the Woodside property is more than a billionaire's personal theme park. With a woodworking Buddhist priest at the design helm, the estate also reflects the fact that the West Coast's explosive information industries are a Pacific Rim phenomenon, as "Zen" in their way as archery or motorcycle maintenance. Whether the computer industry can embody the Buddha's insight into compassion and emptiness, however, is another question—a silicon koan we are all stuck with now.

THE ELECTRIC ONION

Every Sunday, the Sepulveda Unitarian Universalist Society gathers inside a ribbed and shingled bulb known by locals and congregation alike as the Onion. This charming dollop of sacred architecture lies on a leafy five-acre plot in North Hills, one of the various townships that flow seamlessly together in the broad sprawl of the San Fernando Valley. The Onion began its life under the Reverend Paul Sawyer shortly after the Unitarian and Universalist denominations joined forces in 1961. With the exception of Throop Church in Pasadena, Universalism never had much of a foothold in California, but Unitarians, with their similarly progressive sentiments in politics and metaphysics, had thrived in the state's often liberal Christian climate since the days of Thomas Starr King, the most famous and gifted orator of nineteenth-century California.

When the Sepulveda community first purchased their plot in North Hills, the only structures on the property were stables. The congregation met under bamboo awnings in the open air and went elsewhere during the occasional rain. When it came time to design the church, the congregation considered enlisting the celebrated Los Angeles modernist Richard Neutra but settled instead on a Hungarian architect named Frank Ehrenthal, who had fled a war-torn Europe for an expatriate life in Southern California. Ehrenthal designed the Onion at a time when the forward-looking and triumphant spirit of postwar modernism, in the guise of the International Style, was transforming American houses of worship. With-it architects were pouring old wine into new bottles, and even conservative Christians found themselves praying beneath rocket-finned spires, abstract stained-glass windows, and oddball angular roofs. With its deeply liberal and humanist creed, Unitarian Universalism was particularly ripe for modernism's progressive agenda. The Sepulveda Unitarian Universalists leaned hard to the left, and involved themselves in civil rights, the nascent peace movement, and local fair-housing struggles. Ehrenthal lived for a spell with various members of the congregation, and his structure is informed by their sense of engaged community and open-minded innovation.

The Onion's distinctive shape was influenced by the squat cones of West African villages and the famous domes of Russian Orthodoxy, but its earthbound informality is rooted in Californian soil. The cedar shake shingles that originally lined the building—and which unfortunately did not survive a recent renovation—were clear nods to the Craftsman aesthetic that characterized California architecture's earliest organic turn. The building's three-tiered round interior also resonated with Reverend Sawyer's radical vision of an inclusive, nonhierarchical church, one whose very design would foster dialogue, face-to-face contact, and participatory performance. Sawyer was caught up in Los Angeles's thriving arts and culture scene, and he wanted the Onion's "church in the round" to open its doors to the innovative theatrical and musical performances that he believed fleshed out the life of the spirit. Under his exuberant guidance, the Onion hosted jazz services, absurdist plays, and poetry readings by the likes of Robert Duncan, the Bay Area's Gnostic modernist.

The Onion reached a participatory peak of sorts in February 1966, when Ken Kesey's Merry Pranksters came to town in their nutso bus and threw one of their notorious Acid Tests inside the church's three-ringed bulbous hall. Sawyer had met Kesey at a Unitarian convention held the previous year at Asilomar, a lovely state park in Monterey. The theme of the conference was "Shaking the Foundations," and Sawyer thought Kesey, who at one point stomped and burned an American flag, shook them pretty well. (Other ministers agreed, and were not amused.) When the Pranksters piled into their bus and headed down to the Southland from the Bay Area in early 1966, Ken Babbs, Kesey's second in command, called Sawyer up on the spur of the moment. Without informing his congregation, Sawyer agreed to host

THE ONION/SEPULVEDA UNITARIAN UNIVERSALIST SOCIETY, NORTH HILLS

ABOVE: PIANO, KEN KESEY'S FORMER RESIDENCE, LA HONDA
RIGHT: KEN KESEY'S FORMER RESIDENCE, LA HONDA

the event the following night, and soon a tribe of freaks clad in thrift-store collage packed the Onion with flickering lights, electronic sound, movie projectors, and a crowd of crazy celebrants.

The Acid Tests emerged from the wild parties Kesey threw in La Honda, a small community in Portola Valley where the novelist and his family moved after leaving Stanford, where Kesey had written *One Flew Over the Cuckoo's Nest* and participated in government-sponsored psychedelic research. Kesey had decided that expanding consciousness was more interesting than writing novels. With his parties and charismatic indirection, Kesey let the psychedelic cat out of the bag, democratizing an experience that had previously been confined to military labs and elite circles. For the more public Acid Tests, Kesey and the Pranksters deployed about as much media technology as they could get their hands on—film projectors, electronic sound effects, strobes, black lights, and one of Donald Buchla's early synthesizers. Most of this gear would eventually become standard issue at rock clubs like the Fillmore West and the Avalon Ballroom, where a new breed of media wizards fashioned the psychedelic art of the light show. The Pranksters recognized that media were tools of perception that could not only amplify the molecules in people's heads but also seed social space with synchronicities and unexpected encounters. Far beyond the boundaries of religion, the Acid Tests and the psychedelic music scene they helped spawn crafted improvised rituals of enchantment and uncanny communion.

As Acid Tests went, the Onion fete was a mellow affair. Kesey himself had already fled to Mexico to escape a marijuana bust, and the Grateful Dead—the Prankster house band who went on to lead America's only mass psychedelic revival—were also no-shows. At Sawyer's insistence, the Pranksters did not spike the Kool-Aid, or anything else, with LSD. The worst thing that happened was that Hugh Romney, the clown-prince poet later known as Wavy Gravy, tossed a batch of burned pineapple chili down the toilet and clogged the plumbing. All this was in stark contrast with the legendary Acid Test the Pranksters threw the following weekend in Watts, an affair whose lysergic mayhem helped kick California's psychedelic culture into high gear. Babbs fed Paul Sawyer so much LSD that night that when the reverend came to preach the next morning, he was still high.

The North Hills Acid Test underscored two important things about the Pranksters' Day-Glo children's crusade: that the Acid Tests were not just about LSD, and that they possessed a distinct religious dimension. Usually, Ken Kesey and his crew are seen as heretical countercultural rebels; even within psychedelic culture, their wild ways are typically contrasted with the self-consciously mystical trips of East Coast acid gurus like Timothy Leary and Richard Alpert, later reborn as Ram Dass. Kesey was no preacher, and he led the Pranksters obliquely, a "non-navigator" who often spoke in riddles: "Feed the hungry bee," "See with your ears and hear with your eyes," "Nothing lasts." But despite the madcap partying that surrounded him, Kesey nonetheless chose, in the middle of 1965, to descend upon a pretty square gathering of Unitarians. Sawyer, for one, recognized Kesey as "a prophetic figure, a deep and caring man whose mission was to open up life in a deep religious sense." Perhaps Kesey was simply making a more radical and democratic spiritual

FAR LEFT: THE FILLMORE, SAN FRANCISCO

LEFT: JERRY GARCIA ICON, THE FILLMORE, SAN FRANCISCO

wager than Leary did—one that placed its bets on a theater in the round rather than a pulpit.

In his book *The Electric Kool-Aid Acid Test,* Tom Wolfe picked up on Kesey's spiritual vibe, but he also noted how elusive it was. For one thing, the Pranksters were always pulling the rug out from under their own shtick. "That in itself was one of the unspoken rules. *If you label it* this, *then it can't be* that. . . ." This refusal to label or describe reflected Kesey's own West Coast fidelity to radical experience, coupled with a snappy distrust of anything you might say about that experience. Wolfe speculated that all religious movements begin, not with a new idea, but with "an overwhelming new experience," a Gnostic flash that, in the Prankster case, was furnished by the confounding majesty of LSD. The trick, for a Jesus or a Kesey, is to keep the experience alive as more and more people hop on the bus. Within Christianity, this vision of original spontaneity has long been reflected in the periodic call to renew the simple immediacy of the early Church—a desire that intensely motivated the first Unitarians.

Babbs and Kesey were in a graveyard when they first hit upon the idea of the Acid Tests, and their great notion was to communicate the profundity of LSD to everyone without setting up dogma or a charismatic cult. In their hands, a strange and goofy fete became the vehicle of Mystery. It was a dangerous wager, and ultimately, perhaps, a doomed one. But the fact remains that experiential spirituality was a marginal path in American life until the spread of LSD and other hallucinogens offered large numbers of people reliable access to powerfully uncanny and transcendental states of consciousness. How "spiritual" these mind-states are remains a vexing question, and the Pranksters were wise to sidestep the issue. But in their cultivation of weird synchronicities and instinctive creativity, the Pranksters carried on the paradoxical Christian bid to cultivate gratuitous grace.

FULTON

OUR FATHER OF DARKNESS

Along with thick fog and ridiculous hills, nothing defines the visual experience of San Francisco as much as its Victorian homes. Exuberantly thrusting their cantilevered turrets into the air, frosted with ornate lintels and gingerbread detail, these buildings help intensify San Francisco's air of enchantment and excess—especially when they are tarted up with the rainbow hues still favored by some of the city's denizens. But the painted ladies, with their Gothic spires and steeply pitched roofs, can also look a bit like wicked witches. One of the spookiest Victorians in the city is the Westerfield House, a gaunt and moody Italianate palazzo that looms over the northwest corner of Alamo Square, and whose present owner purchased it partly out of a childhood love of *The Addams Family.* Locally known as the Russian Embassy, the building was constructed in 1889 for a local bakery king and earned its nickname a few decades later when a group of Czarist Russians ran a social club out of the place. Guglielmo Marconi broadcast the first radio transmission on the West Coast from the palazzo's odd peaked tower, once one of the highest points of the city. In 1965, when the neighborhood was a roughneck slum, a group of young people formed San Francisco's first hippie commune beneath the Westerfield's leaky wooden roofs. Members of the Calliope commune painted weird sigils on the walls and attracted scores of bikers and speed freaks, as well as a bemused Tom Wolfe.

In 1966, a brilliant underground filmmaker from Los Angeles took over the house, unpacking his Oz books, camera gear, and occult paraphernalia. The filmmaker in question was Kenneth Anger, a fierce little gay man who had been reworking film into a fetishistic dream theater since he shot his first sixteen-millimeter short, *Fireworks,* in 1947. Anger was a visionary, but like some California visionaries, he was drawn to the dark side. A native Angeleno, Anger claims to have appeared in the 1936 Hollywood version of *A Midsummer Night's Dream* as a child, and he has sustained a love-hate relationship with Tinseltown throughout his life and work. Anger's 1954 masterpiece *Inauguration of the Pleasure Dome* plumbed silent-movie gestures in its hallucinogenic evocation of a costumed pagan freak-out; later he wrote the bilious exposé *Hollywood Babylon.* With his lifelong obsession with Aleister Crowley, Anger also reflected the energetic footprint that Britain's notorious sex magician and self-professed Beast had left on Los Angeles. By the time of Crowley's death in 1947, the Los Angeles area was probably the world's most active center of Thelema, Crowley's religion and philosophy of True Will. Jack Parsons's Thelemite Agape Lodge was centered in Pasadena, and most of the heavies in the Ordo Templi Orientis, Crowley's quasi-Masonic order, lived in Los Angeles. Crowley's former secretary, Israel Regardie, also wrote occult books and practiced psychotherapy in the city. Before Crowley's star rose again during the occult boom of the 1970s, the Southland kept his apocalyptic religion of "magick" cooking, with Thelemite sorcerers reportedly gathering for steamy sex rites in the Arroyo Seco.

When Anger moved into the Westerfield House, he ripped out the ceiling of the tower room to maximize its pyramid power, and started performing magick in the pentagram he painted on the floor beneath. He also began work on his magnum opus, *Lucifer Rising.* In the film, Anger planned to link the dawning Age of Aquarius to the Thelemic belief that a new and convulsive era was dawning, an epoch dominated by the Luciferic energies of the Egyptian god Horus, "the Crowned and Conquering Child." According to Anger, a compulsive self-mythologizer, his unfinished film was stolen in 1967, although scraps of the footage made their way into 1969's *Invocation of My Demon Brother,* the filmmaker's most visceral, hypnotic, and grating work. An eleven-minute kaleidoscope of sigils, flesh, and ritual performance, from pot

RUSSIAN EMBASSY/WESTERFIELD HOUSE, SAN FRANCISCO

smoking to a costumed equinox rite, *Invocation* jump-cuts between burned cats, nude hunks, and footage of soldiers in Vietnam. The magickal will behind this densely layered collage is revealed near the end, when Anger himself floats down the stairs of the Westerfield House in a puff of smoke, revealing a voodoo doll whose sign alerts the viewer: "Zap You're Pregnant—That's Witchcraft." For Anger, the film itself was the invocation, and the auteur was no doubt pleased when his short became a hit on the budding midnight-movie circuit. In flicker houses across the land, thousands of drug-softened minds were swallowing Anger's occult dissemination whole.

Invocation of My Demon Brother is probably the most powerful independent film made in the environs of the Haight-Ashbury in the era of the Summer of Love. That the film was so drenched in spectral darkness tells us something about the psychic tenor of the times. Despite the hippie embrace of spontaneous and sacred play—a spiritual ethos captured in the image of the innocent, flower-bedecked child—the quest for altered states, synchronicities, and erotic creativity had a distinctly sulphurous side. Another demon brother featured in Anger's film was Anton Szandor LaVey, the founder of the Church of Satan, who appears with plastic devil horns on his bald pate. Born Howard Levey in 1930, LaVey was less a freak guru than a *Playboy*-era steak-and-martini man. He hated hippies and LSD, played Wurlitzer organs in strip clubs, and had no interest in mystically dissolving the ego. Though essentially a con man, LaVey had enough psychological frankness and sleazy charm to attract scores to the black masses he held at his house in the Outer Richmond, a place he had, as the song goes, painted black. A more metaphysically sophisticated Satanism would have to wait for the founding, in 1975, of the Temple of Set, a sober religious order registered in California and led by LaVey's estranged disciple Michael Aquino, who served in the U.S. Army as a lieutenant colonel of military intelligence and was posted for many years at San Francisco's Presidio.

The devilish smirk LaVey flashes in *Invocation of My Demon Brother,* however, has nothing on the film's unofficial star. Bobby Beausoleil was a handsome and magnetic young musician from Santa Barbara whom a smitten Anger had anointed with the starring role in *Lucifer Rising*. Beausoleil moved into the Westerfield, which Anger had decorated with disco lights and purple paint, but the two had a falling out in 1967, and Beausoleil took off with Anger's Studebaker and, supposedly, his film footage. Heading back to Los Angeles, Beausoleil plunged into the seedy netherworld of soft-core porn and drug dealing. One of his drug sources was Gary Hinman, a UCLA grad student who practiced Nichiren Buddhism and brewed mescaline in the basement lab he ran in the hippie haven of Topanga Canyon. Beausoleil sold some of Hinman's mescaline to Satan's Slaves, a motorcycle crew who claimed the drugs were bunk. Beausoleil returned to Hinman's property, and finding the man uncooperative, beat, stabbed, and ultimately killed him. Beausoleil was not alone that night: assisting him were Mary Brunner and Susan "Sadie" Atkins, the latter of whom once stripped in a coffin during one of LaVey's witchcraft sleaze shows in San Francisco. But the man who first brought all three murderers together, and who may have lopped Hinman's ear off with a ceremonial sword, was the most nefarious California devil of all: Charles Manson.

Decades after his conviction, Manson remains an all-purpose archetype. For some, he represents the bad hippie supreme, living proof that the Summer of Love was a twisted illusion, or at least the brief calm before a storm of nihilism and license. For others, Manson stands as the ultimate cult leader, a crafty Rasputin whose hypnotic powers of mind control presaged later California cult catastrophes like Heaven's Gate and the mass suicides at Jonestown. And for a few fans, Manson remains a misunderstood hero, an avatar of outsiderdom unfairly crucified for other people's crimes. Even today, freelance historians argue over how much responsibility Manson should bear for the brutal Tate-LaBianca murders, which occurred shortly after Beausoleil's arrest for Hinman's murder, though few doubt that the orgiastic LSD-fueled psychodramas Manson orchestrated and the apocalyptic fantasies he nursed helped set the stage.

Though hardly a conventional guru, Manson was a magnetic chameleon whose feral, tricksy charisma bloomed in the overheated spiritual atmosphere of the West Coast. He learned Scientology techniques and jargon in prison, visited Esalen, and morphed into Jesus during acid trips in the Haight. Proclaiming that "sex is religion," he plumbed the depths of carnal magic and enchanted many young seekers—especially girls—with inspired raps that twisted together God, sex, the Devil, and the Now. He also wrote trippy folk songs, which brought him into contact with important musicians in Los Angeles, like Neil Young and Dennis Wilson of the Beach Boys. In the Southland, Manson may also have

FOUNTAIN OF THE WORLD, SIMI VALLEY

associated with a number of darkside occult groups; many pixels have been spilled speculating about his connection to the Process Church of the Final Judgment—rumored to have sacrificed more than animals—and a renegade lodge of the Ordo Templi Orientis headquartered near the University of Southern California.

Perhaps the most curious fringe mystics that Manson encountered in the Southland were the remnants of a midcentury California group called the Wisdom, Knowledge, Faith, and Love Fountain of the World. Robed, hirsute, and barefoot, the mystic Christian sectarians lived in a craggy box canyon to the west of Spahn Ranch, the dilapidated B-movie cowboy set that Manson and his largely female troop occupied in the bouldery foothills of the Santa Susana Mountains. Manson gave some money to the group and was particularly impressed by one of their meditative practices, which involved strapping oneself to a cross made from telephone poles that stood atop a skull-shaped sandstone outcrop. In this way, devotees were able to commune with the departed spirit of their teacher, a chain-smoking longhair named Krishna Venta who established the group there in 1948. Venta claimed to be a 244,000-year-old cosmic Christ,

LEFT: INTERIOR WITH SKULL, BARKER RANCH, DEATH VALLEY NATIONAL PARK

RIGHT: BARKER RANCH, DEATH VALLEY NATIONAL PARK

but more worldly records peg him as a San Franciscan named Francis Pencovic, who had a rap for passing bad checks. Venta preached a New Age message of love and service, but in 1958, some disgruntled ex-followers, convinced that the master had excessively applied his doctrine of "love in action" with their wives, set off twenty sticks of dynamite in the colony's monastery, killing themselves, Venta, and seven others.

Today the only trace of Box Canyon's sectarian past is a fallen archway with a Dantesque proclamation, a few crumbling graffitied walls, and a large fallen cross. Even less remains of Spahn Ranch, whose false fronts and outlaw shacks burned down in a 1970 wildfire as Manson's trial was under way. But the Manson Family's final hideaway still stands, maintained by four-wheel-drive clubs, on a remote desert plateau that borders one of the bleakest places in the western hemisphere. Manson first visited the Death Valley area in late 1968, when visions of dune-buggy armies danced in his head. At the time, miners still worked claims in the Panamint Range, and Manson managed to worm his way into one of their haunts, a humble oasis in the bone-dry desert hills called Barker Ranch. The Family spent the nights playing music and burning away whatever barriers remained between their minds and bodies. During the day, Manson reportedly hunted for a hole that he claimed would lead to an underground paradise, a fantasy perhaps fed by Death Valley's odd subterranean system of freshwater springs. Manson also grooved to the coyotes that served as his power animal, scavengers who embody the teaching that "total paranoia equals total awareness."

Following the grisly murders of August 1969, Manson holed up in Barker Ranch for what would be his last stand. Despite the lawless isolation of the area, Manson's personal power was checked by a local miner and veteran named Paul Crockett. A student of Theosophy, Rosicrucianism, and especially Scientology, Crockett parried Manson's psychic jujitsu and was able to "deprogram" a few of his minions. Finally fleeing Barker Ranch under the cover of darkness, Crockett alerted sheriffs to Manson's freaky survivalist sex cult. The raid on Barker Ranch went down on October 12, Aleister Crowley's birthday. Manson was captured when an officer saw a few strands of hair hanging out of a tiny medicine cupboard that the shrimpy antichrist had managed to squeeze into. Manson's nearby backpack contained dozens of movie-star magazines, a canvas money bag, and a copy of Robert A. Heinlein's 1961 sci-fi classic, *Stranger in a Strange Land*. The novel tells of a polyamorous religious sect led by a psychic messiah from another world. Though a few months remained in the year, Manson's arrest and subsequent trial marked in many minds the real end of the 1960s.

CAUTION
RADIOACTIVE
MATERIALS
NOTICE
This is a research facility that is known to,
and authorized by,
the Contra Costa County Sheriff's Office,
all San Francisco DEA personnel,
and the State and Federal EPA authorities.

DOORWAY, ALEXANDER SHULGIN'S LABORATORY, LAFAYETTE

WEIRD SCIENCE

EYES ON THE SKY

These days, you are more likely to find the term *visionary* applied to scientists, inventors, or pugnacious entrepreneurs than to religious seers. This is especially true in California, where earth-bound visionaries have long thrived within the state's famed culture of innovation—an often subsidized blend of brawny research institutes, economic opportunism, and technology-driven industries like aerospace, IT, and biotech. Despite its focus on profit, the business of technoscience raises deep questions about space, time, and mind, and so remains laced with spiritual import even as it refashions the workaday world and makes some people very rich. But the most visionary of the sciences—in the spiritual as well as the literal sense of the term—remains the least practical: astronomy. Here, too, California has sometimes led the way, reshaping and unsettling our place in the universe with cosmic insights that depend on marvelous machines.

California's cult of the stars began with a miserly millionaire named James Lick. Born in Pennsylvania in 1796, Lick moved to South America, where he amassed a small fortune building and selling pianos. When the Mexican-American War broke out, Lick pulled up stakes and sailed to San Francisco, where he arrived in 1848 with a pile of Peruvian gold doubloons and six hundred pounds of chocolate. Residents snatched up the confection so quickly that Lick convinced his friend Domingo Ghirardelli, from whom he bought the chocolate, to move from Lima to San Francisco. As a businessman, Lick did even better than Ghirardelli, transforming his doubloons into a real estate empire that stretched across the state and at one time included the entire island of Santa Catalina. He also built San Francisco's Lick House, an extravagant hotel that took up nearly an entire city block, with the exception of one corner reserved for a Masonic temple.

Lick became the wealthiest man in San Francisco, but he wore shabby clothes and pushed frugality to the edge of the absurd. When Lick finally gazed into the maw of death, he decided to memorialize himself by spending his fortune. A freethinker and declared "unbeliever in the dogmas of Christianity," Lick was fascinated by the ancient sciences of Egypt and decided to build a marble pyramid in the heart of San Francisco, a monument more massive than the royal tomb at Giza. But he soon changed his tune, and the city would have to wait nearly a century before a similar structure, the Transamerica Pyramid, poked its tapered needle into the downtown skyline. Instead of a pyramid, Lick decided to leave an enormous bequest for an observatory that would house the most powerful telescope on the planet. In 1887, over a decade after Lick's death, the observatory opened on Mount Hamilton, a remote 4,250-foot peak in Santa Clara County named for a Methodist minister. The site was chosen for its calm and crisp atmospheric conditions, and the Lick Observatory became the world's first continuously occupied mountaintop astronomical station. It was also the only such institution to bury the remains of its principal funder beneath the telescope, where Lick's body was interred after being moved from a Masonic vault in San Francisco.

The Lick telescope boasted a thirty-six-inch refractor lens cast in Paris—ten inches broader than its closest rival at the time. During his first evening on the device, astronomer Edward Emerson Barnard discovered the fifth moon of Jupiter, while James Keeler later used the telescope to investigate the cloudy nebulae that infest the Milky Way, discovering that half of these dusty blobs of light were spirals. (More recently, and with a vastly more powerful telescope, astronomers at the Lick Observatory spearheaded the discovery of scores of extrasolar planets.) Another important figure to visit the observatory in its early years was the young George Ellery Hale, a Chicago native from a wealthy Anglo-American family who studied solar phenomena and went on to found the Mount Wilson Observatory in 1904.

THE GREAT 36-INCH LICK REFRACTOR,
LICK OBSERVATORY, MOUNT HAMILTON

LEFT: LICK OBSERVATORY, MOUNT HAMILTON

RIGHT: HALE SOLAR LABORATORY, PASADENA

This complex lies on top of a sheer outcrop high in the San Gabriel Mountains, north of Pasadena. Hale chose the site for atmospheric conditions that were, in those days, superb. But he also drew inspiration from the travel writer Robert Curzon, who offered romantic descriptions of the monasteries of the Levant, balanced on rocky promontories surrounded by views of distant peaks. As such, the main residence on the property was dubbed the Monastery. The Pasadena architect Myron Hunt, who later designed the Rose Bowl, added mystic insignia to the walls, some of the glyphs Egyptian in flavor. The night the Monastery opened, Hale and his fellow astronomers lit candles and proceeded from a nearby cabin to the residence, where they built a roaring conflagration in the massive granite fireplace.

The Monastery's air of religious devotion was echoed in Bertram Goodhue's design of the California Institute of Technology, the vocational school on the valley floor that Hale helped transform into a world-class scientific research university. As much a Gothic-Moorish fantasy as a historical revival, the Pasadena campus is lined with cloisters, where young novitiates of reason shuffle along beneath bursts of Spanish Renaissance and occasionally nutty decor. Hale's own pursuits were housed in the Robinson Laboratory of Astrophysics, which was topped by a twenty-inch telescope built to test early designs for the two-hundred-inch telescope Hale placed on Mount Palomar. A large solar icon in deep relief floats on the latte-colored wall beneath the small white dome.

More humanist than mystic, Hale nonetheless appreciated the mythological resonance of cosmology and playfully dubbed himself a "sun worshipper." Hale was great friends with the University of Chicago Egyptologist James Henry Breasted and visited King Tutankhamen's tomb shortly after it was cracked open in 1922. After retiring from the directorship of Mount Wilson, Hale commissioned the firm of Kaufmann, Coate, and Johnson to build what he called a "solar laboratory" on the grounds of his private home in Pasadena. Along with the spectrohelioscope Hale fashioned himself, the lab included bas-reliefs of the Egyptian pharaoh Ikhnaton, a bust of Nefertiti, and a solar image copied from a tomb in Thebes, signifying immortality. It was the perfect hobby shop for a gentleman sun worshipper.

Of course, the visionary import of astronomy does not lie in bas-reliefs but in insights that transform our experience of the actual universe we inhabit. California's most cosmic breakthrough along these lines occurred on Mount Wilson, when another Anglo-American astronomer, named Edwin Hubble, cast his eye on the pulsing light of distant variable stars called Cepheids. Born in Missouri, Hubble had attended Oxford on a Rhodes Scholarship, and returned to the States with the accent and arrogant manners of a pipe-smoking English don. When the young astronomer pointed his camera at a Cepheid in the pinwheel nebula Andromeda, he discovered that the light source lay well over a million light years away—much farther than the size of the Milky Way. Against reigning opinion, Hubble came to the remarkable conclusion that our galaxy is not alone, but is only an outpost in a vast cosmos filled with galaxies. In 1929, as Hubble began to assemble a map of our suddenly expanded universe, he uncovered an even more mind-blowing fact: the galaxies are fleeing from one another at a constant rate of expansion, as if they are riding the surface of an inflating balloon. This discovery ran counter to the vision of a static universe offered—against his own hunches—by Einstein. In 1931, Einstein hustled all the way to Pasadena to meet Hubble, and soon retracted what he called "the greatest blunder of my life."

Hubble's deep glimpse into the cosmos helped make the crusty astronomer and his Angeleno wife, Grace, the toast of Hollywood, where the couple befriended figures like Aldous Huxley and Charlie Chaplin. Half a century later, the Hubble Space Telescope commemorated the cosmic reach of his vision, which almost instantaneously thrust humans into a vastly more bizarre universe than the one previously defined by the boundaries of the Milky Way. For those riding the edge of modern consciousness, this new and vertiginous cosmic stage, magnificent and rather unsettling, could not be ignored. In a 1930 poem, the poet Robinson Jeffers, always sensitive to the inhuman grandeur of the cosmos, registered the chillier implications of Hubble's discovery. When the astronomer gazed through the "observatory eyeball," he wrote, "space and multitude came in / And the earth is a particle of dust by a sand-grain sun, lost in a nameless cove of the shores of a continent." But for Jeffers, as for others, such loneliness was balanced by the sublimity of creation itself, of that pregnant moment when

all that exists
Roars into flame, the tortured fragments rush away from each other into all the sky, new universes
Jewel the black breast of night; and far off the outer nebulae like charging spearmen again
Invade emptiness.

SPACE BROTHERS

Californians did not invent the modern flying saucer. But they did pioneer the occult and mystic interpretations of these furtive craft, which in their modern form were first glimpsed in June 1947 by the pilot Kenneth Arnold, who saw nine silver disc-shaped objects skipping through the air over Washington State's Mount Rainier in an erratic formation Arnold compared to flying geese. In the ensuing decade, most ufologists believed that flying saucers were nuts-and-bolts contrivances from other planets, and therefore demanded the objective reports and evidentiary tactics of science. But what if the UFO was a space-age return of the apocalyptic revelations of old? A year before Arnold's famous sighting, an artist and budding witch named Marjorie Cameron saw a strange craft in the skies over Pasadena; a member of Jack Parson's magical Agape Lodge, Cameron later said she believed it was the "war engine" that Aleister Crowley predicted in his prophetic Book of the Law. The same year, on October 9, a bat-winged airship passed over San Diego, and a local medium named Mark Probert established contact with its crew. According to Probert, who also channeled teachings from a five-hundred-thousand-year-old Tibetan named Yada Di' Shi'ite, the *Kareeta* was an antigravity machine piloted by peaceful representatives of an advanced culture. Probert's claims were soon repackaged by his friend N. Meade Layne, founder of California's Borderland Sciences Research Foundation. Layne argued that the "ethereans" who piloted the ship were higher-dimensional beings who had lowered their vibrations in order to contact our world and help our benighted souls evolve.

Whatever its visionary dimension, California's cosmic saucer lore paralleled the exploding power of the state's technoscientific institutions and aerospace industry. Cameron's occult partner Jack Parsons, for example, was a rocket scientist at Pasadena's Jet Propulsion Labs, where the native Californian played a critical role in the development of the rocket fuel that would eventually land astronauts on the moon. The most famous UFO contactee of the era, a Polish immigrant named George Adamski, worked at a four-stool café that lay at the foot of Mount Palomar's famous observatory. Adamski's career as a space oddity began on November 20, 1952, when he claimed to have encountered a golden-haired Space Brother named Orthon in the desolate Mojave Desert. As in the 1951 Robert Wise movie *The Day the Earth Stood Still,* the space being chastised humans for mucking around with nuclear weapons and poisoning the planet. As Adamski recounted in his best-selling books, this meeting sparked a series of adventures that found the fry cook voyaging to Venus, examining odd mechanisms, and ogling blonde space babes. The visionary overtones were hardly surprising: Adamski was an old hand at the freelance prophet game, having founded a monastery in Laguna Beach twenty years earlier called the Royal Order of Tibet.

For all its comic-book corn, the UFO craze gave a shot in the arm to the Theosophical fancies that dominated California's occult imagination. The old Ascended Masters gained a postwar, quasi-scientific solidity that crackled with the urgency of revelation. By the close of the decade, thousands of contactees and desert mystics were gathering for the Interplanetary Spacecraft Convention, an annual convocation held in the Mojave Desert, east of the San Bernardino Mountains, alongside a giant rock called, fittingly, Giant Rock. The man behind these gatherings was George Van Tassel, a former aerospace engineer and test pilot who had worked for Howard Hughes and Lockheed before moving to the high plains north of Twentynine Palms in 1947. He built a café and small airstrip next to Giant Rock, hoping to beckon weekend pilots to the enormous boulder. Van Tassel also cleaned out the small caverns tucked away at the base of the rock, where a German prospector had earlier hollowed out a home before blowing himself up along with a cache of dynamite during World War II. Van Tassel turned

INTEGRATRON, LANDERS

INTEGRATRON
DEDICATED to RESEARCH

one grotto into a meditation chamber where he teamed up with other mediums in order to establish contact with alien minds. During these sessions, Van Tassel began channeling the Elvis Presley of the Space Brothers: Ashtar, "commandant quadra sector, patrol section Schare, all projections, all waves."

Ashtar is with us today; from Kauai to Santa Fe, his Command still rocks the New Age mike. But Van Tassel's most powerful legacy is a building—or, rather, a machine disguised as a building. On the night of August 24, 1953, the engineer awoke to discover a spaceman at the foot of his bed. Introducing himself as Solganda, the extraterrestrial led Van Tassel to a nearby spaceship hovering just a few feet off the ground. Giving Van Tassel the standard warning about nuclear annihilation, Solganda then explained that the meager human life span was the problem. As Van Tassel later put it, "By the time we grow old enough to know how to live, we die." To remedy this catch-22, Solganda provided intricate plans for the Integratron, a device that would retard aging. Van Tassel would spend the rest of his natural life trying to complete Solganda's plans.

The Integratron is a thirty-eight-foot-high rotunda designed to produce a high-voltage electrostatic field. The underlying principle holds that the human cell is essentially

THE STAR CENTER, UNARIUS ACADEMY OF SCIENCE, EL CAJON

a polarized battery, and that by exposing our bodies to the correct range of electromagnetic energies, we can recharge our cells. When fully functioning, the Integratron was supposed to generate these energies with a rotating studded aluminum ring, fifty-five feet in diameter, that was attached to the exterior base of the parabolic dome. No other metal was used in the construction of the building, and its gorgeous planks of Douglas fir were fitted together with traditional joinery. Unfortunately, after struggling for twenty-five years to finance his time machine, Van Tassel died in what some might call predictably mysterious circumstances, taking his final plans with him.

Like many visionary ufologists, Van Tassel saw his desert science as the fulfillment of religious prophecy. Despite the Integratron's technical debt to Nikola Tesla and a fringe science device called the Lakhovsky Multiple Wave Oscillator, Van Tassel believed his machine was a twentieth-century reconstruction of the Tabernacle of Moses. The technical specs given in the book of Exodus describe rings and staves that Van Tassel interpreted as coils and condensers, while the Tabernacle's celebrated "ark" looked forward to the Integratron's electrostatic "arc." In this sense, Van Tassel's visionary building is both a machine and a temple. Although the Integratron's full powers remain to be tapped, the two sisters who currently own the property take full advantage of the exquisite acoustic properties of the parabolic upper chamber. During half-hour sound baths, a small orchestra of crystal singing bowls immerses visitors in resonating and reverberating frequencies that reveal the human spine to be a tuning fork.

Elsewhere in Southern California, Van Tassel's blend of science and prophecy took more explicitly religious forms. In 1956, an expatriate British psychic named George King founded the Aetherius Society in Los Angeles. A disciplined meditator and yoga practitioner, King started channeling "transmissions" from Ascended Masters who belonged to a "multi-dimensional, interplanetary, intergalactic organization of beings." Devoted to service, the Aetherians used batteries and antennae to store and transmit the cosmic power of prayer to people and places in need. Though King died in 1997, his followers continue to gather at the society's Moorish stucco compound in Hollywood, where they pray, meditate, and listen to recordings from "Mars, Sector 6" that were taped before the "primary terrestrial channel" passed away.

The Aetherians radiate an undeniable charm, but the most colorful of California's saucer societies is undoubtedly the Unarius Academy of Science. Founded by Ernest and Ruth Norman in 1954, Unarius initially drew from the same well of San Diego saucer lore as Probert and the Borderland Sciences Research Foundation. But Unarius burst into bloom when Ruth—known to her followers as the Archangel Uriel—took over the group following her husband's death in 1971. Flamboyance incarnate, Uriel moved the academy to its present location in downtown El Cajon, where the organization created a headquarters that resembles a Roman villa by way of Buck Rogers. Classical statues, colorful dioramas, and trailing philodendrons are set against sky-blue

Welcome Space Brothers!
The land that you are now visiting was purchased in 1973 by the Cosmic Visionary Uriel to serve as the future landing site of thirty-three spaceships from the Interplanetary Confederation. These ships will land one atop the other, forming a permanent structure that will become a university for planet Earth.
The Space Brothers, highly trained in all scientific disciplines, will remain on Earth to advance the knowledge of a new science of life, of logic and reason, sparking
This land has serv
backdrop for many
throughout the years, as a
man, and Isis and Osir
The Arrival, Roots of the Earth-
popular with the media
and as a locale that was
with Uriel.
"Planet Earth's future is
said Uriel, "and you
are part of that future!"
The Future City of Planet Earth
This model of the Future City of planet Earth is patterned, as near as possible, to the cities existing on the higher spiritual Worlds of Light, the design and details having been related by the higher minds living thereon. Like the cities on the inner worlds, the future cities of Earth will be constructed especially to provide beauty, peace, tranquility, and a feeling of upliftment to the resident or visitor.
The city is laid out in a circular design, surrounded by an alabaster wall that will be about 100 feet high. The history of the earth people is depicted on the wall, each section
Sculptured gardens with elegant fountains, beautiful statuary, and numerous reflection pools will abound in this city. Residents will find great joy in creating and maintaining the colorful parklands and gardens, which will be filled with every conceivable plant and flower, creating a veritable paradise.
Monorails, gliding silently overhead, and sidewalks, moving like flat escalators, will be the means of transportation for the residents. There will be no automobiles, buses, or trolleys, as we have now, and

frescoes and visionary canvases, while harp music and the coos of caged birds soften the air. Everywhere you see the bright eyes of Uriel, beaming from devotional paintings or glossy ceramic busts. Uriel brought a sense of cosmic theater to the group's annual Conclave of Light, where Unarians dress up in bargain-bin spacewear and act out the karmic dramas that forced their incarnating souls to leave higher planets like Vulna or Dal and descend to Earth. Uriel also attracted many followers with her rich use of multimedia. In addition to a stream of books and pamphlets detailing the group's "fourth-dimensional science," Uriel helped create nearly a hundred videos and a handful of full-length films by the time of her death in 1994.

Though the Unarians profess admiration for Buddhism and its model of human evolution, they insist that the academy has nothing to do with religion. Nonetheless, the group's collective imagination centers on the millennialist belief that the Space Brothers will soon descend to our degenerate Earth, a place Unarians sometimes call "the garbage dump of the universe" or "the insane planet of robots." Uriel first got the word that emissaries from the Pleiades were going to be looking for a landing spot in 1967, and immediately purchased seventy-three acres of chaparral southeast of El Cajon. A variety of arrival dates proclaimed by Uriel came and went, but no ships landed at the site—a large dirt parking lot beside a shoddy wooden sign that reads: "Welcome Space Brothers!" Nonetheless, the Unarians still insist that the Pleiadeans are on their way, along with thirty-two huge saucers that will land on top of one another, forming the central tower of an "interplanetary learning center" called Star Center One. After the missionaries hip us to the evolutionary plan, Earth will be able join the Interplanetary Confederation of Planets as its thirty-third and final member. As for the rolling hills surrounding the site, they will be blasted flat when the crystal city comes.

The saucer faith has always been a blend of optimism and fear, a *Popular Science* version of the Book of Revelation set in the postwar shadow of pollution and nuclear annihilation. If the latest signs in the heavens are any indication, then faith in the neon New Jerusalem of the Space Brothers is waning. In March of 1997, thirty-nine members of the California-based saucer sect Heaven's Gate killed themselves in a Spanish Revival mansion in the wealthy San Diego suburb of Rancho Santa Fe. Web developers and *Star Trek* fans, the ascetic followers of Marshall Applewhite believed their souls would escape the illusory nightmare of material reality by hitching a ride on a spaceship riding the tail of comet Hale-Bopp, then sailing through the cosmos. They were seeking not renewal but escape—a final exit from the malfunctioning Holodeck of earthly existence.

Three years later, the backside of Giant Rock split off from the ancient boulder and fell to the side, exposing the white granite beneath. A local Anglo shaman named Shri Naath Devi, who had organized a healing session at the site only days before, claimed the event indicated that Mother Earth had received their prayers and that a vibrational shift was under way. But within days, the gleaming rock was covered with scabrous graffiti. After being a Native American holy ground and a saucer sanctuary, Giant Rock has now become a desecrated haunt of neo-Nazis, meth heads, and teenage alcoholics, long past looking for redemption from above.

LEFT: EARTH CITY OF THE FUTURE, UNARIUS ACADEMY OF SCIENCE, EL CAJON

BELOW: GIANT ROCK, SAN BERNARDINO COUNTY

SCIENTOLOGY

SCI-FI GNOSIS

With seeds of future science planted in its fertile mystic soil, California allowed a thousand mutant mind flowers to bloom. One of the most powerful and controversial is the Church of Scientology, an organization devoted to the cosmic implications of Dianetics, a self-help "technology" invented, and brilliantly promoted, by L. Ron Hubbard. Although some of the most important Scientology centers lie outside California—in Florida and on the high seas—the institution's sectarian heart beats in Los Angeles, which cradles the largest concentration of Scientology practitioners and properties in the world. Here the Church wears a Janus face: both proselytizer and pariah, Scientology is simultaneously the most integrated and most marginalized of Los Angeles's major new religious movements. While big-name stars heap praise (and lucre) on the organization, hackers and ex-members use often devious means to attack the secretive and extremely litigious church. But despite their labors, Scientology's mix of self-improvement techniques, sci-fi cosmology, and corporate culture has wormed its way into Southern California's cultural landscape with the tenacity of fast-food chains and eucalyptus trees.

In the Southland, the Church of Scientology defines itself in part through its visibility, its architecture of power. The International Celebrity Centre, for example, is housed in a particularly opulent expression of prewar Hollywood style. The Chateau Elysée was built by the widow of the silent-movie director Thomas Ince in 1929, during the last gasp of early Hollywood's Babylonian decadence. A massive confection of turrets, high balconies, and hipped roofs, with a drawbridge outside and trompe l'oeil ceilings within, the faux French castle embodied Tinseltown's ambitious grab at luxury, lordship, and dream. Over the next few decades, scores of movie stars—including Bette Davis, Clark Gable, Ginger Rogers, and Humphrey Bogart—made the residential hotel their home and playpen. Eventually, the Chateau fell on hard times, and was slated for demolition when the Church of Scientology bought it in 1973. Hubbard renamed the building the Manor House and proclaimed it the perfect place to attract movie stars, politicians, and sports figures—the "top strata of beings" that had become a central focus of the Scientology mission. In contrast to rank-and-file Scientologists, todays glitterati are treated to lengthy stays in this plush fantasy castle, where they can "audit" their "reactive minds" in style and submit their bodies to Hubbard's patented Purification Rundown in the basement gym. Given the high-profile endorsements of Scientologists like Tom Cruise, John Travolta, Juliette Lewis, and, to a degree, Beck, Hubbard's spin of the star-making machinery seems a savvy move.

In contrast to the Celebrity Centre's aristocratic grandeur, the main headquarters of the Los Angeles Church of Scientology, which lies just off Sunset Boulevard, resembles a corporate campus from a parallel dimension. Here men and women dressed in suits or uniforms, their hands clutching strangely bulky briefcases, hustle between buildings painted in various shades of aqua and set behind crisply mowed lawns, palm trees, and a brick-paved street officially renamed L. Ron Hubbard Way. The only visible signs of cosmic aspiration are the different Scientology logos that decorate the various buildings, such as the striped pyramid that dominates the glass facade of the Hubbard Dianetics Foundation, its triangular shape echoing the low flattened pyramid that tops the boxy structure.

A widespread icon of sacred science, the pyramid is also a Dianetics trademark owned by the Church's Religious Technology Center, which enforces orthodoxy by controlling licenses to Hubbard's copyrighted technologies and trademarks, including, it should be mentioned, the terms Scientology and Dianetics. When it comes to spiritual liberation, in other words, the church means business. It wields the law like a corporation, requiring new members to sign liability wavers before clambering onto the Bridge to Total Freedom, a spiritual mirror of corporate advancement.

CHURCH OF SCIENTOLOGY CELEBRITY CENTRE INTERNATIONAL, HOLLYWOOD

The church has also registered its most esoteric teachings as trade secrets. This enables it to use the strictest intellectual-property regulations against online critics attempting to publish the material, which includes fantastic space-opera scenarios about volcanoes and nuclear weapons that ordinary Scientologists don't hear until they have forked over a couple hundred thousand dollars.

The fact that Hubbard's cosmology sounds a lot like science fiction may have something to do with the science fiction that Hubbard churned out at a jaw-dropping rate during his salad days. An impressive collection of his early publications, with their lurid, eye-popping covers and tales of Nietzschean supermen, can be seen at the L. Ron Hubbard Life Exhibition, located in the heart of tourist Hollywood on the first floor of yet another commercial building owned by the Scientologists. Here guides lead visitors through displays that document, in breathless and exaggerated tones, Hubbard's early travels and adventures, his supposedly glorious service in the U.S. Navy, and his later work as an apostle to the world. The high point of the visit is a large glass case filled with E-meters: bulbous portable machines outfitted with knobs, analog needle displays, and electrodes that resemble tin cans. Scientologists use their E-meters to clear their reactive minds; like the genre of science fiction itself, the devices fuse technology and the psyche.

One phase of Hubbard's life not covered by the museum also reflects the mixture of mysticism and techno-science that gives Scientology its particular gloss. During the 1940s, Hubbard befriended Jack Parsons, a lead scientist at Pasadena's Jet Propulsion Labs and the master of an occult lodge devoted to Crowleyian magick. Parsons was a huge science-fiction fan who befriended local authors like Jack Williamson and, possibly, Robert A. Heinlein, whose classic *Stranger in a Strange Land* resonates with Crowley's Thelemic themes. Parsons saw Hubbard as a soul buddy of sorts, and before Hubbard ran off with Parsons's wife and ten thousand dollars of his money, he helped the rocket scientist perform the Babalon Working, a complex ritual of Enochian magic designed to vaporize Christianity and open the starry gates to the Thelemic apocalypse that will usher in the Age of Horus.

Crowley's magickal teachings may have informed Hubbard's subsequent creation of Dianetics, a do-it-yourself psychotherapy technique that made its sensational appearance in the science-fiction magazine *Astounding* in 1950. Scientology, Hubbard's later religious development of the secular Dianetics, is definitely a mystic technology, rephrasing a Gnostic approach to self-realization in a psycho-cybernetic lingo that would heavily influence later California self-help groups like est. According to Hubbard, buried deep within our dysfunctional personalities are immortal beings called Thetans. Long ago, bored with supreme power, we Thetans decided to amuse ourselves by constructing the universe of space-time and then injecting ourselves into its material confines. Then we became imprisoned in the game world, falling prey to its delusions and dysfunctional programs, which Dianetics auditing and higher Operating Thetan teachings can help overcome.

Scientology claims to liberate the suffering self by reigniting its cosmic powers and seeing through the illusion of the material world. But this Gnostic suspicion about ordinary reality can also lead to a far less triumphalist vision, one laced with anxiety, Kafkaesque comedy, and a deep empathy for all the confused souls who must endure our shoddy house of cards. Such, in any case, was the life's work of the science-fiction writer Philip K. Dick, who died in Orange County in 1982 at the age of fifty-three. Dick struggled psychologically and financially through most of his ragged career, but today his peculiarly powerful tales about fragmented identity, corporate simulacra, and divine invasions are recognized as some of the most compelling and profound in science fiction. What is less often recognized is that Dick was a deeply regional writer. He spent nearly his entire life in California, and reflected its culture of plastic promises and psychic anomie in the funhouse mirror of his mind. Dick lived for decades in the Bay Area, where he hung out with leftists, obsessively tossed the I Ching, gobbled speed with young freaks, and befriended James Pike, the renegade Episcopal bishop who attempted to contact his dead son through séances. Following a suicidal breakdown in 1972, Dick moved to the reactionary wastes of suburban Orange County, where he befriended a small coterie of science-fiction writers and continued an increasingly desperate search for God and girls. He lived out his last days in the distant shadow of Disneyland, the ultimate example of the false worlds that, as a writer, he felt compelled to build and destroy.

Dick was a true visionary, but not in the sense that his fictions predicted the future (although they sometimes did). Dick was a visionary because, like the prophets of old and the schizophrenics of now, he experienced intense, sometimes veridical, and always baffling visions. In 1963, while living in isolated Point Reyes, he glimpsed a horrible metal visage in the sky, an evil god who later became the title character in *The Three Stigmata of Palmer Eldritch,* a novel flush with the Gnostic themes that would come to the fore in later fictions like *Valis* and *The Divine Invasion.* But Dick's most extraordinary visions occurred in the Southland, in the humble apartment he shared with his wife and child in Fullerton. In February 1974, the sight of a delivery woman's Christian fish necklace triggered a long vacation from reality that included prophetic dreams, intense synchronicities, and the reception of messages hidden in Beatles songs. Time went out of joint, and once Dick saw the architecture of ancient Rome settle over Orange County. His spirit ranged across the map, but his most consistent themes were Gnostic and Christian, and he often felt himself to be in telepathic contact with a secret follower of the early Church.

Sometimes Dick felt that he had been plugged into VALIS, a sentient grid of cosmic information that had invaded our fallen and ersatz reality in order to redeem us, and reality, from the forces of oppression he called the Black Iron Prison. Other times he thought the Russians were manipulating his mind with radio waves. Dick's visions, along with the million or so words of the exegesis that he wrote trying to parse their meaning, provide no easy resolution. Though some commentators have diagnosed a temporal lobe epilepsy, the sublimity and strangeness of Dick's experiences, whose ecstasies were more than matched by intense confusion and pain, render such organic explanations superfluous. Besides, the works Dick created from his experiences—especially the sublime *Valis*—represent the agonizing triumph of vision over rational explanation. Something profound and unsettling happened in Dick's cruddy digs in Fullerton. But if Dick was a postmodern prophet, he was also a deeply Californian one: restless, unresolved, with one foot in trash culture and the other in a vast, empty cosmos. To the degree that Dick's writings illuminate our lot, they teach through shared suffering and humor, not through salesmanship or manipulative control.

LEFT: HUBBARD DIANETICS FOUNDATION, LOS ANGELES

BELOW: PHILIP K. DICK'S FORMER RESIDENCE, FULLERTON

VISITOR

MIND LABS

In 1995, the CIA decided to axe one of the oddest secret research programs ever sponsored by the U.S. government. Graced with the popcorn-worthy name of Stargate, the program was devoted to testing the sort of paranormal or PSI powers advertised at psychic fairs. In particular, Stargate researchers focused on remote viewing—the ability to mentally visualize and describe a distant place or object, like a toy hidden in a box a mile away, or a nuclear submarine chugging through the depths of the North Sea. The Stargate program lasted over twenty years under a variety of names and sponsors, a length of time that suggests, at least, that the researchers had their official sympathizers. Though PSI claims are notoriously difficult to assess, it bears mentioning that the independent statistician who analyzed Stargate's findings for the CIA in 1995 recommended that the program be continued.

Whatever nuggets Stargate contributed to U.S. military intelligence, the program played a significant role in the institutionalization of California consciousness. Stargate began in 1972 at the Stanford Research Institute, a facility in Palo Alto, sponsored by Stanford University, that continues to do high-octane research and development work for the government and private corporations. Russell Targ and Harold Puthoff, a physicist who once worked for the National Security Agency, were both SRI researchers who specialized in laser technology. The two men also happened to be fascinated by the hidden powers of the mind, and convinced the CIA—who knew that the Soviets were pursuing PSI studies—to support an in-depth program of applied remote viewing. Puthoff and Targ focused on so-called gifted individuals like the New York artist Ingo Swann, whose astral travels to Jupiter were supposedly confirmed by the Mariner 10 spacecraft. Puthoff and Targ also studied the psychokinetic abilities of Uri Geller, the spoon-twisting diva of 1970s parapsychology, and they published their positive results in the august journal *Nature*.

The SRI boys were introduced to Geller by the Apollo astronaut Edgar Mitchell, another conscript in the consciousness revolution. In 1971, after performing covert ESP experiments in space, Mitchell became the sixth human being to stroll along the lunar strand. On his return journey, Mitchell experienced an influx of divinity, coupled with the certain knowledge "that life in the universe was not just an accident based on random processes." Leaving NASA, Mitchell plunged into "inner space" and founded the Institute of Noetic Sciences in California in 1973. A secular research organization devoted to bridging science and spirit, IONS eventually shifted its focus to alternative healing modalities and mind-body practices like *chi gong* and distance healing. Mitchell remains on board at the institute, which is privately supported by its fifty thousand members. In 2000, IONS opened a retreat and research center south of Petaluma, on a two-hundred-acre spread of lonely brown hills peppered with gnarled live oaks.

The relatively high status of figures like Mitchell, Targ, and Puthoff shows just how far the consciousness movement went in 1970s California, when new paradigms spread beyond the countercultural fringe. Puthoff, for example, was not just an expert in lasers and quantum mechanics with a passing interest in telepathy. He was also an advanced Scientologist, an Operating Thetan who had supposedly cleared his mind of the reactive programs that shroud the spiritual superman within. Ingo Swann and many of SRI's psychic subjects were also Scientologists, and some of SRI's protocols were, apparently, based on Hubbard's high-level techniques. Like Scientology itself, the Stargate program reframed occult experience for a postwar, mind-ops world.

Puthoff and Targ were not the only SRI researchers tantalized by the more scandalous wings of California mind science. Douglas Engelbart was, without question, the most visionary researcher at SRI, a pioneer of human-computer

STANFORD RESEARCH INSTITUTE, MENLO PARK

interaction whose Augmentation Research Center transformed our fundamental metaphors of computerized communication. In a famous 1968 demo at ARC, videotaped by Merry Prankster Stewart Brand, Engelbart first demonstrated much that our wired world now takes for granted: the mouse, the hyperlink, the graphical user interface, videoconferencing. Engelbart realized that the computer offered us not just a machine to program but also a space to explore—particularly when the computer in question was networked with other machines. ARC helped give birth to cyberspace when it and UCLA became the first nodes on the Arpanet, the predecessor of today's Internet.

Engelbart's remarkable vision was guided by a sense of cognitive possibility rooted in the co-evolution of technology and human consciousness. Such interests may also explain all the pot smoked around ARC, as well as Engelbart's personal devotion to the Erhard Training Seminars, that blustering juggernaut of the human-potential movement better known as est. A large group seminar devoted to the intentional reprogramming of the self, est was cobbled together by Werner Erhard, a former car salesman, out of bits and pieces of Zen, Scientology, "psycho-cybernetics," and Dale Carnegie's *How to Win Friends and Influence People.* Erhard launched the training at San Francisco's Jack Tar Hotel in late 1971, attracting scores of lost hippies who wanted to straighten out while still "getting it"—*it* being the ineffable suchness announced by the Zen master's hitting stick, which in Erhard's hands became the est leader's insistence that you can't leave the conference room to pee. The program also presented a practical and potent "technology" of human interaction and self-awareness, one that Engelbart not only embraced on a personal level but also insisted on applying to the collaborative work at ARC. Given the intense feelings aroused by est's in-your-face recruitment strategies, Engelbart's move proved controversial, and ultimately led to the dissolution of the lab.

Parapsychology and meta-programming trainings like est encourage a quasi-scientific or technical approach to the human mind, including nonordinary states of human consciousness. But perhaps the most reliable technology of altered states lay in the chemistry of consciousness—in other words, in psychoactive drugs. Some of the most important psychedelics were first synthesized in Europe, but the proving ground for modern psychedelic culture lay on the West Coast, and especially California. Years before Timothy Leary began dosing Harvard grad students, Aldous Huxley penned *The Doors of Perception,* his literate account of a mescaline trip that began in the Hollywood Hills and ended with a visit to the Rexall Drug Store in Hollywood. Soon afterward, Los Angeles–based psychologists and psychiatrists like Oscar Janiger, Betty Eisner, and Sidney Cohen were exploring inner space with movie stars and intellectuals in a therapeutic, spiritually informed context. When Merry Pranksters and mystic hippies started gobbling LSD in far less controlled settings, they helped drive such therapy underground.

Another victim of the war on psychedelic drugs was the hard science of consciousness: psychopharmacology. How do these molecules work, and might newly invented compounds produce new insights? One pharmacological researcher who still keeps his beakers bubbling is a native Californian named Alexander Shulgin, who was born to a pair of public-school teachers in Berkeley in 1925. After studying pharmacology at UC Berkeley, Shulgin got a job working for Dow Chemical, whose legendary slogan, later taken up by ironic hippies, was "Better Living through Chemistry." In 1960, Shulgin whipped up his first batch of the hallucinogen mescaline sulfate, and life definitely got better. Fascinated by the personal insights that psychoactives provide, Shulgin began inventing and experimenting with novel compounds, which he saw as research tools capable of probing powers already latent in the mind. After testing the compounds on himself and a small group of fellow psychonauts, he would publish his results and recipes.

Despite the times, and his unwavering commitment to sandals, Shulgin was no hippie. He was friends with Drug Enforcement Agency chemists and a member of the exclusive, right-leaning, all-male Bohemian Club. As a researcher, he had no interest in making street drugs, although in 1967, one of Shulgin's compounds, a potent, long-acting mind-bender called DOM, showed up in the Haight-Ashbury as the notoriously squirrelly STP. In later decades, Shulgin inventions like 2C-B, 2C-T-7, and 5-MeO-DIPT wowed ravers and psychonauts alike. But Shulgin's greatest gift to the world was his 1976 synthesis of a long-forgotten phenethylamine called MDMA, or Ecstasy, now one of the most popular recreational drugs in the world. Impressed by MDMA's empathic powers, Shulgin shared the compound with a spiritually minded Oakland psychologist named Leo Zeff, who postponed retirement in order to spread the good news through a national network of therapists working underground with

INSTITUTE OF NOETIC SCIENCES, PETALUMA

psychoactives. But despite MDMA's clear potential for serious soulwork, the Food and Drug Administration scheduled the drug once it had become popular in clubs, making it illegal. Eventually, the DEA forced Shulgin to relinquish the license that allowed him to work with scheduled drugs. However, the ban has not prevented the good doctor from continuing to tinker with new classes of psychoactive drugs or from analyzing the active alkaloids in the scores of psychoactive cacti that dot the twenty-acre homestead he shares with his wife and coauthor, Ann, in the unincorporated hills of Contra Costa County.

Shulgin's parents purchased the sloping, grassy estate as a weekend retreat in the 1930s, when the valley below boasted more almond trees than people. After a house on the property burned down in the 1950s, Shulgin's son made a fort in its unburned basement, tucked into the hillside beneath towering pines. A few years later, Shulgin transformed the fort into the private lab he continues to use today. Beneath a roof made of two-by-fours, aluminum sheeting, and corrugated plastic lies a rank alchemist's den of grimy bottles, loopy glassware, and racks of crosshatched tubing made out of cheap gas pipe. This is the place that launched a million trips. The windows are thick with ivy and spiderwebs, while dried leaves and pine needles blow in through the door. The chimney attached to the brick fireplace, a godsend on chilly evenings, is propped up against the hillside with a weathered beam. Despite the exacting work performed here, the messy drift of matter holds sway, a reminder, were one needed, that the ultimate laboratory of the human mind lies beyond our gadgetry, in the great seething organic world.

ALEXANDER SHULGIN'S LABORATORY, LAFAYETTE

PRIVATE
ROAD

VIRGIN OF GUADALUPE APPARITION,
WATSONVILLE

LADYLAND

MAGIC IS AFOOT

Every Samhain, the Celtic equinox festival that falls near Halloween, a group of witches holds a public ritual in San Francisco called the Spiral Dance. Probably the largest such Sabbat held in North America, the ceremony honors the ever present dead with festive altars, earnest prayers, and a sweaty-palmed line dance that loopily snakes its way through a large auditorium. First staged in 1979, the Spiral Dance now attracts a few thousand attendees, drawn mostly from the Bay Area's aggressively diverse community of Wiccans, Druids, heathens, radical faeries, ceremonial magicians, technopagans, goths, geeks, and eco-mystics. Facing the dark night that swallows us all, the Spiral Dancers celebrate with the homespun pageantry characteristic of Neopagans everywhere. Perhaps the greatest sign of the event's religious power is how ordinary, in the best sense of the term, it seems. Beneath the dragon cloaks and the masks of feather and bone, regular folks, with kids in tow, gather to spin meaning from the rhythms of mortal life.

For a religious movement so focused on ancient ways, Neopaganism is a comparatively recent phenomenon. Contemporary Wicca can be traced to the British witchcraft covens popularized—and, it seems, largely invented—by an antiquarian and nudist named Gerald Gardner in the 1940s and 1950s. With the rise of the counterculture, Gardnerian Wicca and other homegrown earth religions blossomed across America. California proved exceptionally fertile ground, and some of its witches were directly responsible for the emergence of feminist Wicca and, to a lesser extent, the close identification of the Goddess with the planetary biosphere, and hence with environmental causes. Such developments should hardly be surprising in a region named for an earthy Amazon queen, or one so deeply informed by the heathen Transcendentalism of John Muir. Some Wiccan priestesses have even characterized California's physical territory as the mystic body of the Goddess, with her second chakra located in Los Angeles, her spine along the Sierras, her breasts dangling over Santa Cruz, and her crown chakra erupting at Shasta.

Among the many female pioneers who shaped California's religious landscape, Zsuzsanna Budapest stands out for her portrayal of the Goddess as a sacred embodiment of the life cycles of women. A native of Hungary who fled the Russians in 1956, Budapest eventually found her way to Los Angeles, where she started working at a women's center. On the winter solstice of 1971, Budapest founded the Susan B. Anthony Coven Number 1, named after the early suffragette leader. Like many Wiccans, Budapest claimed to be heir to a family witchcraft lineage, though the form it took in California certainly reflected the essentialist ideas of countercultural feminism, which proclaimed that all women share a core sense of self rooted in their biology. As Budapest outlined in her 1975 tome *The Feminist Book of Lights and Shadows,* later renamed *The Holy Book of Women's Mysteries,* the Dianic tradition offered rites of passage designed to honor all phases of a woman's natural life. It was also a separatist and largely lesbian affair, its magic available solely to women until the "equality of the sexes is achieved." Budapest's political intransigence was understandable—during the same year that she published her book, she was arrested for reading tarot cards, a violation of a local ordinance against foretelling the future. Budapest believed she had been set up because of the store she ran in Venice Beach, a witchcraft shop called Feminist Wicca. Budapest fought the law under the slogan "Hands Off Wimmin's Religion." She lost the case, though eventually the California Supreme Court overturned all such ordinances.

In 1975, an extended network of witches in the Bay Area formed the Covenant of the Goddess partly to protect themselves from the sort of harassment that Budapest had faced. Organizing Neopagans is like herding cats, but COG successfully created an umbrella group that allowed a number of covens and individuals to incorporate as a nonprofit

SOLSTICE FIRE RING, OCEAN BEACH, SAN FRANCISCO

DIANA, SUTRO HEIGHTS, SAN FRANCISCO

religious organization under the banner of Goddess worship. Attempting to honor the increasingly decentralized nature of American Wicca, COG consciously structured itself after the bylaws of America's Congregationalist Churches. Meanwhile, the Goddess was growing into an increasingly politicized archetype, thanks in part to the work of a UCLA archaeologist named Marija Gimbutas. Gluing her thesis together from potsherds and figurines, Gimbutas argued that prehistoric Europe was a peaceful, matriarchal society that worshipped a deity she came to identify as a single great-hipped Goddess. Running with Gimbutas's already rather speculative claims, many witches forged a political origin story that pit mellow tribes of Goddess-loving egalitarians against marauding Indo-European warriors with patriarchal sky gods and nasty Bronze Age weapons.

UCLA also produced perhaps the most influential witch in American history. Miriam Simos was a young Jewish woman who discovered Gardnerian Wicca in an experimental anthropology class and went on to practice witchcraft with Budapest. Simos later moved to the Bay Area, where she published her best-selling book *The Spiral Dance* in 1979 under the name Starhawk. A powerfully written work of Wiccan theory and praxis, *The Spiral Dance* was packed with liturgy and spells and feminist politics, and it spawned hundreds of covens across the land. Starhawk's subsequent books offered an ever more evangelical blend of Goddess worship and political activism, linking Wicca's affirmation of nature and the (female) body to a recognizably Bay Area blend of demands for human rights, peace, and environmental regulations. *Dreaming the Dark* details the mix of rituals and direct action that Starhawk and other witches performed during a celebrated three-week blockade of California's Diablo Canyon Nuclear Power Plant in 1981.

Like most Neopagans, Starhawk and the Reclaiming Collective she helped found did not follow Budapest's separatist approach to the mysteries. On the other hand, the lesbian undercurrent of the Dianic tradition did help deepen the connection between the Neopagan movement and California's queer and increasingly vocal sexual cultures. In 1978, the independent scholar Arthur Evans, who had come to San Francisco after abandoning a PhD program at Columbia University, published *Witchcraft and the Gay Counterculture*. The book argued for the existence of a hidden tradition of ecstatic pansexual pagan rites, centered on the Great Mother and a horned consort, that ran all the way through European history back to the shaman days. Evans had already begun to re-create such Bacchic fetes in the flesh when a similarly Dionysian inspiration seized the soul of Harry Hay, the Angeleno gay rights pioneer who had founded the homosexual Mattachine Society in Silver Lake at the impressively early date of 1950. Along with a handful of other men exploring the sacred dimension of gay experience, Hay called for the first Radical Faerie gathering at an Arizona ashram in 1979. Whipping up an infectious blend of gay eros, magic ritual, and feral campy chaos, the Radical Faeries proved highly successful and soon spread their wild ways throughout the West Coast and the rest of the pagan nation.

Given their need to rejigger witchcraft to reflect homosexual experience, gay and lesbian Neopagans had to confront the fact that the Craft was more of a creative religious invention than the authentic expression of an unbroken stream of traditional practices. Gardnerian Wiccans claimed to represent a surviving witch cult, but during the experimental days of the counterculture, this view came to be seen by many Neopagans as both historically inaccurate and unhelpful. One person to skillfully attack the British myths was a Neopagan intellectual from Southern California named Isaac Bonewits, who received the first and only BA given by UC Berkeley in the field of magic and thaumaturgy. In San Francisco, Aidan Kelly and others embraced the contingency of Neopagan ritual, freely composing the poetic liturgy for an eclectic and influential coven of "bootstrap witches" called the New Reformed Order of the Golden Dawn. The loopiest countercultural example of this ad hoc Goddess worship was a self-published book called *Principia Discordia: Or How I How I Found Goddess and What I Did to Her When I Found Her,* a slapstick sutra of Dada encyclicals, collage cartoons, and mystic hot dog jokes compiled by two men who claimed to have encountered a simian emissary of Eris, the Greek goddess of chaos, in an all-night bowling alley in Whittier, California, in 1958—or possibly 1959.

Another crucial development in Neopagan Californiana was the Society for Creative Anachronism, a medieval-reenactment fellowship that began in Berkeley in 1966 when a group of history majors, swordsmen, and J. R. R. Tolkien fans gathered for a costumed tournament in Diane Paxson's backyard one lovely day in May. They had fun, and today the membership of the SCA stands in the tens of thousands. Though the group attracts as many Christians and atheists as witches, the SCA does mirror Neopaganism's potent brew of historical research, playful fantasy, and living theater. In 1971, Paxson and some of her extended family network moved into a rambling gray-shingled house in the Berkeley Hills they called Greyhaven, which became a nexus of sci-fi fandom and Goddess religion. With her sister-in-law, Marion Zimmer Bradley, Paxson developed seasonal rituals and formed an all-female coven called the Dark Moon Circle. Bradley went on to pen the best-selling and justly celebrated *Mists of Avalon,* which mixed Goddess juice into the Matter of Britain. Though it reflected little of actual Celtic religion, Bradley's fantasy helped spread Goddess spirituality into the American mainstream during the 1980s, a rapprochement perhaps reflected by the author's own decision to return to the Episcopal Church sometime before her death in 1999.

Science fiction and fantasy literature resonate with Neopaganism because, like the rituals and beliefs of modern Wiccans and Druids, these genres are expressions of the creative imagination in a cosmological key. But the Neopagan imagination is also, crucially, a reimagining of the actual material world of temples and nature. Some of the most interesting architecture devoted to the Goddess lies in the wine country, on the site of a former Baha'i school in the town of Geyserville. A ten-acre New Age retreat center, the Isis Oasis Sanctuary contains a number of structures, including a theater, a guest pavilion, and a sauna fashioned from an old redwood wine barrel. The sacred heart of the sanctuary is a small, cheery Isis temple where the Egyptian goddess is worshipped as the avatar of the earth mother. A fanciful scarab, painted in Haight-Ashbury hues, stands watch over the entrance to a small meditation room decorated with astrological symbols and statues of Bast and Anubis, the psychopomp of the dead. The altar includes a few feathers from the white peacocks who live at the retreat center's animal sanctuary, a noisy convocation of ocelots, emus, and rare Technicolor birds. A goat named Frodo, painstakingly bred by Mendocino County Neopagans to resemble an actual unicorn, also lives at the Sanctuary. The founder of Isis Oasis, Loreon Vigne, loves exotic beasts, and originally collected and bred them in San Francisco. When the city passed an ordinance banning such menageries, Vigne was forced to move from her home, which lay on, of all places, Isis Street.

TEMPLE, ISIS OASIS SANCTUARY, GEYSERVILLE

Temples are common to all religions; Neopagans differ from most in making sacred space wherever they can find it, whether in redwood groves or public parks or suburban basements. For decades, the witches in the Reclaiming Collective have celebrated the winter solstice on the sands of San Francisco's Ocean Beach, where, after calling the spirits of the four directions, they plunge naked into the frigid surf before merrily dancing around a bonfire. A mile or so up the coast, on the same crowning outcrop that supports the famous Cliff House, lie the remains of Adolph Sutro's garden estate, once dotted with classical statues that the onetime San Francisco mayor hoped would bring some high culture to benighted San Francisco. One of the two statues that still stand is a small copy of a Roman image of Diana, the Virgin Huntress. The mayor would no doubt be shocked to learn that his Diana is now regularly bedecked with flowers from the fell hands of local witches.

One of the most creative Neopagan transformations of the California landscape was enacted by the Church of All Worlds, an influential polytheistic group whose founders moved from the Midwest to Mendocino in the late 1970s. Initially inspired by Ayn Rand and Heinlein's *Stranger in a Strange Land,* CAW developed an eco-conscious earth religion based in part on cofounder Tim Zell's LSD-fueled revelation that the planet Earth is a single organism. This was a prescient version of the Gaia hypothesis later described by the British scientist James Lovelock, whose own vision of the planet as a self-regulating entity came in a "flash of enlightenment" in Pasadena in 1965. In 1990, Zell, now known as Oberon Ravenheart, helped bring some of this Gaian consciousness to bear on an elaborate re-creation of the Eleusinian mysteries, an ancient ritual initiation held near Athens, Greece, for roughly a thousand years. CAW staged its mysteries in Pinnacles National Monument, whose spiraling monoliths of volcanic rock formed when magma spewed out of a rift that opened in the San Andreas Fault twenty-three million years ago. Using the Homeric Hymn to Demeter as its core text, CAW led twenty initiates through an elaborate ritual theater from dusk to dawn, a rite that culminated in a spectral plunge into the underworld, represented at Pinnacles by a network of caves that snake beneath bedrock boulders the size of single-family homes.

Students of the earth mysteries claim that volcanic regions create powerful vortexes of psychic energy—a claim that presumably extends to rift zones like the San Andreas Fault, and that would therefore tell us much about California. Such volutes of telluric energy may also help explain the mysterious labyrinths that have appeared over the last few decades in Sibley Volcanic Preserve, an undeveloped series of hills and gulleys that surround Round Top, the tallest volcanic formation in the Oakland Hills. Historically, we probably owe the labyrinth to the Minoans on Crete, and the design later became a feature of some medieval cathedrals, where it came to symbolize the journey of the

LABYRINTH, SIBLEY VOLCANIC REGIONAL PRESERVE, OAKLAND

soul. Recent attention to the calming and meditative effects of the labyrinth's spiral dance have encouraged its spread around the world, with scores in the Bay Area alone, including two prominent Chartres-style designs at San Francisco's Grace Cathedral. But none of California's labyrinths can match the haunting serenity of the ones in the Sibley preserve, which are well maintained and regularly host gatherings of witches and warlocks and other feather-clad wonder workers. The largest and most impressive of these mazes was built in the center of a deep quarry by Helena Mazzariello, a Montclair sculptor and psychic; the rest were constructed anonymously. Originally, Mazzariello laid out her stones in a classic seven-circuit Cretan design, with the opening to the south. Later, some unknown innovator added on to the labyrinth, extending the opening from the south to the northwest, where the entrance lies today. As with most of the park's stone designs, the motivations behind this unauthorized addition are unknown. But it may reflect the geomantic orientation of California itself, lodged in the northwest climes of the great dame Earth.

IN GUAD WE TRUST

In 1993, during the month of June, Anita Contreras knelt down beside a lake in a leafy public park to pray for her children. Then she looked up into the trees and saw the Virgin of Guadalupe, or the image of the Virgin, revealed in the knotted bark of a live oak. Soon thousands of pilgrims were flocking to the site, which lies in Watsonville, a small strawberry-growing town in the lush farmlands north of the Salinas Valley. Though such enthusiasms often dissipate quickly, the Watsonville site has persevered, despite its somewhat awkward location on public land. The oak is now surrounded by an altar and a fence, and the lakeside grotto that encompasses the spot has been terraced into a lovely outdoor chapel, a small amphitheater of curved benches and votive-candle racks. The foot-high figure is not very easy to pick out from other suggestive knots in the trees, which is why a white box included on the sprawling altar contains a mirror, enabling those in the know to cast a beam of sunlight onto the Virgin's miraculous silhouette.

Though they are rarely acknowledged by the Vatican, apparitions of Mary continue to occur worldwide. Besides popping up in the visionary flesh, as at Fatima and Lourdes, the mother of God has also graced objects as quotidian as tortillas and grilled cheese sandwiches with her image. But Contreras did not see just any Mary: she saw the Virgin of Guadalupe, the official patron saint of the Americas and the most important female deity in the New World. Fittingly, the story of the Virgin of Guadalupe's original appearance also concerns an image that emerged spontaneously from local flora. On December 9, 1531, an Indian peasant named Juan

VIRGIN OF GUADALUPE SHRINE, WATSONVILLE

Diego passed by the hill of Tepeyac, which now lies within the environs of Mexico City. Barely a decade had passed since Cortez had conquered the Aztecs, but the Spaniards had already managed to raze the temple that once crowned the hill, a pyramid dedicated to the serpent-skirted earth mother Tonantzin. As Diego walked by, he heard birdsong so beautiful that he felt he must be dreaming. A voice called him. He ascended the hill and found a brown-skinned woman standing in clothing radiant as the sun. This being claimed that she was Mary, and that she wanted a church dedicated to her on the site. But when Diego told this to Bishop Juan de Zumarraga—who destroyed twenty thousand idols in his career—the Indian was not believed. The Virgin told Diego to try again, but Zumarraga wanted proof. So the Virgin told Diego to gather roses blooming at the top of the mesquite-covered hill. Diego stashed the flowers in his *tilma,* a peasant shawl woven from the agave maguey, which also gives us the intoxicating beverages pulque and mescal. Diego took the roses to Zumarraga, and when he dumped the offerings out of his tilma, the rough cloth was stained with the image of Our Lady of Guadalupe. It is this very cloak, it is said, that hangs in the modern basilica at Tepeyac and draws millions of pilgrims a year.

The pilgrims come to Tepeyac because the Virgin of Guadalupe is an enormously sustaining figure, an avatar of justice and grace and perseverance. This is particularly true for Chicanas like Anita Contreras, who work hard and worry about their kids and live in places like Watsonville—a poor town with a large, struggling migrant population. Eight years before the Virgin appeared to Contreras, over a thousand local workers, mostly Mexican American, launched a grueling eighteen-month-long strike against the Watsonville Cannery Company. One of the most important labor campaigns of the 1980s, the Watsonville strike ultimately succeeded, although, ironically, most of the factories soon moved to the same regions of Mexico that many of the migrants hailed from. A few years after the Virgin came, labor unrest again erupted when the United Farm Workers—which Cesar Chavez first organized, under the banner of Guadalupe, in the 1960s—struggled to bring thousands of local strawberry pickers into the union.

For California's Chicanos, the Virgin is a multi-dimensional figure, as political and cultural as she is religious. While John Paul II gave "the Mother of the Americas" the stamp of approval by dedicating a chapel in Saint Peter's Cathedral to her, the Virgin's image also graces gangster biceps, skateboards, and taqueria calendars. Many Chicanos who keep their distance from the Church still embrace Guadalupe, whose mestiza blend of Spanish and Indian, Catholic and pagan, resonates with people navigating America's modern melting pot. The Virgin lives large in East Los Angeles, for example, which contains the largest concentration of ethnic Mexicans outside Mexico City. Here most of her manifestations are Catholic, while others hover in the no-man's zone between sacred and profane. In the corner of the parking lot of Self Help Graphics and Art, a visual-arts center serving East Los Angeles, a statue of Guadalupe stands atop a pagan pyramid in a lovely grotto of yuccas maintained, more or less, by local women. The figure, which once was used for religious processions in the neighborhood, is decorated with a mosaic of broken crockery, the work of an eccentric New Mexican artist with more than a little of the Watts Towers' Simon Rodia in him. Although the center never officially sanctioned the religious use of the shrine, locals have sometimes formed spontaneous vigils around the figure, serving up posole and prayers. At the same time, Self Help Graphics has also found itself in trouble with Guadalupe's most ardent devotees, who loudly objected to a digitized image of the Virgin in a rose-colored bikini created by a Chicana artist associated with the organization.

RIGHT: CATHEDRAL OF OUR LADY OF ANGELS, LOS ANGELES

BELOW: VIRGIN OF GUADALUPE, SELF HELP GRAPHICS & ART, EAST LOS ANGELES

Don des Dames

California's Chicano arts are a rich stew of sacred symbols, pop culture, and grassroots politics. Although a secular outpost, Self Help Graphics was founded with the help of a Franciscan nun named Sister Karen Boccalero. In 1972, the center also joined with Galería de la Raza, in San Francisco's Mission district, to bring Mexico's Day of the Dead to California. Like the Virgin of Guadalupe, the Día de los Muertos is a mestizo affair, a Catholic Saints Day draped over an Aztec festival that celebrated the periodic return of the dead to our world. In Mexico, the day is a family affair, and generally a rural one. But the California festivities thrive in the modern urban milieu, where traditional elements like altars and *calacas*—the skeletons that probably descend from Aztec skull masks—are woven into a sort of street theater devoted to satire, political struggle, and community memory. In San Francisco, where Halloween is basically a civic holiday, the event also draws scores of Neopagans, who come to celebrate the rites of Samhain with a Latin tinge.

The Virgin seems at home in America's funky mix of commerce and cultural miscegenation. At the same time, the Church has recently coaxed her away from the margins of popular faith into the heart of Roman Catholic power. Although some prominent Catholic scholars continue to insist that Juan Diego did not exist, the peasant was beatified by Pope John Paul II in 1990 and canonized a decade later. Inside Mexico, Diego's ascent toward sainthood may have had something to do with the 1992 decision by the country's government to abolish some of its strong anticlerical laws. In the United States, the ascent of the Virgin can be charted at the Cathedral of Our Lady of Angels, a brassy peach-colored modernist hulk designed by the Spanish architect José Raphael Moneo and consecrated in downtown Los Angeles in 2002. In one of the cathedral's many soulless and awkwardly asymmetrical chapels, off the north ambulatory, you will find a three-foot-tall Baroque statue of the Virgin. A silvery reliquary around her neck contains a snippet of Diego's actual tilma, along with some tiny nuggets of unidentified but presumably holy material. The tilma tuft—the only bit outside of Mexico—was given to the archdiocese in the 1940s but was stuck in an archival museum for decades. Shortly after the new cathedral opened its massive doors, Cardinal Mahoney sent the miniscule patch on a twenty-one-city tour before installing it in the chapel.

Alongside the north wall of the cathedral property, near date palms and gory statues, stands another Guadalupe shrine: a framed digital reproduction of Diego's tilma, surrounded by the mural work of the Mexican-born artist Làlo Garcia. Garcia was also responsible for the twelve-foot-high mural of the Virgin on the other side of the wall, which directly faces the southbound lanes of Highway 101. Some Angelenos call this image Our Lady of the Freeways, but even from her peculiar perch, the Virgin shines. Everywhere she presents the same profile: cloaked by stars, cradled by the moon, held aloft by a seraphim. Her hands are cupped, as if she holds a gift, and she looks to the side with a compassionate reserve, intimate but unsentimental, like the angels in Wim Wenders's *Wings of Desire*. Technically speaking, the image on Diego's tilma does not simply represent the Virgin but actually *embodies* her, and reproductions of that image thus carry a special power. Some compare the Virgin to a hieroglyph, a fusion of image and Logos, but the best characterization of the figure lies in the Eastern Orthodox concept of the icon. Within the Byzantine Church, holy images of saints are considered not mere pictures, but literal portals into sacred reality.

It is hardly accidental, then, that the Virgin of Guadalupe rears her head in one of California's most intensely traditional Byzantine chapels. Archimandrite Boniface Luykx first brought the Holy Transfiguration Monastery to Mendocino's Redwood Valley in the mid-1970s. Though it belongs to a Roman Catholic diocese, the contemplative monastery, also known as Mount Tabor, draws from the liturgy, architecture, and spiritual traditions of Eastern Christianity. Its gorgeous wooden buildings, with their weathered shingles and exposed beams, seem to reflect a recognizable Californian style of organic architecture, but they actually derive from the old wooden churches that dot the Carpathian Mountains in Ukraine. Mount Tabor's monks hew to a life of poverty, fasting, and intercessory prayer, and observe some of the hoariest, and most haunting, rites of Christendom. Within the small church, a gorgeous icon screen cloaks the sanctuary from the nave, its gilt images of holy personages intentionally similar to a thousand other Byzantine icons across the world. Facing this traditional iconostasis is a wall covered with Orthodox icons of Mary, as well as one large image of the face of the Virgin of Guadalupe. Even in this place of strict tradition, which is about as Old World as they come, the Empress of America, with her brown skin and Aztec lineaments, nurtures her devotees.

HOLY TRANSFIGURATION MONASTERY, REDWOOD VALLEY

BLUE LOTUS TEMPLE of SOUND & LIGHT

KALIFORNIA

Before Christopher Hills died in 1997 at the age of seventy, he was a radiant light of the New Age, a tireless explorer of energy fields and subtle vibrations. His investigations initially drew him to hatha yoga, and in 1970, he brought hundreds of yogis and scientists together in New Delhi for the first World Conference on Scientific Yoga. A few years later, seeking the optimum environmental vibes, the Englishman settled in the richly forested mountains above Santa Cruz. There he founded the University of the Trees and published a very thick book called *Nuclear Evolution,* which exhaustively weaves together cellular consciousness, chakras, and the colors of the rainbow. Hills was more than a cosmic light worker, though; he also codiscovered and developed the superfood spirulina, a high-protein blue-green algae he touted as the quickest way to get sunlight into the cells. Though Hills's claim that the green goop could help alleviate world hunger did not exactly pan out, spirulina brought him and his multilevel Light Force Company millions of dollars.

In 1989, shortly before the Loma Prieta earthquake wreaked havoc in Santa Cruz County, Hills poured the concrete foundation for a private home and retreat center near the mountain town of Boulder Creek. Initially called the Garden of Forgiveness, the landscape temple was keyed to the vortex energies of Hills's forty-four-acre property, whose towering redwoods he compared to giant antenna. The only thing missing from Hills's spiritual playground was a partner to share it with. In an intentional act of magic, Hills crafted a lengthy description of the *dakini* of his dreams and asked the Goddess to manifest this being in flesh. Shortly thereafter, Hills met Penny Slinger, a British artist and performer who fit the bill. A magnetic sacred sensualist, Slinger had been studying Tantra since the early 1970s and penned the million-selling manual *Sexual Secrets* with her former partner Nik Douglas. In 1994, just a few years before Hills's death, Slinger moved into the estate, which is now known as the Goddess Temple, a place, she says, "dedicated to the goddess by a wizard, and now both a shrine to her and a living testimonial to that man."

The private temple home greets visitors with a hermetic motto emblazoned on the side of a peaked redwood portico: "Neh-Wey Sev-Ia-Nakh," which means "As above so below" in Aramaic. A large gong stands in the main foyer, alongside a large wooden pietà Hills received—still consecrated—from an English nunnery. The hallways are lined with Slinger's paintings of Arawak maidens and the goddess Kali, the fearsome Hindu deity that she believes brought her and Hills together. At the southeastern end of the building stands an octagonal "wizard's tower," its golden spire complementing the vibrating waves of lapis-blue ceramic tiles that cover the rest of the roof. The tower overlooks a steep meadow surrounded on all sides by magnificent groves of redwoods, including one called, fittingly, the Magnificat. Near a large gazebo dubbed the Kuan Yin Shrine stands an elaborate metalwork dragon gate, which leads into a "Magical Kingdom" of sacred groves, sweat lodges, and weathered yoni shrines. The highest spot on the property is called the Eighth Domain, after the energy field that exists beyond our seven chakras. More dependable energy fields are massaged in the Blue Lotus Temple of Sound and Light, a digital editing studio and blue-screen soundstage accessed through a pair of narrow Balinese temple doors.

Slinger's approach to Tantra—feminist, erotic, cyberdelic—is by no means unusual in her neck of the woods. Orthodox scholar-practitioners like Georg Feuerstein even use the term "California Tantra" to distinguish such Shaktified spiritual hedonism from its Indian namesake, a vast and complex body of ritual practices whose lustiness has been rather oversold in the West. While few orthodox adepts would ever consider California Tantra an authentic expression of the tradition, this wayward path is traditional as far as the

BLUE LOTUS TEMPLE OF SOUND AND LIGHT, GODDESS TEMPLE, BOULDER CREEK

Golden State itself goes. Over a century ago, a self-styled yogi named Pierre Arnold Bernard founded the Bacchante Academy in San Francisco. Bernard, who was probably born in California around 1875, taught self-hypnotism, hatha yoga, and love secrets to his largely female clientele. Bernard claimed to have received Tantric initiation in India, and he almost certainly picked up some tips from Swami Ram Tirath, an ascetic yogi and poet from the Punjab who traipsed around northern California in the early 1900s and compared Bernard to "the Tantrik High Priests of India." Whatever his authentic powers, Bernard was also a bit of a flimflam man, and he could not resist dubbing himself the Omnipotent Oom. After the 1906 earthquake, Oom relocated his studio to New York, where he founded the First Tantrik Order of America. Despite a string of scandals surrounding his purported "love-cult," Bernard introduced scads of wealthy New Yorkers to yogic practices like mantra and *pranayama,* or breathwork, while also spinning their heads with a philosophy of carnal bliss that proclaimed the sex drive to be the animating spirit of the world. The body was the real temple for Bernard, and true religion "the worship of man's invisible power."

Here Bernard misspoke, for Tantra—in both its traditional and California flavors—is more accurately seen as the worship of *woman's* invisible power. Shakti lies at the root of Tantra's gendered universe, a feminine power often identified with the earth energies tapped by geomancers like Christopher Hills. Tantric deities like Tara and Durga may ultimately descend from the great Goddess that some believe represents the foundation of human religious consciousness. Such power is not all sweetness and light. No male god in the world's pantheons, for example, can match the bloodthirsty spectacle of Kali, the Tantric goddess of dissolution and death who so fascinates Penny Slinger. The black-skinned goddess is often pictured straddling a dead (but erect) Shiva, her red tongue thrust out between fangs, her nude form accessorized with blades and garlands of skulls

RIGHT: TEMPLE ROOM, GODDESS TEMPLE, BOULDER CREEK

FAR RIGHT: YONI TREE, KALI MANDIR, LAGUNA BEACH

and decapitated mustachioed heads. In the West, Kali's air of heresy and sexual empowerment has made her an important icon for California Tantrists, feminist Neopagans, and even some aficionados of sadomasochism. Such appropriation is not altogether out of the ballpark; left-hand Tantrists in India also walk on the wild side of social taboo, and the Kali-worshipping Thuggee cult even practiced human sacrifice with their kidnap victims during the British Raj. But most orthodox South Asian devotees of the goddess embrace Kali as a bountiful and forgiving mother, with the same sweetness that Mexican grandmothers bring to Guadalupe.

In 1986, Elizabeth Harding, a Viennese woman living in Los Angeles, flew to Calcutta on a spiritual quest. Harding was a follower of Ramakrishna, and she wanted to visit the Kali temple at Dakshineswar, a curvilinear, multidomed compound on the edge of the Ganges, where Ramakrishna had lived and prayed and swooned in sacred ecstasy. Harding, whose subsequent photograph of the Kali shrine became one of the most widely distributed images of the dark goddess, wanted to read more about Kali, and when she could not find a good book in English, she decided to write one. In 1993, when her book *Kali: The Black Goddess of Dakshineswar* was going to be released, Harding thought it appropriate to stage a formal Kali *puja*, or ritual, in Southern California.

A priest from Dakshineswar, Sri Haradhan Chakraborti, agreed to fly to America, and also arranged to have a Kali image carved from basalt and shipped to Laguna Beach, where Harding, who worked in the software industry, was living. Once Sri Haradhan had ritually awakened the statue, Harding and her fellow Laguna Beach devotees faced a choice: either commit the figure to the sea or ritually feed her every single day with food, prayers, and offerings. No one in the loose-knit group knew how to perform traditional pujas themselves, but they took up the call, founding the Kali Mandir in 1995. Formal Kali shrines are nearly nonexistent in America, and soon the neighbors were complaining about the "religious noise" caused by the crowds of singing, conch-blowing acolytes who gathered every dark moon. The Kali statue was then moved to its current location, a modest yellow cottage nestled in the serpentine folds of Laguna Canyon, near a school where the group's popular yearly gatherings are held. Kali Mandir hopes to one day buy the school, which not only boasts the space the temple needs but also lies near a Native American burial site and the auspicious confluence of nine scrub canyons.

With the exception of tiny personal spaces reserved for Harding and one monk who lives on site, Kali Mandir is given over to the goddess, who stands in the main room flanked by Durga and Shiva, with a radiant yantra at her back and her right foot thrust forward—the indication that she is showing her more benign, right-hand aspect. Framed images of Ramakrishna and the mother temple at Dakshineswar hang nearby, as does a reproduction of the Virgin of Guadalupe. Kali is always hungry for flowers, and the half acre outside the house is given over to roses, dahlias, hibiscus, sweet peas, and other future offerings. Alongside the carport stands a tree with a large vaginal cleft. Such naturally occurring yonis make great Shakti shrines, and early on Harding dedicated the tree to Manasa Devi, the queen of the snakes. Not long after the dedication, a king snake nestled itself at the foot of the tree around an image of Ramakrishna, and then reared its upper body in apparent imitation of a cobra.

Kali Mandir is the most welcoming American temple devoted to the world's darkest goddess. But this modest sanctuary also represents a quiet revolution in the modes of Hindu worship in America. In general, Hindu religious centers established by whites are started by gurus and their single-minded devotees. But Kali Mandir has no guru, no doctrine, and no formal congregation. Instead, the temple is simply committed to performing a traditional Kali blessing "in the mood of Ramakrishna," and then leaving the door open for whoever comes. According to the presiding *pujari,* an Anglo-Mexican fellow from Tijuana named Bhajanananda Saraswati, Kali Mandir is designed to create "a grid of authentic practice" that will ground the loose energies surrounding goddess worship and Tantra in the West. The temple avoids animal sacrifices and scandalous Tantric practices, and this in turn attracts a wider and more moderate range of devotees, from Hare Krishnas to orthodox Christians to wandering sadhus who sport seven-foot-long dreadlocks. Kali Mandir also beckons scores of ordinary Indians. Although the temple is run by whites, three-quarters of its visitors are South Asians with ties to diverse regions in India. This sets Kali Mandir apart from most Hindu temples established by South Asians in the West, which generally attract a single ethnic or language group. In other words, Kali continues her work of dissolution by eroding the difference between South Asians who want to preserve their cultural identity in America and white Americans who want to dissolve their identities into the dark night of sweet devotion.

KALI MANDIR, LAGUNA BEACH

We're

FREYA ALTAR, GREYHAVEN, BERKELEY

DIY

THE ALCHEMY OF TRASH

The Beat movement that so defined California's postwar cultural scene is best remembered for its poets and writers. Bohemian malcontents like Gary Snyder, Allen Ginsberg, and Michael McClure fashioned prophetic voices out of trauma and delight, and planted the seeds of a hip, experiential spirituality that would bloom in the hippie era. But an equally significant dimension of Beat creativity focused on the plastic arts, particularly collage and assemblage: works of sculpture and paper that mixed and matched fragments scavenged from the cultural landscape and its clutter of signs, commodities, and trash. In the 1950s and '60s, artists like Bruce Conner, Jess, Wallace Berman, George Herms, Edward Kienholz, and Helen Adam appropriated images, objects, and materials into mordant celebrations of the dreamlike detritus surrounding them. Raiding lowbrow sources with Jungian glee, Jess and Adam made surrealist paste-ups out of comic books and magazine ads, while Conner, Kienholz, and Herms used the flotsam of the day to construct fetishistic and sly assemblages.

Soul work was vital to most of these artists, and the creative work of cobbling and collage partly grew out of a spiritual urge to reflect and redeem the environment around them, to both witness and sacralize a broken postwar world. As bohemians making art far from the galleries of New York, they were also driven by pragmatic concerns. Like the thrift-store racks that would furnish clothing for the Pranksters and hippies, found materials—a.k.a. junk—were affordable. But economics never offers complete explanations. The marvelous monstrosity that William Randolph Hearst built at San Simeon—a gumbo of architectural fragments and European museum pieces piled up in elegant disarray—showed that even the wealthiest Californians had a yen to sample and slam together different times and places.

The most monumental assemblage artist in California was neither a wealthy media baron nor a hipster. Simon Rodia immigrated to America from southern Italy at the end of the nineteenth century and labored in coal mines and quarries until he found himself scrounging out a living as a tile setter in Watts, then a rural neighborhood south of downtown Los Angeles. For thirty-odd years, Rodia poured his soul into three giddy, thin-ribbed towers and the walled, wedge-shaped compound that encloses them. Rodia worked without assistance, constructing his spires out of chicken wire, cement, and steel rods he bent into shape on the trolley tracks for the Pacific Electric Red Car line that lay just beyond his property. He built without plans, scaffolding, or fancy tools, constantly varying his designs, making it up as he went along. To decorate the myriad concrete struts and surfaces, Rodia applied a riotous mosaic of refuse: smashed tiles, terra-cotta pots, corncobs, cookie jars, and seashells he found combing the South Bay beaches he reached by the Red Car. A nearby bottling plant furnished loads of green 7-Up glass, which he pressed into mortar beside cobalt-blue shards of Milk of Magnesia bottles. Sometime in the 1930s, Rodia even sacrificed a 1927 Hudson touring car to his great work.

Rodia abandoned Watts in 1954, eleven years before a traffic incident sparked a legendary week of armed revolt in the neighborhood. When a subsequent owner decided to turn the site into a taco joint, the city condemned Rodia's marvel. A group of art lovers joined forces to protect the towers. A stress test proved the remarkable steeliness of Rodia's intuitive engineering, and the site was preserved, eventually passing into the city's hands. Watts Towers now stands as the most celebrated example of untrained visionary architecture in the United States, a roadside companion of Antonio Gaudi's Sagrada Familia in Barcelona.

Is Watts Tower a sacred space? Though the overall compound most resembles a three-masted ship, the towers also clearly borrow from the spires and flying buttresses of the cathedrals Rodia saw as a child. One spire is topped by a headless angel, a sign, perhaps, of Rodia's own ambivalent religious feelings. The artist did not seem to

HEADLESS ANGEL, WATTS TOWERS, WATTS

In Rodia's work, Duncan recognized a fellow scavenger of beauty. Duncan was a lifetime companion of the collagist Jess, and echoed his lover's working methods by peppering his poetry with citations and textual fragments, many lifted from hermetic and mystical literature. He saw Rodia's work as a cathedral "dedicated to itself," a collage of "disregarded splendors" that were "resurrected against the rules." Beyond religion, Rodia's ecstasy of broken bottles and colored dishes realized the sacred independence of the human imagination, "risking height."

Despite Rodia's personal isolation, Watts Towers has cast its spindly shadow on a broad range of California folk arts. In 1958, the towers were featured on the cover of a beatnik comedy record by Bay Area sound collagist Henry Jacobs. Almost twenty years later, Rodia's crockery mosaic was echoed on the rear wall and Guadalupe shrine at Self Help Graphics and Art in East Los Angeles. Rodia also influenced a visionary African-American junk artist named Noah Purifoy, who founded the Watts Towers Art Center in the early 1960s. Following the 1965 riots, Purifoy and a friend collected charred wood and melted neon signs from the rubble and then doled the material out to a handful of artists, including some whites; the resulting show, *66 Signs of Neon,* toured college campuses before a lack of institutional interest returned most of the works to the junk heap. In 1987, Purifoy moved to the high-desert town of Joshua Tree, where he erected scores of fantastic assemblages and luxuriously ratty environments on his two-and-a-half-acre plot of land. The artist died in 2004, and his witty and mournful wonders, with names like *Cathedral* and *Mondrian,* just flake away in the baking dust.

Sixty miles southeast from Joshua Tree lies Slab City, a community of squatters and nomads that is also home to the only folk-art environment in California that matches the scale and sovereign vision of Watts Towers. Set between the stinky Salton Sea and the jagged upthrust of the Chocolate Mountains Gunnery Range, Slab City occupies the concrete foundations of an otherwise vanished U.S. Marine Corps base; it annually attracts a couple thousand snowbirds, veterans, and impoverished misfits with the prospect of a rent-free parking lot. In 1985, a Vermont jack-of-all-trades named Leonard Knight rolled into the village with a three-hundred-foot-tall hot-air balloon packed into the modified dump truck he called home. Knight, a born-again Christian, had sewn the bag himself in order to create a giant floating billboard for God, but when his repeated attempts

care for Catholicism much, but he was known to sometimes preach at local Pentecostal meetings. Scholars of the towers now believe that church ceremonies were held in the delicate gazebo he built, and that baptisms were performed in the small font once identified as a bird bath.

Though many homes and gardens built by outsider artists in America are obsessively Christian, Rodia's creative aspirations reach beyond any established faith, an ambition that the generally taciturn man alluded to once when he described the towers as "taller than the Church." During a tent revival hosted by a Mexican immigrant group called the Cry of Christian Freedom, Rodia once offered a sermon called "True Freedom: Freedom of Spirit and Soul." Perhaps his spiraling mastheads and speckled prow represent an ark of true deliverance from a lonely life of poverty and anomie, an individual vehicle of the spirit that transcends art and devotion alike. In his poem about Rodia, "Nel Mezzo Del Cammin Di Nostra Vita," the Bay Area poet Robert Duncan also recognized the alchemy of trash represented by the towers:

> scavenged
> from the city dump, from sea-wrack,
> taller than the Holy Roman Catholic church
> steeples, and, moreover,
> inspired; built up from bits of beauty

failed to get the balloon aloft, he abandoned the project and turned to creating Salvation Mountain. Making adobe with straw and local clay, Knight shaped an artificial hill on the edge of a low plateau and coated it with massive amounts of paint, much of it scavenged and, later, donated. With colors resembling a DayGlo children's book, Salvation Mountain includes pine trees, waterfalls, flags, and a yellow-brick road that leads to the top of the mountain. Blue fluttering creatures intended to signify birds look like angels instead, a redemptive vision of nature that becomes especially palpable in the post-apocalyptic environs of Slab City. Along with myriad flowers, which Knight shapes by slamming his fist into a bucketload of adobe, the artist created the General Sherman tree stump, an elegy for a massive sequoia famously felled, under a different name, back in the 1850s. As with many works of Protestant folk art, the mountain and the various "Salvation Wagons" littered about the site are also plastered with Scripture, it being Knight's sworn mission to broadcast the slogans of God. Hence the pink and cherry-red proclamation that underscores the single white cross that tops the mountain: "God Is Love."

The sentiment seems indisputable to many who have made the pilgrimage to Slab City and met the kind and bright-eyed Knight. According to the artist, though, Knight was a hard-swearing reprobate until 1967, when he broke down on a suburban lawn in Lemon Grove, east of San Diego, and recited the sinner's prayer like a mantra. Twenty minutes later he was weeping and filled with the Holy Spirit. About as independent a Christian as they come, Knight is an exemplar of Harold Bloom's contention that the American Jesus is actually a Gnostic Jesus, a figure of the inner light, of direct companionship. Knight firmly believes in the promise

LEFT: BAPTISMAL FONT, WATTS TOWERS, WATTS

RIGHT: "TWO SIMILAR BELIEF SYSTEMS FACE TO FACE," NOAH PURIFOY SCULPTURE GARDEN, JOSHUA TREE

LOVE
JESUS I'M
A SINNER PLEASE
COME UPON MY
AND INTO
MY HEART

LEFT: SALVATION MOUNTAIN, SLAB CITY

RIGHT: TIRE TREE, SALVATION MOUNTAIN, SLAB CITY

of 1 John 2:27: "The anointing you received from Him remains in you, and you do not need anyone to teach you." He shuns churches and has shooed away televangelists who want to use Salvation Mountain for a backdrop. He has no use for fundamentalist arrogance. When his Christian critics ask him how many people his artwork has saved, Knight's answer is simple: "None. Jesus saves."

Despite its geographical isolation, Salvation Mountain has become a far richer medium for Knight's gospel truths than a giant balloon could ever have been. Knight still honors his earlier vision, though. To the south of the mountain, he is constructing a large, bulbous grotto that resembles a hot-air balloon only slightly less than Watts Towers resembles a schooner. The precarious ceiling of this huge, crumpled earthship is supported by branching candy-colored trees made of tractor tires and adobe; along with off-kilter telephone poles and bales of hay, these pillars support a structure that will hopefully never be put to a stress test. In contrast to the mountain proper, the grotto features a more explicit alchemy of trash: portholes in the walls are furnished by automobile glass, along with the occasional car door, while a donated satellite dish outside waits for a home in the composition. As Knight puts it, "The whole thing is made of throwaway junk." The humbleness of materials, though, makes Knight's triumph all the greater, a success that delights him simply because it spreads the word of God. A small shelter that abuts the entrance to the grotto, patterned after a Native American hogan, is filled with sports trophies and newspaper stories about Knight. But he doesn't say too much in interviews about the meaning of his work. Mostly, he lets the mountain, and the Spirit, do the talking.

THOU SHALT RENEW

Jewish tradition includes myriad arcane commandments, but the mitzvah that drives the autumn holiday of Sukkot, or the Feast of Booths, is rather simple: build a sukkah and dwell in it. Though Sukkot is not as widely celebrated by American Jews as more packaged holidays like Hanukkah, many families and institutions construct these temporary outdoor shelters shortly after Yom Kippur, in preparation for a time of joy that makes up somewhat for the heaviness of the High Holidays. For most, to dwell means to take meals and hang out with friends, although some observant Jews sleep in their sukkahs as well. The most important element of the structure is its loosely thatched roof, often made from palm fronds or hedge cuttings: tradition asks that it offer protection from the sun but remain open to the stars and, therefore, the rain and snow. Temporary and vulnerable, the sukkah commemorates the forty years the Israelites lived as nomads in the desert, dependent wholly on God. But the holiday also derives from the ancient harvest celebrations of Israel, and its essential ritual elements are flora: a citron fruit and a bundle of three plants called the *lulav,* which is shaken during prayers in the same six cosmic directions revered by Native Americans.

American sukkahs are in the main rather humble affairs, falling somewhere between sheltered picnic tables and the backyard forts kids like to build. Walls are constructed out of plywood, canvas, or even blue tarp; many people buy prefab sukkah kits, which may feature galvanized conduit or special "SukkahScreens." In the Northeast especially, the holiday often resembles a combination of Thanksgiving and the trimming of the Christmas tree, as families decorate their booths with corncobs and zucchini and crayon artwork from school.

Rather more exotic and colorful sukkahs can be glimpsed every fall in the backyards of the Bay Area, and especially Berkeley, where a loose tribe of Jews creates nomad shelters that would fit in comfortably at a Rainbow Gathering or at Burning Man. On the attached deck of one Berkeley abode, an almost psychedelic collage of tapestries carves out a languid, inviting space charged with a distinctly regional assemblage of icons: peacock feathers and a hookah, a Buddha and a dream catcher, Mexican votive candles and Middle Eastern amulets against the evil eye. Many of Berkeley's sukkah dwellers also take the call to celebration seriously, partying as much as they dwell and pray. According to Avram Davis, the director of a local Jewish meditation center and the regular host of a most merry sukkah, the Feast of Booths is one of the few Jewish holidays devoted wholly to joy. "All the other laws are under that banner."

Berkeley's colorful nomad fetes radiate the wild fire of Jewish Renewal, a movement that emerged from the collision of American Jewish life with the countercultural longings of the 1960s and '70s. The rebellious movement's most important early leaders were the rabbis Shlomo Carlebach and Zalman Schachter-Shalomi, both of whom were trained in the passionate orthodoxy of Lubavitch Hasidism but left the black hats for more tie-dyed tribes. Shlomo, as Carlebach preferred to be known, was a colorful and randy character who composed popular neo-Hasidic folk songs. In 1969, he moved from the East Coast to San Francisco to organize a *havurah,* or commune, called the House of Love and Prayer, a mystic hippie collective of Jews hungry for social change and the sacred hallowing of ordinary life through the mindful observation of orthodox law. Shlomo's followers founded a similar community in Los Angeles, a city that by then had come to host the third-largest number of Jews in the world.

Rabbi Zalman was a Kabbalistic innovator who visited California many times a year, reveling in its spirit of inclusion. In 1974, Zalman led High Holidays at Reverend Cecil Williams's Glide Memorial Church and invited a neo-Sufi choir to join in the service. Although the rabbis whom Zalman ordained are not always recognized by the

SUKKAH, AVRAM DAVIS AND SARA SHENDELMAN RESIDENCE, BERKELEY

three main denominations of American Jews, their quality and intensity have deepened the influence of Jewish Renewal over the decades. In the 1980s, the San Francisco Renewal rabbi Michael Lerner spearheaded Tikkun, a movement and magazine dedicated to seeding a "politics of meaning." Lerner's original notion was that the American right wing had made headway because it provided a spiritual basis lacking in the liberal left; Tikkun aimed to provide progressive activism with a specifically Jewish sense of sacred engagement with the world. Lerner's Commonweal organization, established in the Marin County enclave of Bolinas, has since made great strides toward humanizing modern medicine and raising awareness about the health implications of the toxins that pervade our environment. Lerner's pragmatic struggles are nonetheless grounded in ideas hatched up by a sixteenth-century Jewish Kabbalist named Isaac Luria, who described our reality as a created world shattered by the simultaneous emanation and concealment of the Godhead at the beginning of time. *Tikkun ha-Olam* is the commitment to repair the resulting broken vessels of cosmic light.

The thirsty spiritual tribes that propelled Jewish Renewal also wandered beyond the borders of Judaism proper. From Allen Ginsberg and Ram Dass on down, Jews have played a disproportionate role in the alternative spiritual movements born of the counterculture, adding a critical—and often funny—dimension to the evolving experiment with the self. The psychological sophistication and pragmatism of American Buddhism can be attributed in part to the contribution of Jews, who, according to the book *The Jew in the Lotus,* make up something like 30 percent of its leadership. The Buddhist landscape in California has been shaped by notable "Ju-Bu" teachers like Jack Kornfeld, Roshi Bernie Glassman, Mel Weitsman, Norman Fisher, Wes Nisker, and Sylvia Boorstein, who cofounded Marin's Spirit Rock Meditation Center with Kornfeld and wrote the memoir *Funny, You Don't Look Buddhist.* At the end of the day, however, most of these teachers owe far more of their spirituality to the Far East than the Near.

For other Jews drawn to meditation, the Buddhadharma is already implicit in Torah, and reveals itself there if the word of God is given room to breathe. As a teenager in 1970, Avram Davis left for India, frustrated at the difficulty of finding juicy spiritual teachers in the *shuls* and temples of America. He dove into India's freewheeling seeker scene and hung out with sadhus and Buddhist monks near Sarnath,

ABOVE: SUKKAH, SARA NICOLETTI RESIDENCE, BERKELEY

RIGHT: EMANU-EL SISTERHOOD RESIDENCE/ SAN FRANCISCO ZEN CENTER, CITY CENTER, SAN FRANCISCO

plunging into visionary consciousness while continuing to pray to God and practice davening, the ritual body bob of the Orthodox. Returning to the States, Davis donned robes and lived as a wandering ascetic, begging and doing odd jobs. Craving spiritual retreat, he took refuge in the Prince of Peace Abbey in Oceanside, north of San Diego, where he murmured the Birkat HaShachar while the Benedictine monks performed their morning office. Davis studied with Zalman and Shlomo, and eventually came to found the independent meditation center Chochmat HaLev in Berkeley. Although created to fan the still, silent flame within mystic Judaism, Chochmat's Friday-night Shabbats now roil with the exuberant funk of neo-Hasidic celebration. Such unexpected upwellings of tribal verve are part of the legacy of Jewish Renewal, which engages tradition not as a solid edifice but as a sukkah: a temporary structure that's open to the changing elements.

The tension between mystical tradition and open reinvention is a delicate balance, however, especially when the mystical tradition in question is tucked deep inside a religion whose orthodox core remains closed to outsiders. Perhaps the most controversial development in Jewish mysticism since the 1980s has been the explosive growth of pop Kabbalah, principally through Rabbi Rav Berg's absurdly successful Kabbalah Centre, which some critics condemn as the new Scientology. Berg lived as an Orthodox Jew in Brooklyn before moving to Israel in the early 1960s, where he studied with the Kabbalist Rabbi Yehuda Zvi Brandwein and eventually took over Brandwein's organization. Today the Kabbalah Centre packages an exuberantly New Age self-improvement regime within a consumerist framework of debased Kabbalistic magic. The center makes a portion of its considerable income on cancer-besting "Kabbalah water" and $415 copies of the Zohar, a medieval Kabbalistic text whose spiritual blessings Berg claims can be milked simply by scanning one's eyes uncomprehendingly over the text. The Kabbalah Centre's most popular "tool," though, is a twenty-six-dollar red wrist string that protects against the evil eye, and which the institution unsuccessfully attempted to trademark.

The Kabbalah Centre is a multimillion-dollar family-run operation with major centers in Miami, New York, and London, but the Los Angeles branch has, unsurprisingly, been the heart of the operation since it opened in 1989. Although traditional Kabbalah is not restricted to Orthodox Judaism, and forms the backbone of the modern occult tradition, it remains a rather hush-hush affair. But Berg broadcasts the lore, proclaiming, for example, that the seventy-two Names of God—esoteric monikers buried in the acrostics of the Pentateuch—are a "technology for the soul" available to all. By stripping Kabbalism of Judaism, not to mention mystery, Berg has subjected it to the overexposure endemic to modern media. This rush to the virtual light may explain why so many celebrities, including Demi Moore, Britney Spears, David Beckham, and Courtney Love, have dipped their toes in Kabbalistic water. Madonna, that most numinous of pop stars, has been a student of Berg since the late 1990s, and has publicized her climb up the Tree of Life by sporting T-shirts with cheeky slogans like "Kabbalists Do It Better" and "Cult Member." Berg is clearly adept at ministering to the peculiar spiritual maladies of celebrities, and this has made him one of the most successful gurus in Los Angeles. When his manual *The Red String Book: The Power of Protection* came out in the fall of 2004, it seemed quite fitting that Berg announced the news with a large billboard ad, hovering over the Sunset Strip like a rainbow of promise.

PRETZEL LOGIC

Among the various Asian spiritual practices that have made their way into the West, none today holds the commanding aura of hatha yoga. Once chided for their pretzel postures and weird dietary practices, yogis are now thoroughly mainstream, and certainly no weirder than steroid-popping bodybuilders. For millions of Americans on the go, yoga has become the perfect one-stop holistic shop: an "ancient" spiritual path that lends meaning and depth to the chore of exercise, focusing the mind while keeping the body vital—and sweetly cut, to boot. In India, the physical asanas of hatha yoga—which have more modern origins than are generally believed—are traditionally seen as only one aspect of a rigorous process of psychospiritual alchemy aimed at supernatural liberation. In the United States, these same postures now often float free, shorn of metaphysics or moral strictures but still gleaming with spiritual juice. This process of secularization has been lamented by some traditionalists, but it can also be seen as the reflection of America's spiritual pragmatism. Without worshipping gurus or subscribing to arcane cosmologies, individuals reach the marrow on the mat.

Californian yoga teachers have played a dominant role in transmitting yoga postures and pranayama to Americans. The stage was set with the more philosophical yoga taught by early visitors like Vivekananda and Swami Rama Tirtha, and with the energetic Kriya Yoga that Yogananda introduced to his many followers. The state's first strictly hatha yoga studio launched in 1947, when a Latvian woman named Indra Devi opened a Hollywood salon to great acclaim. Devi had lived in India, where she studied with Tirumalai Krishnamacharya, an innovator and master who also schooled the celebrated teachers B. K. S. Iyengar and Pattabhi Jois. Initially, Krishnamacharya refused to allow a foreign female into his ashram, but she convinced the master's patron, the maharaja of Mysore, to pull some strings. Within a year, Krishnamacharya was encouraging Devi to teach, providing her with information that made its way into her 1953 best seller, *Forever Young, Forever Healthy.* The title alone reflected Devi's Southern California orientation, as did her popularity with celebrities like Gloria Swanson, Olivia de Havilland, and Christopher Isherwood. She was no snake-oil salesman: the "First Lady of Yoga" lived to the ripe age of 102.

Long before Devi opened her Hollywood studio, a health nut named Walt Baptiste started offering yoga stretches and pranayama at the Center for Physical Culture, which he opened in San Francisco in the 1930s. Baptiste had picked up the practices from his uncle, a follower of Yogananda, and they led him to reframe physical fitness as a vehicle of conscious evolution, part of a larger quest to be "infinite in every capacity." Baptiste was also a hardcore bodybuilder, one of a number of California strongmen, many of whom gathered at Santa Monica's Muscle Beach, who revolutionized the American physique in the 1930s and '40s. Along with Jack LaLanne's studio in Oakland, Baptiste's center was the only place around that offered resistance weight training. In 1949, Baptiste won the Mr. America contest. A couple of decades later, long after he had opened San Francisco's first yoga studio with his wife, Magana, Mr. America became Yogiraj—or "King of Yoga," the title given to Baptiste by Swami Sivananda, the august head of the Yoga Vedanta University in Rishikesh, India.

Since the 1960s, the Bay Area has fostered scores of vital yoga centers, but Los Angeles remains the Benares of American yoga, the hot spot where the ancient practice has been most transformed within the pressure cooker of commerce, celebrity, and gilded body consciousness. Los Angeles boasts over one hundred yoga studios, and the oldest one still in operation is the Center for Yoga, which was founded in 1967 by Ganga White, a Sivananda student and one of the most creative teachers of the era. White pushed yoga into the counterculture, demonstrating snaky postures at the Human Be-In and later consulting on movies like *Billy Jack.* Though schooled in India, White was no strict

YOGA TREE HAYES, SAN FRANCISCO

ABOVE: BIKRAM'S YOGA COLLEGE OF INDIA, WORLD HEADQUARTERS, LOS ANGELES

RIGHT: INSIGHT YOGA, PASADENA

traditionalist, and he offered an eclectic, independent mix of styles at his center, which hosted important early visits by Iyengar and Pattabhi Jois. In 1980, White developed his own series, a sequence and style he called Flow—now a common term in studios across the land. Besides referencing his own name (Ganga means something like "swift-goer"), the term also suggested the regional ethic of going with the flow—the flow in this case being a vigorous moving sequence of poses. Flow struck a chord, and the video that White made with Tracey Rich in 1989 helped launch the yoga-video boom.

The Center for Yoga continues to mirror the American transformation of yoga, although these days that transformation has as much to do with business as methodology. In 2004, over a decade after White had sold the center and set up the White Lotus Foundation in Santa Barbara, the Center for Yoga became the most venerable Los Angeles studio to be absorbed into Yoga Works, a national chain of yoga studios centered in Santa Monica and headed by two snazzy former Internet entrepreneurs. Such chains are probably an inevitable development, and not necessarily a tragic one. When Yoga Works acquires independents, it does lower salaries and enforce harsh noncompete requirements, but it also offers deep pockets, marketing muscle, and a comprehensive teacher-training program. Though the spirit of American yoga lies in the quirky diversity of its studios, Yoga Works reflects the fact that American yoga has morphed from a faddish mystic path into a mind-body fitness regime regularly offered by gyms, corporations, and community centers.

In any case, Yoga Works can't hold a candle to the brazen empire building of Bikram Choudhury, the Speedo-sporting glitz king who started teaching Hollywood's athletes and movie stars in 1973. Known as "sweaty yoga," Bikram's regime involves performing a series of twenty-six poses inside a humid room heated to a suffocating 105 degrees. Bikram has franchised his method into a network of fifteen hundred studios across the globe and has also managed to copyright his specific sequence of poses, which he claims is the only "authentic" yoga around. Even the practice studio in his Los Angeles world headquarters looks different from your typical corner yoga shop. It is a huge, shockingly bright room paneled entirely with mirrors—a stark contrast to the scrappy, vaguely devotional atmosphere fostered by studios like Yoga Tree, a mom-and-pop chain found in San Francisco. In a bit of Angeleno synchronicity, the Bikram headquarters lies next door to an indoor batting joint. Given that Choudhury and his wife sponsored the first yoga championships in the country, the man probably appreciates the athletic juxtaposition. Yoga competitions are held in India as well, but the message of Bikram's mat meet in this hustling city is clear: yoga breeds success.

Seconding this notion, albeit in a gentler key, is Gurmukh Kaur Khalsa, a radiant teacher in her golden years who has opened the largest urban yoga center in the country. Gurmukh is an acolyte of Yogi Bhajan, a maverick Sikh who started teaching Kundalini yoga to the hippies in the late 1960s and eventually built a billion-dollar corporate empire that encompassed natural food, beauty products, and the lucrative Akal Security firm. Riding the success of their first Golden Bridge studio, Gurmukh and her husband, Gurushabd, built the Golden Bridge Spiritual Village, a million-dollar yoga mall designed with the help of a feng shui consultant. The fourteen-thousand-square-foot Hollywood warehouse once housed A-1 Audio, which prepared and tested equipment for touring rock

bands. The Sikh couple built an entirely new structure inside the building's shell; it features multiple studios, a tea garden, a vegetarian café, a wellness center, and a handful of boutiques and shops, including a toy store. Special attention was paid to the lighting in the practice rooms. The original skylights were kept, but modernized with Mylar lining, styrene diffusers, and photocells to distribute photons evenly across the recycled teak floors.

The Golden Bridge Spiritual Village is a monument to the contradictions of yoga's mystically glazed success, demonstrating that the mainstream embrace of the practice does not necessarily mean the vaporization of its higher aspirations. On the other hand, the corporate scale of such operations may squelch the personality that provides much of the spirit of the traditional independent studio. This spirit is more of an atmosphere of intimacy than a product, an atmosphere that is by no means antithetical to classy design. This is evident at Insight Meditation, one of the Southland's most beautiful studios. When Rick Colella decided to found his own studio, he had already taught at the Center for Yoga and coached the stars, including the Red Hot Chili Peppers, whom he accompanied on, of all things, their Kalifornication tour. Colella was not looking for a place in Pasadena, but he discovered an ivy-covered Gothic chapel built there in the 1920s to serve an adjacent mortuary, which now houses shops and offices. Enlisting the help of James Meraz, who teaches environmental design at the Art Center College of Design, Colella added shoji doors, bamboo floors, and handcrafted Asian furniture to a building whose peaked archways, gabled roof, and stained glass define an archetypical Christian sacred space. This elegant integration of East and West creates an intriguing container for the fusion that is American yoga: not just a fusion of body and soul, or of India and the United States, but of spirituality and the bottom line.

TEMPLE BURN

In Gary Snyder's *Mountains and Rivers without End,* the old Beat writes about visiting "long gone Lake Lahontan," a flat dry lake bed now called the Black Rock Desert. Turning the truck onto the playa, "heading for know-not," Snyder drives into this trackless waste east of the Sierra Nevada Mountains and coasts to a halt on its "crazed cracked" surface. And there he is:

> Off nowhere, to be or not to be,
> all equal, far reaches, no bounds.

Snyder's quintessential playa moment continues to reverberate today, though in a very different, more frenetic key. Since 1990, the Black Rock Desert has played host to the annual Burning Man art festival, which is about as crazed and cracked as it gets. Over the course of a week, tens of thousands of freaks and free spirits from around the world, but especially from the Bay Area, build, cruise, and destroy a temporary city whose crowning landmark—a giant man made of wood, neon, and fireworks—is immolated during the final weekend. Outside the centralized vending of coffee, tea, and ice, there is no commerce; rules and shames are few; and opportunities for both ecstasy and physical discomfort abound. The festival's mantra: "No observers."

Though the Black Rock Desert lies in northwestern Nevada, the origins and temperament of Burning Man's festival of know-not are thoroughly Californian. Larry Harvey burned the first Man on San Francisco's Baker Beach in 1985, for reasons that remain intentionally obscure. Over the next few years, the event drew a growing crowd of blue-collar artist-intellectuals, anarcho-Dadaists, fire freaks, and dwellers of San Francisco's postpunk demimonde. Given these roots, it is hardly surprising that today's event does not resemble a typical spiritual gathering, even by West Coast standards. Ironic and hilarious, intoxicated and lewd, the event's Dionysian theater of the absurd could even be said to embody the slaphappy nihilism of postmodern culture itself. Many attendees would also deny that spirituality has any bearing on their rollicking good times.

That said, Burning Man features clear and conscious parallels to traditional sacred revels. Most important are the Eleusinian Mysteries of ancient Greece, whose combination of pageantry, pork roasts, and mysterious sound-and-light shows was crowned with the numinous initiatory experience of a "great light." Writing under a pseudonym in a 1995 issue of San Francisco's *Gnosis* magazine, Harvey noted that, like Burning Man, the Mysteries attracted a largely urban and sophisticated crowd. "Intense, ecstatic, and immediate, the rites did not stress doctrinal belief, but valued outward show and inward feeling." In addition, Burning Man's outward show regularly exploits sacred symbols. Participants cannibalize Christianity, Judaism, Buddhism, Hinduism, shamanism, and the occult for their costumes, camps, sculptures, and performances. The playa has hosted voodoo invocations, Balinese monkey chants, Shabbat prayers, Santería drum circles, Tantric yoga, Wiccan spiral dances, group zazen, and Thelemic rituals. While some of these performances are sarcastic or even blasphemous, many are serious attempts to squeeze the juice from more or less traditional rites and images. But even this distinction between serious and silly breaks down: Burning Man twists authenticity and irony into a Möbius strip, an alchemical conjunction of sacred and profane.

Burning Man can also be seen as a convocation of California's own home-grown spiritual traditions. The festival ties together the pursuit of intense experience and the alchemy of trash, the bohemian embrace of sacred sensuality and the draw to nature unadorned. It kick-starts the Merry Prankster bus into a higher, digital gear. Perhaps most importantly, Burning Man makes a virtue of the exotic eclecticism that has characterized California's spiritual

DUST STORM, BLACK ROCK CITY, NEVADA

imagination since Los Angeles became a carnival of souls a century ago. Burning Man is not just a bohemian theme park; it's thousands of theme parks butting heads, like a flea market of parallel worlds, or the Mos Eisley spaceport from *Star Wars*. In consort with the assemblage artists of the Beat era, Black Rock City's playful schizoid sensibility is based on juxtaposition, on clash and collage. Camps like Elvis Yoga stitch together divergent cultures, while some artists create surreal contrast by placing structures—a huge duck, massive fuzzy dice, a lone bed—against the white void of the outer playa. Costumes are often thrift-store patchworks featuring bold clashes of color, material, and samples of forgotten subcultures. Huge space aliens or interactive sound sculptures are built from scavenged metal or scrap wood or discarded tongue depressors. And though many installations and costumes are devoted to particular themes—the bayou, Bedouins, octopi—these elements inevitably crisscross and collide in the turbulent serendipity of playa life.

Juxtaposition also underlies Burning Man's elliptical approach to spirituality. For his recurrent center-camp piece Twinkie Henge, Dennis Hinkamp used the Hostess treats to construct a small-scale version of the famous megalithic monument in Wiltshire, England. In 2002 and 2003, the playa was blessed with a huge seated Ronald McDonald—a gold-

LEFT: THE MAN, BLACK ROCK CITY, NEVADA

RIGHT: NIGHT, BLACK ROCK CITY, NEVADA

painted inflatable, sporting a Nepalese third eye, that smiled beatifically onto the crowds. Finley Fryer has occasionally presented an incandescent chapel built of recycled plastic. On one level, these pieces show how juxtaposition allows people to invoke sacred forces while sidestepping issues of belief. But their humor is also a doorway into something deeper: a sacred irony, one that rejects all outward forms of the spirit as impediments to the quest. As Krishnamurti claimed, the quest itself may be the biggest impediment of all.

Black Rock City's most powerful sacred spaces, however, leave the festival's brazen irony at the temple door. For the 2000 event, a middle-aged Petaluma art-car artist named David Best dedicated the Temple of the Mind to the memory of a young man on his work crew who had died in a motorcycle accident the week before. In the highest tradition of alchemical trash, Best, who visits dumps religiously, built the structure out of the pressed-wood leftovers from the manufacture of kids' dinosaur puzzles. From these curved and skeletal scraps, Best wove an intricate, almost insubstantial fantasy, a lacy longhouse of Indonesian filigree that called forth reverence and burned like a dream. The following year, he and the temple crew expanded the concept into the extraordinary Temple of Tears, a towering memorial for suicides that was placed in the outer wastes of the playa.

TEMPLE OF STARS, BLACK ROCK CITY, NEVADA

Here the frivolity of Burning Man spontaneously dissolved into a deeply sober but intimate communion with the collective reality of loss. Burners meditated, sang, and wept; they covered the temple's reptilian surfaces with messages and names and photos and offerings destined to burn. As with the temples Best built in subsequent years, the ritual immolation of the Temple of Tears on Sunday night provided the hushed and contemplative flip side to the crass and boisterous spectacle of Saturday night, when the Burning Man himself is burned. Rumors spread that a real body had been committed to the flames; either way, some saw ghosts in the roaring flicker.

In 2004, Best built his most elaborate structure yet, a steeply peaked joss house called the Temple of Stars. Crowds were able to access the temple by climbing two quarter-mile-long walkways that led into the gauzy heart of the central tower. But Best built his most distinctly Californian temple the year before. Leaving the puzzle scraps at home, Best and his crew used papier-mâché to construct the seventy-five-foot-tall Temple of Honor, a triple-tiered Orientalist tower whose supporting columns were topped with squashed and spiky onion domes. Like the Taj Mahal, which is itself a mausoleum, the base of Best's tower was basically a square with canted corners; this device helped dematerialize the structure, lending it an air of insubstantiality that also reflected the flimsy materials that held the temple together. On approach, the marvel of the structure gave way to the marvel of detail. Every surface was covered with large sheets of paper printed in black and white, a densely patterned decoupage of stars, flowers, Islamic geometries, Celtic knots, dharma wheels, and Venetian decoration that would not have looked out of place on Las Vegas's Venetian Resort Hotel, five hundred miles to the south. While the temple lacked the hypnotic intricacy of Best's other playa buildings, this paper mosaic—at once Op Art and Victorian—even more clearly reflected the artist's roots in surrealist collage and West Coast assemblage. But the temple also echoed California's own history of eclectic sacred structures. Best says that one of the temple's primary inspirations was Swami Trigunatita's crazy-quilt Vedanta Temple in San Francisco, whose mélange of multicultural domes and towers blew his mind when he saw it as a child. In California, it seems, even the creative commingling of spiritual traditions has become a tradition.

LUNA, HUMBOLDT COUNTY

LUNA

One of the most inspiring acts of the California spiritual imagination in recent memory began in 1997, when a young woman from Arkansas climbed 180 feet up a coast redwood tree in Humboldt County and decided to call it home for a while. The woman's name was Julia Butterfly Hill, and the tree's name, as media consumers across the globe would learn before Hill returned to earth two years later, was Luna. When Hill made her climb, Luna had clocked about as many years as individual living things can hope for on this planet. A millennium or so ago, when the tree's roots first sank down into the shadowed loam between the ferns and banana slugs, the surrounding land was choked with black bears and butterflies, the skies plump with golden eagles and condors. Occasional human beings may have crossed her shadow, for she stands on a ridge high above the Eel River where the king salmon once thronged like commuters. We cannot know the minds of these people—Mattole, perhaps, or maybe Sinkyone, Lassik, or Nongatl—but we suspect that Luna was not, for them, a commodity, but something like a fold in the continuous fabric of creation.

When Christopher Columbus first bumped into the Caribbean islands, Luna was half a millennium old. Five hundred years again, and she had become, by virtue of her species, a charismatic symbol of California's audacious ecology. She had also become, through the invisible spell of civilization, property—the Pacific Lumber Company's, to be exact. And in the 1990s, the Pacific Lumber Company and its corporate owner, the Houston-based Maxxam Corporation, had dividends to pay. Along with the nearby Headwaters Forest, which was the largest chunk of old-growth forest left in private hands at the time, Luna was on the block. In order to protect the tree, some scruffy young Earth First! activists, not unaware of the symbolic profile of redwoods, took turns sitting on a tarp-cloaked platform they had placed near the top of her trunk, which had been conveniently severed by lightning. When Hill first clambered up, she thought she'd stick it out for a few weeks, but as her devotion and media visibility grew, she decided to hang on until Pacific Lumber agreed to save the tree in exchange for fifty thousand dollars and her prompt descent.

Tree sitting is an established activist tactic, one of a variety of strategies employed by conservationists ever since John Muir and the Sierra Club he founded first began defending California country against the depredations of humanity. The West Coast has long been a hotbed for both the theory and practice of environmentalism, from the direct actions of Vancouver's Greenpeace to the ecosystems philosophy of Gregory Bateson, an early cybernetics researcher who lived at Esalen and died at the San Francisco Zen Center's Green Gulch Farm. The volatile Earth First! campaign for the Northern California redwoods showed the most militant face of the movement, with hundreds of dreadlocked anarchists spiking trees before the group renounced such tactics for intense civil disobedience. There are plenty of pantheistic pagans in Earth First!, but Hill's monastic commitment beamed a more angelic frequency of green spirituality into the heart of the mediaverse. Rarely have voices of protest resonated with such simple authenticity and ascetic grace—communicated, it must be said, through Hill's exhaustive use of the cellular phone. Though Hill insisted in interviews that she was no saint, her spirit was deeply shaped by American religion, and by the American—and Californian—quest to leave religion behind and discover spirit in the world at hand.

Hill's father was a nomadic evangelist who roamed the South when Hill was a child, preaching the joy of Christ more than the torments of hell. When Hill let go of Christianity as

a teenager, she did not give up on prayer or faith. Nor could she free herself from one of the most classic patterns in American religious biography: illness or physical calamity followed by conversion. In August of 1996, a Ford Bronco rear-ended Hill's Honda hatchback, jamming her right eye into her skull and scrambling neurons that would require a year of therapy to rewire. (John Muir also hurt his right eye in a life-changing accident.) During her recovery, Hill heard the sweet and painful call of the spirit and decided to backpack to the world's sacred sites. Arriving in California's Lost Coast, a largely undeveloped area in Humboldt County, she wandered into a grove of redwoods, whose vaulting uplift and arched patterns reminded her, as they have so many, of Europe's great Gothic churches. "When I entered the majestic cathedral of the redwood forest for the first time, my spirit knew it had found what it was searching for," she wrote in her autobiography. She dropped to her knees and laid her face on the duff, breathing in the moldering funk and weeping until she laughed. "Surrounded by these huge, ancient giants, I felt the film covering my senses from the imbalance of our fast-paced, technologically dependent society melt away." She decided to stay in California and, in the words of Dr. Seuss's Lorax, to speak for the trees.

In *The Mountains of California,* John Muir describes a memorable day he spent riding out a windstorm from the top of a Douglas spruce he had climbed. "We all travel the milky way together, trees and men; but it never occurred to me until this storm-day, while swinging in the wind, that trees are travelers, in the ordinary sense." Hill learned a similar lesson one winter day, when a violent windstorm tore through Luna's branches. Whipped about in the gale, tarpaulins rent, Hill felt death lean in. She clung to life, which meant clinging to Luna. With her jaws clenched, Hill gripped the tree with all the might her lithe, elven frame could muster. She cried out to the tree that the Earth First! activists had called into individual being with a name, and heard, she says, a voice speaking back inside her: "Now is not the time for you to be strong, Julia, or you, too, will break. Learn the power of the trees. Let it flow. Let it go." With this bit of Californian Taoism in mind, Hill released her grip and let herself go mad for a spell, whooping and jabbering and moving with the exultant winds.

Luna has since been threatened by more than storms. In 2000, after Pacific Lumber agreed to save the redwood, vandals, who were never caught, chain-sawed a thirty-six-inch-deep cut around much of Luna's base. The tree's structural integrity was quickly restored by guy wires and metal braces, but the redwood still faced the problem of drawing nutrients up from the soil. Biologists and arborists were pessimistic about her chances, even as suggestions of ways to treat the wound—from synthetic resins to beeswax—poured in from around the globe. Hill knew she wanted to use soil. She met a Cherokee bear-medicine worker who lived in Cambridge, Massachusetts, and he passed on native lore about the healing properties of clay, which apparently becomes particularly efficacious when mixed with bear spittle. When they prepared the poultice, Hill and Luna's other caretakers mixed homeopathic remedies into the clay, along with a load of bear drool FedExed to them by sympathetic zookeepers.

More than four years later, Luna continues to thrive, with new growth appearing near the tree's upper boughs every spring. A spontaneous shrine has also grown in the blackened hollows at the base of the tree, an informal collection of power objects—a dream catcher, a cross, a Cretan snake goddess—left by a trickle of unknown (and unauthorized) pilgrims. A red pouch filled with tobacco lies next to shells and stones and a curious miniature teapot. This midden heap of charms shows how much Luna came to shelter, for a time, the informal strains of spirituality that continue to flow outside churches and the institutions of property, and that claim their ultimate source in the living, and now unraveling, earth. An image of a tree is etched into the charcoal surface above the shrine, and a button on the ground simply reads: "Your silence does not protect you."

SHRINE, LUNA, HUMBOLDT COUNTY

HERETICS

When Matthew Fox was a twelve-year-old kid growing up in Wisconsin, he was stricken with polio. The boy spent nearly a year regaining the use of his legs, sometimes under the ministrations of a soft-spoken Dominican named Brother Martin. When Fox recovered, he felt utterly grateful for the universe, and later described his bout with disease as a baptism in mystical awareness—a mind-set he characterizes as the refusal to take things, and especially natural things, for granted. In 1960, Fox joined the Dominican order, and was ordained seven years later. At the time, Catholic thinkers largely ignored the Church's rich mystical tradition, but Fox immersed himself in the worldviews of medieval seers like Meister Eckhart and Hildegard of Bingen, a visionary twelfth-century abbess whose facility with art, altered states, and natural healing shaped Fox's own emerging theology.

Fox called that theology Creation Spirituality. Rooting itself in the voluptuous splendor of the material cosmos, Creation Spirituality affirmed the fundamental goodness of our interdependence with the ever transforming web of life. Creation Spirituality resembled the beliefs of Native Americans and other first peoples, but Fox insisted that it also represented the oldest, most tribal strands of the Bible. Criticizing the church's obsession with original sin, Fox instead stressed the joys of original blessing, and our responsibility to further creation through art, social action, and care for Mother Earth. To put his progressive, ecumenical, and pantheistic inclinations into practice, Fox founded the Institute of Culture and Creation Spirituality in Chicago in the late 1970s, but the organization did not really take off until 1983, when ICCS moved to Holy Names College in Oakland. In the Bay Area, Fox cross-bred his vision of the Cosmic Christ with local strains of green spirituality that drew more from Buddhism, Wicca, and the New Age movement than they did from the Christian tradition.

Fox's frolics in the wide pastures of California nature worship soon attracted the pitiless gaze of Cardinal Joseph Ratzinger, the ultraconservative Vatican watchdog who became Pope Benedict XVI in 2005. Ratzinger was then prefect of the Congregation for the Doctrine of the Faith, once known as the Holy Office of the Inquisition, and he disciplined the liberal fringes of the church with a ferocity born of his conviction that the Church must reject the permissive and open-minded ways of the modern world. One could imagine a no more irritating burr in his side than Father Fox, who called God "our Mother," hired the feminist witch Starhawk to teach at ICCS, and wrote books like *Whee! We, Wee All the Way Home: A Guide to the New Sensual Spirituality.* Fox's Dominican superiors protected him for a time, but in 1988, Ratzinger demanded that the order silence the priest, who then used his free time to travel around Latin America absorbing the leftist enthusiasms of liberation theology. In 1991, the Dominicans ordered Fox to leave ICCS and return to Chicago, but Fox refused and was expelled from the order. While remaining a priest, Fox was forbidden from ever again performing the holy sacraments.

For a self-professed "post-denominational priest," Fox did not stay unmoored to tradition for long. In 1994, after reciting the Nicene Creed in a side chapel of San Francisco's hulking Grace Cathedral, he was accepted into the Episcopal Church. The move made sense. Besides providing High Church authority without a meddling papacy, the Episcopal Church had long nursed a strongly liberal wing—especially in California. Thirty years before Fox became an Episcopalian, the diocese was led by a brilliant and iconoclastic bishop named James Pike, a mediagenic former Roman Catholic who made national news by questioning the infallibility of Scripture, advocating for women's ordination, and encouraging the church to jettison "theological baggage" like the Virgin Birth and the Trinity. Pike's liberal spirit is partly reflected in the design of Grace Cathedral, which was

UNIVERSITY OF CREATION SPIRITUALITY/
WISDOM UNIVERSITY, OAKLAND

UNIVERSITY OF CREATION SPIRITUALITY
IMAGINATION FOR
2141
Wisdom

GRACE CATHEDRAL, SAN FRANCISCO

consecrated during his tenure. The high altar in this huge cathedral—the largest west of the Mississippi—lies in the transept crossing, an unusual scheme that makes the sanctuary accessible to all. Pike had employed a similar arrangement in a Massachusetts church he designed earlier in his career.

Pike's widely publicized opinions drove a number of his fellow bishops to call for a heresy trial. Pike was censured, and he resigned and wandered ever farther from orthodoxy. After a series of spooky visitations, Pike consulted Spiritualist mediums in order to contact his son, who had committed suicide. (One of Pike's mistresses later killed herself as well.) Pike also befriended the science-fiction visionary Philip K. Dick, who considered himself an Episcopalian for much of his life. Pike influenced Dick's classic tale *A Maze of Death* and especially his last novel, *The Transmigration of Timothy Archer.* Like Dick, Pike was obsessed with the origins of Christianity. In 1969, while in Israel tracking down the haunts of the Essenes, the renegade bishop died after his Avis rental car broke down in the parched wilderness near the Dead Sea. All he had in the way of desert supplies was two bottles of Coke.

During his tenure as president of ICCS and later the University of Creation Spirituality, Matthew Fox did not make the consternating waves of a James Pike. The wildest thing that Fox did was to kick-start the Techno Cosmic Mass: a postmodern transformation of the liturgy that features techno music, video screens, and trance-dancing youthful celebrants. Fox got the idea from the Nine O'clock Service, a collective of young, white-robed Anglican ravers from Sheffield, in the United Kingdom, who performed the first American version of their Planetary Mass in the basement of Grace Cathedral for an audience that included Jerry Garcia. Though the British group dissolved in a tawdry sex scandal soon afterward, Fox soldiered on and continues to host Cosmic Masses. "When everyone dances," says Fox, "everyone is a priest."

During the 1990s, the Bay Area hosted one of America's more vital rave scenes. Raves are techno-utopian gatherings of the tribes whose mystic euphoria is fueled, at least in part, by the heart-opening properties of MDMA, or Ecstasy. Fox's Cosmic Masses tried to pour some of that raw exuberance into a drug-free neotraditional container, but his insistence on serving up the Eucharist during the events alienated more paganish ravers, and a deep youth scene never formed. A more galvanizing blend of high church and high energy was concocted by a rave collective called the St. John's Divine Rhythm Society, which threw its events in San Francisco's Episcopal Church of St. John the Evangelist. A Gothic Victorian church with shingled sides and a lovely walled courtyard, the church served a predominantly gay and lesbian congregation and was struggling to survive when the Rhythm Society came knocking. The collective was spearheaded by Bob Jesse, a onetime vice president at Oracle who also founded the Council on Spiritual Practices, a group that promotes "primary religious experience" through a variety of means, including compounds like MDMA. Rhythm Society parties began with low-key rituals like circle dances or songs and ended hours later with St. John's resident organist welcoming the dawn with soaring improvisations on a renovated M. P. Moller mechanical-action organ. More traditional members of the congregation grew critical of the events, however, and in 2002, a mild drug-related mishap gave them the ammunition they needed to force the Rhythm Society out of the church, along with the gay rector who supported the group and enjoyed its upbeat fetes.

One does not have to be a reactionary to question the appropriateness of consuming scheduled substances in a church, regardless of sacred intent. But the flap at St. John's was really a muted reflection of a much larger battle: the conservative assault on liberalism that has come to define American Christianity in the twenty-first century. Facing hot-button issues like homosexual marriage, stem-cell research, and abortion, parishes and seminaries that may once have attempted to gracefully go with the modern flow have hardened into rocks of absolutism and judgment. Under George W. Bush, right-wing Christianity has been born again as an instrument of statecraft, challenging the implicit openness of democracy and American culture with a dogmatic fundamentalism. And while American Catholics remain a moderately liberal lot, the papacy under John Paul II and Benedict XVI has steadily undermined the tolerant spirit represented by the Second Vatican Council, or Vatican II. From the perspective of this dominating and pugnacious orthodoxy, California consciousness—an evolving, open-ended sensibility informed by Asian religion, goddess feminism, the human-potential movement, altered states, modern science, bodywork, and nature mysticism—is, literally, anathema.

That said, one of the most spectacular expressions of the new millennium's muscular Christo-conservatism came out of Hollywood, that bastion of cultural relativism and moral decay. Mel Gibson's blockbuster *The Passion of the Christ* was not only the most galvanizing film to emerge from California in the dawn of the twenty-first century but also one of the most successful. Funded with roughly fifty million dollars that the quasi-Australian actor dug out of his own pocket, *The Passion* earned hundreds of millions of dollars in ticket sales globally and became one of the most successful DVDs ever. *The Passion* was brilliantly promoted, with church groups pushing the film and Gibson fashioning himself as a rebel shunned by elite critics and cowardly Hollywood liberals. Utterly lacking in transcendence, *The Passion* made few converts. Nonbelievers seemed largely revolted by Gibson's brutal portrayal of Christ's last hours, while many critics accused the director of reviving the sort of anti-Semitic sentiments that Vatican II had begun to reverse. But though some evangelicals complained about the Europorn background of some of the film's actresses, *The Passion* was embraced by droves of Catholics and Protestants as a confirmation of their faith in Christ's loving sacrifice. For once a bloody Hollywood film squeezed sacred sense from all the gore.

Matthew Fox called Gibson's film a joyless exercise in necrophilia, a sadomasochistic travesty of Christ's core message of human dignity, compassion, and the affirmation of life. Fox also accused Gibson of spreading the "piety of fascism." After all, the spectacle of martyrs and violent suffering has often been instrumental in fascist and fundamentalist propaganda, and *The Passion* is big spectacle. Gibson is a Traditionalist Catholic, part of a loose ultraconservative movement of believers who reject Vatican II, some to the point of schism. Gibson is also rumored to be a member of Opus Dei, a secretive and reactionary order of Catholics who played the bad guys in Dan Brown's esoteric potboiler *The Da Vinci Code.* Though Opus Dei insists that Gibson is not a member, Jan Michelini, Gibson's assistant director for *The Passion,* is a supernumerary of the order, and was part of the group that showed *The Passion* to Pope John Paul II. Michelini was also twice struck by lightning during filming, an omen not always interpreted as a sign of favor from God.

Not all Traditionalist Catholics have fallen out of communion with Rome, but Gibson apparently has decided to go his own way, making him no less a heretic than Matthew Fox. The proof lies in Gibson's own contribution to the religious landscape of California: a 9,300-square-foot church complex he built in the Malibu Hills called the Holy Family Chapel. A curiously DIY monument to orthodox authority, the chapel is an independent institution that serves a schismatic congregation of Traditionalist Catholics. Gibson is a member of the small group and serves as the chapel's CEO and major benefactor. Every Sunday, a Traditionalist priest enacts a precious and now rather rare ritual: the Tridentine Latin Mass, which was celebrated by Catholic priests for almost fifteen hundred years until Vatican II inaugurated the vernacular mass. The Holy Family services are short, without song, and are not followed by coffee and donuts. A strict dress code is posted, as well as a list of traditional requirements for taking communion—an act that is here received on one's knees.

For all the hyperorthodoxy of its liturgy, the Holy Family Chapel is itself a rather subdued affair. The off-white interior is understated, with plain statuary, and features, as of this writing, no images of the Stations of the Cross—the fourteen stages of Christ's passion that served as the storyboard for Gibson's film. The style of the chapel is, of course, Mission Revival. The terra-cotta hue, tile roofs, and round archways hearken back to California's first encounter with the Christian God and the restless Europeans who pursued—or fled—his kingdom to the ends of the earth. But in third-millennium California, the architecture of the Holy Family Chapel does not invoke colonial history so much as the McMansions that have come to blanket Southern California with the ubiquity of the clone armies of *Star Wars.* Such blandly themed suburban citadels reflect both a privilege of means and a poverty of soul, and they now infest California's hills and canyons—the once unredeemed wilderness where the old pagans, near naked and now long gone, walked and gathered in the golden sun.

HOLY FAMILY CHAPEL, AGOURA HILLS

CODA

SUNDOWN

When I was growing up on the north coast of San Diego, sunset served as the holiest moment of the day. The fall of light inspired real religion: the rituals of a greater order we perform without thinking, with flesh in time. When the great blazing ball dropped toward the horizon, it seemed like everyone—soccer moms, surfers, Mexican gardeners, Republican developers—would stop, pull their cars over, and fall silent for a moment, drinking in the Maxfield Parrish displays that are the great gift of smog. I particularly loved the view from the cliffs above Swami's, the Encinitas point break that lies beneath the bleached minarets and palm trees of the Self-Realization Fellowship. The ashram's air of faded Orientalist glory, combined with the dense palm groves, only magnified the exotica of dusk, as the honeyed light oozed along the flaked gold that touched the compound's white walls and fairy-tale domes.

Sunset over the Pacific is California's supreme icon, a natural logo emblazoned on thousands of T-shirts and license plates. As with all symbolic icons, this image suggests a myth, and the myth in question is simple to state: the West heads west. The jury is still out on the value of this world historical process. But whether you see Western civilization as destiny or a cancer, as an unprecedented flowering of human potential or a bloody disaster, its mad technological will lurched after the sun from the bogs of Europe until it found itself here, on the

SUNSET, REDONDO BEACH

sandy banks of the Pacific. And here is where Walt Whitman stood, at least in his imagination, when he chanted his best and truest poem about the Golden State, "Facing West from California's Shores." In the poem, Whitman's expansive poetic "I" broadens to encompass humanity itself, a single being that moves westward from Asia until finally arriving at the sea:

> Facing west from California's shores,
> Inquiring, tireless, seeking what is yet unfound,
> I, a child, very old, over waves, toward the house of
> maternity, the land of migrations, look afar,
> Look off the shores of my Western sea, the circle almost
> circled.

Here the poet, like so many Californians "a child, very old," finds himself at the end of migrations. But even as he faces home again, sensing California's Pacific Rim connection to Asia and its ancient ways, Whitman grows anxious. He ends the poem by asking a question that goes to the heart of the region's restless spiritual imagination: "But where is what I started for so long ago? / And why is it yet unfound?"

Almost one hundred years later, the Beat poet Lew Welch offered an answer of sorts, or at least suggested that we might have to stop asking the question. In "The Song Mount Tamalpais Sings," a hymn to the gentle peak that overlooks the Marin Headlands, north of San Francisco, Welch follows Whitman's lead:

> Human movements,
> but for a few,
> are Westerly.
> Man follows the Sun.
>
> . . .
>
> Or follows what he thinks to be the
> movement of the Sun.
> It is hard to feel it, as a rider,
> on a spinning ball.

Welch is clearly not sure how he feels about the myth of the West. He embraces its power but recognizes the illusions, optical and otherwise, it rests upon. He closes his poem "at the feet of the final cliffs / of all Man's wanderings." But the almost smug acceptance that makes up his final refrain is tinged with defeat: "This is the last place," he cries. "There is nowhere else we need to go."

As the "last place," California has inevitably carried a heavy symbolic load. Successive waves of incomers have reimagined its potential, until the land itself has become a palimpsest of dreams. California has also trashed as many fantasies as it has conjured, and today its natural disasters, polluted sprawl, exploding population, and dreadfully narcissistic pop culture have become as clichéd as its earlier points of light. In the American imagination, California's shores stage both the fulfillment and decline of the West, its final shot at paradise and its perilous fall into the sea. That is why the California dream encompasses both Arcadian frontier and apocalyptic end zone, Eden and Babylon. As Christopher Isherwood put it, "California is a tragic land—like Palestine, like every promised land."

California's tragicomedy also shapes the state's central symbol of the sun. All religions have their public and esoteric sides, and California's visible creed is captured in the radiant, restorative power of Sol. The sun is California's pie in the sky, the guarantor of endless summer, which is itself a natural symbol for the fullness of experience that is the great lust of California consciousness. But endless summer is a fable, of course, a dream used to sell tract homes and rock 'n' roll 45s. Though winter may barely descend on the most populous regions of the state, twilight certainly does, what Jack Kerouac called, in a description of 1950s San Francisco, "the late afternoon of time." The California sunset can be seen, then, as the inevitable dwindling of all pagan Utopias, a confirmation of how difficult it is to stay on the sunny side, whether through youth or beauty or perpetual bliss.

There is a psychospiritual aspect to the sunset as well. As a symbol of the self, the sun can be seen as the waking ego, the individual agent of reason and responsibility who strides through the choices of the day. In many ways, California consciousness has sought to question and undermine this quotidian ego, dissolving the self into the larger frameworks of mind and body and the wilderness within and without. Seekers dive into the great sea of unconsciousness, where, as Herman Melville wrote of the Pacific, lie "millions of mixed shades and shadows, drowned dreams, somnambulisms, reveries." For well over a century, countless Californians have embraced the nonrational as if it were a mystic portal into a deeper freedom, opening their arms to everything from nature mysticism to psychedelic rapture, from Pentecostal fire to the "choiceless awareness" of the deeply meditating mind. In so doing, California has become a testing ground for Freud's famous claim that the mystic turn is simply a regression to the fetus's "oceanic" immersion in the womb. Was the good doctor right? Or might such dips also open up more evolved and integrated states of consciousness, intensifying those universal bonds that must lie within and between us all?

The answer, of course, is yes to both. California consciousness is a paradox. California has witnessed and inspired some of the worst excesses of modern spirituality: paranoid messiahs, manipulative sex-and-drug cults, and the murky and profoundly silly confusions that infest the New Age. But if California consciousness has sometimes fallen far, it is because it has also reached—and gotten—so high. The adepts of California's new edge have drawn the spiritual marrow from the old bones of religion, and used this energy to catalyze postreligious forms of healing, art, and cosmic connection. In contrast with established religions, California consciousness affirms the modern condition, in all its vertiginous freedom. But it also seeks to transcend the narrow materialism of secular rationality, even as it reconciles spirit with a cosmic sense of the material world. Awakening today is a physical matter, rooted in the body of sensation and the ecological realities that pin us to this spinning ball. But consciousness also continues to surf the cusp of novelty, discovering a Promethean sensibility that is not content with limitations, earthly or otherwise. Spirituality means transformation, a metamorphosis that may well be necessary if we are to gracefully weather our times, this dark night of the world soul.

For there is a larger story to the California sunset, one that goes beyond mere spirituality. Today we are in the midst of one of the most turbulent and disturbing periods of change humans have ever known. The biosphere we depend on is passing through a severe and possibly disastrous shuddering, while molecular engineering, brain implants, neuropharmacology, and media technology are shattering our basic sense of self. Modernity is always in crisis—that's what modernity means. But nowadays the lights are winking out on some of our deepest assurances—about progress, about reason, about gender, about the boundaries between nature and technology, about the very definition of human being. California has had a front seat on these transformations, not just because it is a haunt of harbingers, but because so much of the anxious science fiction we now inhabit was born or nurtured in the Golden State: freeways, fast-food chains, cinema, TV, aerospace, biotechnology, designer drugs, teenage tribes, satellites, personal computers, the Internet. In short, California is the petri dish of posthumanity.

These transformations in matter and culture challenge our conventional ideas about who and what we are, and they demand a spiritual response. In some ways, the rise of religious fundamentalism, in the United States and abroad, makes sense. In the face of unnerving possibilities, people understandably seek fixed truths and clear definitions, which provide ballast at a time when everything threatens to both collapse and converge. But though California has minted conservative Christian leaders whose blistering attacks on liberal culture can match any in America, the core Californian response to our global transformation is to plunge onward and upward. The essential temperament of the spiritual tradition I have outlined here is progressive and evolutionary rather than reactionary. It fundamentally rejects fundamentalism. California's unusual spiritual culture can thus be seen as a prophetic and paradoxical reflection of the crisis of our times, at once reflecting it and providing, or at least attempting to provide, visionary alternatives to our considerable blight.

The very eclecticism and recombinant creativity of religion in the Golden State reflects an intuition that mere ecumenism isn't enough on the global stage. While some great resonating crystal of Unity may bind us all, the spiritual sources that individuals actually draw from in their daily lives are valuable precisely for their differences and even contradictions. The spirituality of the future is not a cathedral of absolutes, even if it finds in its heart an unwavering faith in going forward. The spirituality of the future is a bazaar, a commingling and collaborative environment of integration, peer-to-peer networks, and creative exchange. California's spiritual legacy reflects a fragile prophetic history of this condition, which is perhaps better thought of as a process: an open-ended, unpredictable, and perpetual flow through a landscape of possibility and threat that itself continues to change. The rootlessness of California is a call to rootlessness, the state's shattering and reassembling of traditions a single teaching about the loss of tradition and the collectively improvised tactics that must follow. This process is the moving core of California's edge consciousness. Like the streams of mind and time, it is the flow you go with, past all reason.

SELECTED BIBLIOGRAPHY

Adler, Margot. *Drawing Down the Moon.* New York: Penguin, 1997.

Anderson, Walter Truett. *The Upstart Spring: Esalen and the American Awakening.* Reading, MA: Addison-Wesley, 1983.

Banham, Reyner. *Los Angeles: City of Four Ecologies.* New York: Harper & Row, 1971.

Bardini, Thierry. *Bootstrapping: Douglas Engelbart, Coevolution, and the Origins of Personal Computing.* Stanford, CA: Stanford University Press, 2000.

Bean, Lowell, ed. *California Indian Shamanism.* Menlo Park: Ballena Press, 1992.

Beardsley, John. *Gardens of Revelation: Environments by Visionary Artists.* New York: Abbeville Press, 1995.

Beers, Terry, ed. *Unfolding Beauty: Celebrating California's Landscapes.* Berkeley, CA: Heyday Books, 2000.

Boutelle, Sara Holmes. *Julia Morgan, Architect.* New York: Abbeville Press, 1995.

Brading, D. A. *Mexican Phoenix: Our Lady of Guadalupe.* New York: Cambridge University Press, 2001.

Cándida Smith, Richard. *Utopia and Dissent: Art, Poetry and Politics in California.* Berkeley: University of California Press, 1995.

Carter, John. *Sex and Rockets: The Occult World of Jack Parsons.* Venice, CA: Feral House, 1999.

Chadwick, David. *Crooked Cucumber: The Life and Zen Teaching of Shunryu Suzuki.* New York: Broadway Books, 1999.

Cox, Harvey. *Fire from Heaven.* Reading, MA: Addison-Wesley, 1995.

Curran, Douglas. *In Advance of the Landing: Folk Concepts of Outer Space.* New York: Abbeville Press, 1985.

Davis, Avram. *The Way of Flame: A Guide to the Forgotten Mystical Tradition of Jewish Meditation.* San Francisco: HarperSanFrancisco, 1996.

Davis, Mike. *City of Quartz: Excavating the Future in Los Angeles.* New York: Verso, 1990.

———. *Ecology of Fear: Los Angeles and the Imagination of Disaster.* New York: Metropolitan Books, 1998.

Dick, Philip K. *Valis.* New York: Vintage, 1991.

Dulcinos, Donald. *Pioneer of Inner Space: The Life of Fitz Hugh Ludlow, Hasheesh Eater.* Brooklyn: Autonomedia, 1998.

Dunaway, David King. *Huxley in Hollywood.* New York: Harper & Row, 1989.

Duncan, Robert. *Selected Poems.* Ed. Robert Bertholf. New York: New Directions Books, 1997.

Epstein, Daniel Mark. *Sister Aimee.* New York: Harcourt Brace Jovanovich, 1993.

Evans, Christopher. *Cults of Unreason.* New York: Farrar, Straus and Giroux, 1973.

Fields, Rick. *How the Swans Came to the Lake: A Narrative History of Buddhism in America.* Boston: Shambhala, 1981.

Frankiel, Sandra. *California's Spiritual Frontiers: Religious Alternatives in Anglo-Protestantism, 1850–1910.* Berkeley: University of California Press, 1988.

Freudenheim, Leslie Mandelson, and Elisabeth Sacks Sussman. *Building with Nature: Roots of the San Francisco Bay Region Tradition.* Santa Barbara: Peregrine Smith, 1974.

Friedman, Lenore. *Meetings with Remarkable Women: Buddhist Teachers in America.* Boston: Shambhala, 1987.

Fuller, Robert C. *Religion and Wine: A Cultural History of Wine Drinking in the United States.* Knoxville: University of Tennessee Press, 1996.

———. *Stairways to Heaven: Drugs in American Religious History.* Boulder: Westview Press, 2000.

Gebhard, David. *Robert Stacy-Judd: Maya Architecture and the Creation of a New Style.* Santa Barbara: Capra Press, 1993.

Gebhard, David, and Harriette Von Breton. *Lloyd Wright: Architect.* New York: Hennessey & Ingalls, 1998.

Gidlow, Elsa. *Elsa, I Come with My Songs: The Autobiography of Elsa Gidlow.* San Francisco: Booklegger Press, 1986.

Gifford, Edward, and Gwendoline Harris Block. *California Indian Nights.* Lincoln: University of Nebraska Press, 1990.

Gorightly, Adam. *The Shadow over Santa Susana: Black Magic, Mind Control, and the "Manson Family" Mythos.* San Jose: Writers Club Press, 2001.

Greenwalt, Emmett. *California Utopia: Point Loma: 1897–1942.* San Diego: Point Loma Publications, 1955.

Gutiérrez, Ramón, and Richard Orsi, eds. *Contested Eden: California before the Gold Rush.* Berkeley: University of California Press, 1998.

Hale, Dennis, and Jonathan Eisen, eds. *The California Dream.* New York: Collier, 1968.

Heimann, Jim. *California Crazy & Beyond: Roadside Vernacular Architecture.* San Francisco: Chronicle Books, 2001.

Heizer, Robert, and Albert Elsasser. *The Natural World of the California Indians.* Berkeley: University of California Press, 1980.

Heizer, Robert, and M. Whipple, eds. *The California Indians: A Source Book.* Berkeley: University of California Press, 1971.

Hill, Julia Butterfly. *The Legacy of Luna: The Story of a Tree, a Woman, and the Struggle to Save the Redwoods.* San Francisco: HarperSanFrancisco, 2000.

Hine, Robert V. *California's Utopian Colonies.* New Haven, CT: Yale University Press, 1966.

Hogan, Elizabeth, ed. *The California Missions.* Menlo Park, CA: Sunset Publishing, 1993.

Hort, Gertrude, R. B. Ince, and W. P. Swainson. *Three Famous Occultists.* London: Rider & Co., 1939.

Huxley, Aldous. *Ape and Essence.* New York: Bantam, 1948.

———. *The Perennial Philosophy.* London: Chatto & Windus, 1969.

———. *After Many a Summer Dies the Swan.* Chicago: I. R. Dee, 1993.

Isherwood, Christopher. "Los Angeles." In *Exhumations: Stories, Articles, Verses.* New York: Simon and Schuster, 1966.

———. *The Wishing Tree: Christopher Isherwood on Mystical Religion.* Ed. Robert Adjemian. San Francisco: Harper & Row, 1987.

———. *My Guru and His Disciple.* Minneapolis: University of Minnesota Press, 2001.

Jackson, Carl. *Vedanta for the West: The Ramakrishna Movement in the United States.* Bloomington: Indiana University Press, 1994.

Jeffers, Robinson. *The Selected Poetry of Robinson Jeffers.* Ed. Tim Hunt. Stanford, CA: Stanford University Press, 2001.

Karman, James. *Robinson Jeffers: Poet of California.* Brownsville, OR: Story Line Press, 1995.

Kennedy, Gordon. *Children of the Sun.* Ojai, CA: Nivaria Press, 1998.

Kerouac, Jack. *The Dharma Bums.* New York: New American Library, 1958.

Kirker, Harold. *California's Architectural Frontier.* Santa Barbara: Peregrine Smith, 1973.

Klages, Ellen. *Harbin Hot Springs: Healing Waters, Sacred Land.* Middletown, CA: Harbin Springs Publishing, 1991.

Koenig, Gloria. *Iconic LA: Stories of LA's Most Memorable Buildings.* Glendale, CA: Balcony Press, 2000.

Lachman, Gary Valentine. *Turn Off Your Mind: The Mystic Sixties and the Dark Side of the Age of Aquarius.* London: Sidgwick & Jackson, 2001.

Lewis, James R., ed. *Odd Gods: New Religions and the Cult Controversy.* Amherst, NY: Prometheus Books, 2001.

Longstreth, Richard. *On the Edge of the World: Four Architects in San Francisco at the Turn of the Century.* Berkeley: University of California Press, 2003.

Lutyens, Mary. *Krishnamurti: Years of Awakening.* New York: Farrar, Straus and Giroux, 1975.

Maffly-Kipp, Laurie. *Religion and Society in Frontier California.* New Haven, CT: Yale University Press, 1994.

McCoy, Esther. *Five California Architects.* New York: Rheinhold Publishing Corporation, 1960.

Michaels, Leonard, David Reid, and Raquel Scherr, eds. *West of the West: Imagining California: An Anthology.* San Francisco: North Point Press, 1989.

Miller, Donald. *Reinventing American Protestantism: Christianity in the New Millennium.* Berkeley: University of California Press, 1997.

Miller, Russell. *Bare-Faced Messiah: The True Story of L. Ron Hubbard.* London: Michael Joseph, 1987.

Muir, John. *The Mountains of California.* Garden City, NY: Doubleday, 1961.

Muir, Leo. *A Century of Mormon Activities in California.* Salt Lake City: Desert News Press, 1952.

Plagens, Peter. *Sunshine Muse: Art on the West Coast, 1945–1970.* Berkeley: University of California Press, 1974.

Prothero, Stephen. *Purified by Fire: A History of Cremation in America.* Berkeley: University of California Press, 2001.

Rius. *The Myth of the Virgin of Guadalupe.* Austin, TX: American Atheist Press, 1987.

Robertson, David. *Real Matter.* Salt Lake City: University of Utah Press, 1997.

Ross, Joseph E. *Krotona of Old Hollywood, 1866–1913.* Montecito, CA: El Montecito Oaks Press, 1989.

Schuller, Robert H. *My Journey: From an Iowa Farm to a Cathedral of Dreams.* San Francisco: HarperSanFrancisco, 2002.

Schulze, Franz. *Philip Johnson: Life and Work.* Chicago: University of Chicago Press, 1996.

Shulgin, Alexander, and Ann Shulgin. *PIHKAL: A Chemical Love Story.* Berkeley, CA: Transform Press, 1991.

Simmons, John K., and Brian Wilson. *Competing Visions of Paradise: The California Experience of 19th-Century American Sectarianism.* Santa Barbara: Fithian Press, 1993.

Singleton, Gregory H. *Religion in the City of Angels: American Protestant Culture and Urbanization, Los Angeles, 1850–1930.* Ann Arbor: UMI Research Press, 1979.

Snyder, Gary. *Mountains and Rivers without End.* Washington, DC: Counterpoint, 1996.

Starhawk. *The Spiral Dance: Rebirth of the Ancient Religion of the Goddess.* San Francisco: HarperSanFrancisco, 1999.

Starr, Kevin. *Americans and the California Dream, 1850–1915.* New York: Oxford University Press, 1973.

———. *Inventing the Dream: California through the Progressive Era.* New York: Oxford University Press, 1985.

———. *Material Dreams: Southern California through the 1920s.* New York: Oxford University Press, 1990.

———. *The Dream Endures: California Enters the 1940s.* New York: Oxford University Press, 2002.

Stevens, Jay. *Storming Heaven: LSD and the American Dream.* New York: Atlantic Monthly Press, 1987.

Sure, Heng, and Heng Ch'ua. *With One Heart, Bowing to the City of 10,000 Buddhas.* San Francisco: Sino-American Buddhist Association, 1979.

Sutin, Lawrence. *Divine Invasions.* New York: Harmony, 1989.

Tipton, Steven M. *Getting Saved from the Sixties.* Berkeley: University of California Press, 1982.

Urban, Hugh. *Tantra: Sex, Secrecy, Power, and Politics in the Study of Religion.* Berkeley: University of California Press, 2003.

Vale, V., and John Sulak, eds. *Modern Pagans: An Investigation of Contemporary Ritual.* San Francisco: RE/Search, 2001.

Watts, Alan. *The Way of Zen.* New York: Pantheon, 1957.

———. *The Joyous Cosmology: Adventures in the Chemistry of Consciousness.* New York: Pantheon, 1962.

———. *In My Own Way: An Autobiography, 1915–1965.* New York: Vintage, 1973.

Weintraub, Alan. *Lloyd Wright.* New York: Harry N. Abrams, 1998.

Welch, Lew. *Ring of Bone.* Ed. Donald Allen. Bolinas, CA: Grey Fox Press, 1973.

Whitley, David. *Art of the Shaman.* Salt Lake City: University of Utah Press, 2000.

Winter, Robert, ed. *Toward a Simpler Way of Life: The Arts & Crafts Architects of California.* Berkeley: University of California Press, 1997.

———. *Hidden LA.* Salt Lake City: Gibbs Smith, 1998.

Wolfe, Tom. *The Electric Kool-Aid Acid Test.* New York: Bantam, 1968.

Yogananda, Paramahansa. *Autobiography of a Yogi.* Los Angeles: Self-Realization Publishers, 1946.

INDEX

D

E

F

G

H

I

J

K

L

M

N

O

P

R

S

T

U

V

ACKNOWLEDGMENTS

First and foremost, Erik Davis and Michael Rauner would like to thank our parents for supporting us in our work.

Erik Davis also praises the stars for Jennifer Dumpert, who supported me throughout the long haul. Special shout-outs go to Sandi Zarcades and Adam Fisher for massaging the manuscript, to the Woodfield crew for providing inspiration, and to Sylvia Thyssen for being my office pal. My research would not have been possible without input from dozens of individuals, including, in no particular order, David Ulansey, Gregg Rickman, Paul Williams, Robert Winter, Romy Wyllie, David Chadwick, Gene DeSmidt, Dale Pendell, Tom Lane, Molly McGarry, Reverend Heng Sure, Jim Heimann, Victoria Nelson, Adrick Tetrucelli, Richard Rosen, Owen Rowley, Ed Stiles, Echo Heron, J. P. Harpignies, Steven Black, Michael Wenger, Grand Master Julie Scott, Reverend Paul Sawyer, Richard Metzger, Carlos Seligo, Chris Mays, Carolyn Garcia, Jack Petranker, Stefanie Syman, Mark D. Turner, and David Di Sabatino. Thanks as well to the library staffs at the Philosophical Research Library, the Krotona Institute, AMORC, the San Francisco History Center, and the Vedanta Society. None of these people or institutions, of course, is responsible for any errors in the text.

Michael Rauner especially thanks Michael Light and the spirit of Marnie Gillett; these two friends and former employers showed me the most. Early support for this project also came from brother Steve and sisters Julie and Mary, amor Paz de la Calzada, and friends Michael Read, Tanya Kieslich, Greg Jahiel, Bryan Davidson, Leigh Marz, Bill Kouwenhoven, Carin Colleen McKay, Juan Pablo Guiterrez, Cecilia Sterner, Matthew Millman, Luis Delgado, Matt Magaña, Dan Dion, Steven Black, Julia Brashares, Deborah Klochko, Rebecca Solnit, Frish Brandt, Bob Dawson, Berin Golonu, Chris Carlsson, Mona Caron, Adriana Camarena, Mokai and CC DePolo, Paul Catasus, Sue Dempsey, Joy Farina, Heather Serantis, Chris McCaw, Erik and Amy Auerbach, Neil Porter, Nick Kasimatis, Tim McKenna, Jeff Davis, Matt Gonzalez, Jim Dorenkott, Craig Baldwin, and Kathleen Quillian. Thanks also goes to the ATA Gallery, Photo Alliance, YOO Projects, photo-eye, and SF Camerawork.

Erik and Michael both want to acknowledge everyone who gave us access to the locations in this book. Thank you for believing in the project, and for inviting us into your sanctuaries and homes. We would like to especially thank Swami Prabuddhananda, the Tule River Tribal Council, Jim and Stell Miltch and the San Diego Historical Society, Eric Bender and Downtown Properties IX LLC, Fred and Judy Porta and the Friends of the First Church of Christ, Scientist, Berkeley, Alex Vardamis and the Tor Foundation, Xorin Balbes, Loretta Hee, Gordon Tom, Mayer Maisel, Christopher Keanu, Brother Lee and the Self-Realization Fellowship, the Hollywood and Highland Mall, Bishop Charles E. Blake, Reverend Cecil B. Williams, Angelus Temple, Forest Lawn, Reverend Robert H. Schuller, Stan Frisbee, Bill Buck, the denizens of the *Vallejo*, Elke Murphy, Allan Hunt Badiner, Megan McFeely, Jeffery Snyder, Roshi Nelson Foster and the board of Ring of Bone, Terry Adams, Michael Baily, Bill Graham Presents, Dee Stone, Jim Siegel, Steve Groppe, Sasha and Ann Shulgin, Stephanos Polizodes, the Unarius Academy of Science, Joanne and Nancy Karl, Chel Stith, Madrone, Brother James, Penny Slinger Hill, Usha Harding, Diana Paxson, the Watts Towers Cultural Center, Leonard Knight, Zak Zaidman, Avram Davis, Sara Nicoletti, Tim Dale and the staff of Yoga Tree, Larry Harvey and Maid Marian, the crew of Fish Amok, and Stuart Moskowitz and the Circle of Life Foundation. We also thank Shawn Hazen for incorporating our vision into his excellent book design.

Finally, and most emphatically, we want to thank Alan Rapp and Jenn Shreve for introducing the two of us to each other and for shepherding this project from spark to book.

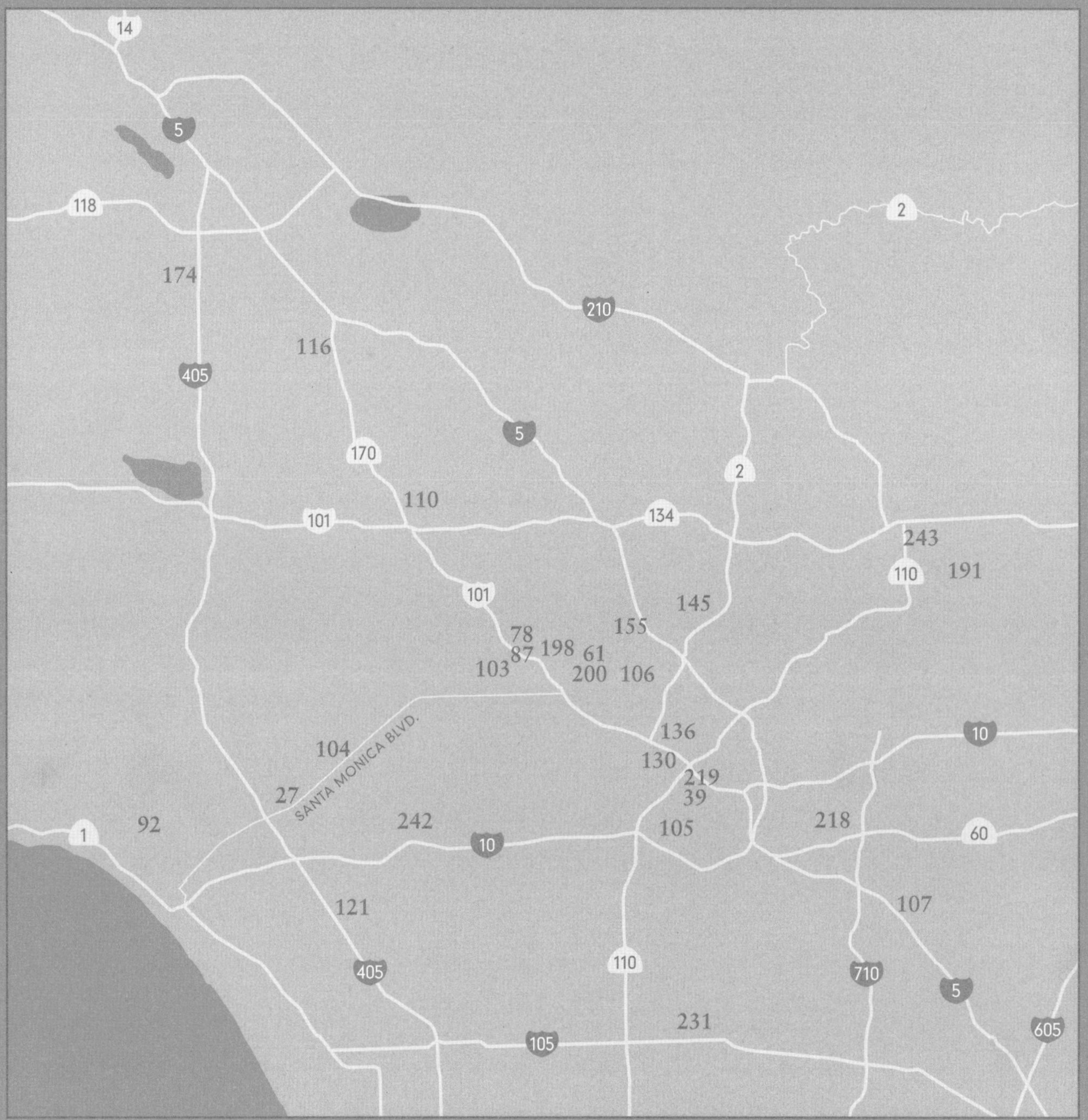
14
5
118
2
174
210
116
405
5
170
2
110
101
134
243
110
191
101
145
155
78
87
198
61
103
200
106
136
10
104
SANTA MONICA BLVD.
130
219
39
27
218
92
242
105
1
10
60
107
121
405
110
710
5
231
605
105